Their Day In the Sun

WOMEN OF THE
1932 OLYMPICS

★

Their
Day
In the
Sun

WOMEN OF THE
1932 OLYMPICS

★

DORIS H. PIEROTH

A SAMUEL AND ALTHEA STROUM BOOK

UNIVERSITY OF WASHINGTON PRESS
SEATTLE AND LONDON

This book is published with the assistance of a grant from the Stroum Book Fund, established through the generosity of Samuel and Althea Stroum.

Library of Congress Cataloging-in-Publication Data
Pieroth, Doris Hinson.
    Their day in the sun : women of the 1932 Olympics / Doris
H. Pieroth.
      p.   cm.
    "A Samuel and Althea Stroum book."
    Includes bibliographical references (p.   ) and index.
    ISBN 0-295-97553-9 (cloth : alk. paper).—ISBN 0-295-97554-7
(pbk. : alk. paper)
    1. Olympic Games (10th : 1932 : Los Angeles, Calif.)
    2. Women athletes—United States—Biography. I. Title.
GV722 1932.P54   1996
796.48—dc20   96-23104
                                              CIP

Contents

★

Preface and Acknowledgments

A research project for the Washington State Aquatics History Foundation led me to Seattle's Helene Madison. The triple gold medal winner at the 1932 Olympic Games in Los Angeles was the state's first medalist. Uncovering the Madison story fired anew my interest in that Xth Olympiad and the entire 1932 women's team.

The more I learned, the more I wanted to know—who they were, how they became athletes, what 1932 meant to them, what they became after their "day in the sun." I had the pleasure and good fortune of talking and corresponding with eleven of those remarkable people, and I cherish the memory of those contacts.

The history of women's sports holds few accounts of individual women athletes of the late twenties and early thirties. I have sought to bring the women of '32 to the forefront and to focus on their Olympic era. I have included some description of 1932 competition to give a stronger sense of the women as athletes and some sense of the enthusiasm they generated.

As is often true in ferreting out the history of women outside the leadership ranks, the documentary evidence is thin excepting for the Olympic Games themselves. I made judicious use of contemporary press accounts. These included wire service releases, local and national news coverage and personal profiles, nationally syndicated political and entertainment columns, and the like. Sports journalism, in full bloom, provided the major source of information about the athletic events themselves. I corroborated and substantiated accounts wherever possible and found a high degree of press accuracy and reliability.

In addition to interviews with the Olympians themselves, oral sources include interviews with some of their family members, other members of their sponsors' teams, a coach, other 1928 and '36 Olympians, and contemporary witnesses of the '32 Games. A list of interviews is on page 174. I used the excellent interview transcripts in the oral history collection in the library of the Amateur Athletic Foundation's Ziphron Resource Center in Los Angeles.

Given the vagaries of memory and the possibility that the importance of an event or one's role in it may become either inflated or diminished over time, recollections were corroborated with other sources wherever possible. Remarkable similarities appeared in recollections of events in individual interviews that were separated by considerable distance and often by considerable time.

In the course of writing this book, I incurred many debts of gratitude. Thanks go to John Torney III for connecting me with the network of Southern California Olympians and others involved in the 1984 Games in Los Angeles. The latter include, especially, Jean D'Amico and Patricia Henry Yeomans, the daughter of the '32 Games technical director Bill Henry. The help of others who gave time in interviews was invaluable: Elizabeth Hoffman, Doris Buckley Johnson, Olive McKean Mucha, Velma Dunn Ploessel, Janice York Romary, Elizabeth Robinson Schwartz, Fred Schwengel, Mary Lou Petty Skok, Maria Cerra Tishman, and Helene McIver Ware.

No historian could write without librarians. This book has benefited from the help of library staffs across the country, including: the Atlanta-Fulton Public Library, Atlanta, Georgia; The Public Library of Cincinnati and Hamilton County, Cincinnati, Ohio; The Kansas City Public Library, Kansas City, Missouri; The Los Angeles Public Library, Los Angeles, California; The *San Francisco Chronicle* Library, San Francisco, California; The San Francisco Public Library, San Francisco, California; The Seattle Public Library, Seattle, Washington; University of Georgia Library, Athens, Georgia; and The Whitinsville Public Library, Whitinsville, Massachusetts.

Librarians and archivists to whom I am especially indebted are: Susan Barnard, Atlanta History Center, Atlanta, Georgia; Elizabeth Kenyon and Mavis Holland, Chisholm Public Library, Chisholm, Minnesota; Marion Washburn, Librarian, International Swimming Hall of Fame, Fort Lauderdale, Florida; Sister Aurelia, Archivist, Sisters of Loretto, Nerinx, Kentucky; Joel Thiele, Malden Public Library, Malden, Massachusetts; Laura Boeckman, The State Historical Society of Missouri, Columbia, Missouri; Michael Salmon, Amateur Athletic Foundation Ziphron Resource Center, Los Angeles, California; Catherine Wright, San Rafael Library, San Rafael, California; Linda Kropf, Shelbina Carnegie Public Library, Shelbina, Missouri; Noel Holobeck, St. Louis Public Library, St. Louis, Missouri; Michael Sutherland, Occidental College Library, Los Angeles, California; Barry Parsons, Library of the *Worcester Telegram and Gazette,* Worcester, Massachusetts; and Nancy Gaudette, Worcester Public Library, Worcester, Massachusetts.

Others who gave invaluable help are Edwin C. Theisen, Jr., Past Commodore and Historian, Detroit Yacht Club, Detroit, Michigan; Camilla Shires, Los Angeles Athletic Club, Los Angeles, California; C. Robert Paul of the United States Olympic Committee and Carla Mae Richards, Executive Director, United States Fencing Association, both in Colorado Springs, Colorado; and Jeffrey Tishman, Sports Archivist, Associated Press, New York, New York.

I am indebted to friends and colleagues whose assistance, interest, and encouragement lasted from beginning to end of this project —Joanne Torney Rehfeldt; Charles and Pauline LeWarne; Suzanne Hittman; Margaret Hall; and Jack Berryman. A patient husband, John Pieroth, lent computer expertise and moral support to the endeavor.

Finally, I thank those without whom there truly would have been no book—those wonderful women of 1932 who gave so generously of their time and enthusiasm: Evelyne Hall Adams, Mary Carew Armstrong, Helen Johns Carroll, Margaret Jenkins, Margaret Hoffman, Annette Rogers Kelly, Elizabeth Wilde Kinnard, Jean Shiley Newhouse, Evelyn Furtsch Ojeda, Ruth Osburn, Eleanor Garatti Saville, and Lenore Kight Wingard.

Introduction

When the International Olympic Committee named Los Angeles the site for the 1932 Games at its meeting in Rome in 1923, no one could have foreseen economic storm clouds ahead. After presenting the case for Los Angeles, William May Garland, real estate baron, civic booster, and member of the IOC, returned home convinced the Games would bring international acclaim to his optimistic and expanding city. Work soon began to renovate and expand the Coliseum in Exposition Park into an Olympic Stadium.

As the twenties gave way to the thirties, organizers faced the task of producing a sports extravaganza in the depths of the Great Depression. They worked against a backdrop of record unemployment in California—nearly 350,000 in the greater Los Angeles area alone. Other nations, their economies in shambles, were reluctant to commit teams to this longest Olympic journey to date.

In mid-April 1932, guarantees of participation and total ticket sales for the Games remained near zero. But the Opening Ceremony on Saturday, July 30, hid all traces of the anxiety that had gripped Olympic organizers only a few months earlier.

Zack Farmer, General Secretary of the Los Angeles Olympic Organizing Committee, resurrected a plan he had proposed earlier for housing all athletes in an "Olympic Village." His idea had been rejected by nations preferring secrecy and opposed to fraternizing among competitors. This time, however, it proved to be the salvation of the Games. Sharp-penciled accounting brought the total cost of feeding and housing an athlete to two dollars a day, a sum beleaguered national Olympic Committees found within their means. Just three months before the scheduled opening, an athletes' village of 500 cottages sprouted on 250 acres in the undeveloped Baldwin Hills section of Los Angeles, just west of the Coliseum.

Organizers persuaded steamship and rail lines to cut fares. Teams could then afford to travel from Europe, Asia, and South America on otherwise nearly empty carriers.

Leaders in the movie colony climbed on the slowly moving Olympic bandwagon, bringing promotion, charisma, and entertainment plans with them. The American press woke finally to begin its coverage, and by midsummer, Olympic items appeared on society pages, in travel columns, in sports sections, and as pictorial spreads in the rotogravure section of virtually every Sunday newspaper. "Olympic fever" swept the country at long last, ticket sales skyrocketed, and the city was ready.

Those Summer Games in Los Angeles introduced highly successful models of organization, housing, staging, and presentation. Every Olympic host city since has sought to equal or surpass them. Thirteen hundred athletes, one-tenth of them women, provided record-setting thrills, controversy, and entertainment for huge crowds of spectators.

The Olympics themselves took on greater importance in the United States that year. Before 1932, and long before they became a television staple, the Olympic Games were viewed as elitist or foreign by many of the Americans who had heard anything at all about them.

The 1932 Games were also pivotal for the future of women in the Olympics and for women athletes in general. As late as April 1931, the International Olympic Committee had seriously considered eliminating women's events. Los Angeles commanded impressive media coverage, and the "Hollywood connection" assured positive publicity in 1932, carrying with it a certain validation.

The women athletes became familiar, popular figures. This stemmed in no small part from the excitement surrounding the performances of Mildred "Babe" Didrikson, the phenomenal all-around athlete from Texas. Generally considered to have been the outstanding individual competitor of the Los Angeles Games, Babe was the preeminent American woman athlete of the pre–World War II years.

Nevertheless, although historians have noted few others from that transitional era that began in the late 1920s, she was not alone.

The United States sent thirty-seven women to compete in Los Angeles—seventeen swimmers, seventeen track and field athletes, and three fencers. The team truly represented a cross-section of America—from New York to California, Washington to Florida, Illinois to Texas, and points in between. The athletes came from public schools, pools and playgrounds, municipal and industrial recreation programs, and from private clubs. They reflected the country's ethnic mix and spanned its socioeconomic spectrum. They emerged from the Games as bona fide athletic stars; their electrifying performances produced a record number of Olympic medals.

When the 1932 Olympians were growing toward their competitive prime, it was still not easy for a woman to be an athlete in the United States—especially in track and field. Even for this transitional generation, going beyond the stereotype of the "ideal woman" constituted a challenge. For all that the 1920s promised in the way of freedom and opportunity, public pronouncements and private expectations still carried conventional ideas of what was proper for women. Short hairstyles worn by some athletes could still provoke outcry, and streamlined swimsuits and track shorts were widely considered indecent. And more important than strictures of dress, many physical education teachers, both male and female, believed that rigorous training and competition harmed women.

Opportunities for American women to participate in sports had begun to grow toward the end of the nineteenth century. By the 1920s women engaged in a variety of sports; but their opportunities were fewer and developed more slowly and inequitably than those for men. Like the New Woman in politics, who also emerged during the twenties, the Athletic Woman had to work within a male dominated world.

While inequality may be implicit in these athletes' story, the intent of this book is not to examine inequality, sexuality, or repression. For the most part, implications of scholarship on the gender struggle in sports appear in the end notes.[1] This is, rather, an account of a select group of women who did challenge what one scholar has termed a "heritage of exclusion."[2]

The Olympians of 1932 can be numbered among those who throughout American history have been willing or driven to go beyond limits set for them. They went against the grain of social convention at a time when women were only gradually beginning to receive general acceptance as athletes. This is their story—who they were, whence they came, how they reached the pinnacle, and their varied routes to Los Angeles. It recounts their Olympic summer—people, places, and events.

Their Day In the Sun

WOMEN OF THE
1932 OLYMPICS

★

1 | Women's Athletic Odyssey

★

For the women athletes of 1932, contradiction marked the path to maturity. They benefited from the legacy of an early wave of popular women athletes in the 1920s, but they also had to deal with continuing general antipathy toward women in sports. A "heritage of exclusion" stemming from an idealized vision of the American woman and an aversion to the concept of competition continued to strike at the heart of what it means to be an athlete.

Intense championship competition for women in any sport drew solid opposition from some influential sources—from both men and women physical education professionals, from the Women's Division of the National Amateur Athletic Federation (NAAF), and from the International Olympic Committee. Protection of women's health, especially their childbearing potential, figured prominently in most arguments. Many of the 1932 Olympians were warned that they put motherhood at risk by taking part in athletics. It had long been so. In mid-nineteenth-century America, popular opinion and medical canon held physical activity to be inimical to women's best interest. When women entered colleges in growing numbers in the last half of the century, their advocates promoted exercise, mainly in the form of calisthenics. They sought thus to counter arguments of frailty lodged against a woman's claim to a place in higher education.[1]

Sports slowly entered college programs toward the end of the century, especially with the introduction of that most American of

1

sports, basketball. Basketball's popularity spread rapidly throughout the country and all sports waxed more prominent in the nation at large. Women, both on and beyond the campus, enjoyed the growth of tennis and swimming and energetically embraced the bicycle craze of the 1890s.[2]

By the turn of the century, the force of some nineteenth-century taboos had waned. The roles assumed by American women during World War I would erase more. After the war, a robust advertising industry contributed to further freedom. The sportswoman became a ubiquitous symbol in advertising wars to promote and sell a wide range of products. This embrace by free enterprise allowed women "to become not merely athletic but athletes—*as long as they underscored their femininity with the right sports and attire.*"[3]

In the twenties, the Golden Age of Sport for men, women made their debut on the sports pages, as golfers, swimmers, and tennis players. Golfer Glenna Collett (Vare) won fame and six United States Women's Amateur titles. She came from a family of wealth, as most golfers in the twenties did, and her "grace and feminine charm" was credited with helping popularize golf with American women. No doubt they helped make Collett popular with the sports press.[4]

Drive, determination, and a competitive nature, not grace and feminine charm, marked Helen Wills's tennis play and earned her the label "Little Miss Poker Face." By 1938 she had won seven United States singles titles and eight singles championships at Wimbledon. Wells won the singles gold medal at Paris in 1924, the last appearance of tennis in the Olympic Games before a long hiatus.[5]

With the possible exception of Suzanne Lenglen, the great French tennis "Goddess," no woman athlete of the twenties captured the imagination of the world as swimmer Gertrude Ederle did. Daughter of the German-American owner of a delicatessen on New York's Amsterdam Avenue, Ederle won two Olympic bronze medals and one gold in 1924. Two years later, on August 6, 1926, she neared immortality as the first woman to swim the English Channel. She made the crossing in 14 hours, 31 minutes—almost two hours under the men's channel record. Ederle's feat, perhaps more than anything else, helped increase the interest in swimming for women.[6] By 1924 competitive swimming for women had occupied a fairly secure niche in the athletic scheme of things.

Women's track and field, although growing in popularity, was another matter. Athletic politics—foreign, domestic, Olympic—kept track and field at the margins of public regard but in the center of controversies that carried over into the lives of the young women who competed in Los Angeles in 1932. Their sports carried a masculine label, putting them at odds with the feminine ideal. Social class, too, constrained track and field, reflecting the belief that masculine events belonged with leisure pursuits of the working class.[7]

Early opportunity in sports had come primarily in physical education programs for middle-class college and university women, but it was for those same women that the strictures of femininity were most binding. Women leaders of those and later programs and of the normal schools that trained them had insisted on decorum. Their students must be "ladies and then athletes." These early leaders erected an enduring barrier to competition for women. The truly talented, competitive, championship-caliber athlete caused distress and concern in women's departments across the country.[8]

Department leaders in the twenties and thirties, whose professional roots trace to early Progressive reformers as well, also maintained a protective belief that sports and recreation should be offered and regulated for society's betterment. A strong feeling of community service lay behind their motto, which became "A Sport for Every Girl and a Girl for Every Sport." For them, competitive athletics held the potential for exploitation of gifted women athletes. They found abuses in men's intercollegiate sports intolerable and competition was anathema.[9]

They insisted on women coaches and women officials, and were tenacious in the fight to control women's sports. Had they been able to include the gifted competitive athlete in their world view, they might have maintained control and taken women's sports along a different path in the twentieth century. As it was, they could not prevail against the takeover of women's sports by the Amateur Athletic Union.

The AAU, which sought to control all amateur sports in the United States, took command of women's swimming at its annual meeting in 1914.[10] Eight years later the AAU Board of Governors turned to women's track and field. They met with supporters and advocates of women's athletics at New York's Hotel McAlpin in April

1922. After much undoubtedly heated discussion, the AAU made its move and assumed jurisdiction over track and field as well as swimming. The first National Track & Field Championships for women took place in Newark, New Jersey, on September 29, 1923.[11]

Creation of the National Amateur Athletic Federation (NAAF) in December 1922 added a new group to the fray. Lou Henry Hoover, wife of then Secretary of Commerce Herbert Hoover, accepted an invitation to lead the women's section and, at her suggestion, the NAAF created an independent women's division. The Women's Division gave women professionals in physical education the opportunity to control a national group beyond the confines of college campuses. From this new platform they continued to voice philosophical opposition to competition.[12]

When Baron Pierre de Coubertin reintroduced the Olympic Ideal in the 1890s, leading the way to creation of the modern Olympic movement, he saw no place for women in the Olympic Games. He envisioned a rebirth of the classical Greek athletic ideal that celebrated the perfect young adult male athlete excelling in the ultimate contest. Coubertin never dropped his opposition to women participating in the Games.[13]

Even so, women did appear in the modern Olympics as early as 1900 in a one-time-only women's Olympic golf tournament. Tennis for women also appeared in 1900 and remained an Olympic sport until 1924. Swimming and platform diving for women were added for the Stockholm Games in 1912. Swimming included only 100-meter freestyle and the 4 × 100-meter freestyle relay. No American woman competed that year.[14]

World War I forced cancellation of the 1916 Games scheduled for Berlin. Antwerp hosted the first postwar Olympics, and the United States sent a team of women swimmers who swept the field. Ethelda Bleibtrey of the New York Women's Swimming Association won the gold medal, setting a world record for 100-meter freestyle. She set another world record in winning the new 400-meter freestyle race, and she anchored the gold-medal-winning relay team. In newly added springboard diving, Americans Aileen Riggin, Helen Wainwright, Thelma Payne, and Aileen Allen shut out the rest of the world.[15]

Fencing for women made its first appearance in the Olympic

Games in Paris in 1924. From the beginning, Europeans wholly dominated in fencing. Individual foil remained the extent of Olympic
fencing until team foil competition was added in 1960.[16]

The number of women's events gradually increased, but the International Amateur Athletic Federation (IAAF), governing body of
Olympic track and field, ruled out track events for women in the
Antwerp Games. They did so again for 1924 in Paris. But the departure of Pierre de Coubertin from the presidency of the International
Olympic Committee after the '24 Games opened the way for women's
track and field as Olympic events.

After Coubertin resigned, the IOC agreed to stage five women's
events on an experimental basis at the Games slated for Amsterdam
in 1928. Competition would be in the 100- and 800-meter races,
4 × 100-meter relay, high jump, and discus.[17]

American awareness of the Games was minimal in 1928, but the
furor caused by the women's 800-meter race no doubt increased it.
The exhausted collapse of some runners at the end of that event re-
vived the issues of health and women's proper role among Olympic
leaders and in the press. Never mind that male athletes, too, were often exhausted, grimacing with pain and gasping for breath at the end
of a race. Men in the sports press corps, among others, could not rec-
oncile a similar state with their concept of what a woman should be
and how she should look. They deplored the 800-meter event.[18]

Although written eight years later, the words of Paul Gallico echo
the feeling of journalists at the time:

> . . . There is no girl living who can manage to look anything but
> awful during the process of some strenuous game played on a hot
> day, . . .
>
> If there is anything more dreadful aesthetically or more depress-
> ing than the fatigue-distorted face of a girl runner at the finish line,
> I have never seen it. . . .[19]

The 800-meter episode spurred the Women's Division of the
NAAF to further action. In an attempt to keep women from competing in the Los Angeles Games, in April 1930 they petitioned the IOC
to drop women's track and field. Their appeal coincided with a desire
to trim the growing program of the Games. In 1929 the new IOC
president, Count Henri de Baillet-Latour, had proposed cutting all

women's events as one means to that end. Track and field, an experiment in 1928, remained particularly vulnerable.[20]

The IOC deferred action until it met in Barcelona in 1931. By that time, a superb women's track and field demonstration at the 1930 Olympic Congress in Berlin had won the support of a key American —Avery Brundage. As president of the AAU and representative to the IAAF, Brundage stood on the threshold of a dominant role in Olympic affairs that would last forty years. The IAAF's committee on women's sports, with Brundage a member, strongly recommended keeping women's events in the Games.[21]

Finally, in April 1931, the IOC called for women's swimming, fencing, and track and field to be part of the upcoming Xth Olympiad. Despite political roadblocks obstructing their route, women *would* compete in Los Angeles.

In the history of women's sports, the 1932 Olympians comprise a discrete, defined cohort of pioneer athletes. Their competitive time came just as the bright, illusive promise of the twenties was curtailed by the Depression; it ended with the approach of World War II, which deferred the Olympic Games. They made the most of their opportunities, and their acceptance and popularity in 1932 helped to assure the place of women in future Olympics. While there were postwar threats to exclude women, they appear more as stratagems in Cold War Olympic politics than serious attempts to revert to the past.

Those thirty-seven talented women shared a love of sports and of competing, combined with the focus, determination, and discipline to take them to world-class status. For the most part they received confirmation from the wholehearted backing and cooperation of their families. Where parents may have been opposed, neutral, or passive, another significant person—perhaps a truly dedicated coach—provided support.

Some coaches were volunteers or teachers in the schools who gave hours far beyond their compensation. Some worked in park or playground programs, others in private or semi-private clubs. Not all the private clubs had bona fide, dependable coaching staffs, but sponsors did undertake and underwrite most provisions and opportunities for competition.

Few if any of the coaches had been deeply involved in the philo-sophical debates on women's athletic competition, and they had no reservations about working with women athletes. The young women themselves had the desire, inclination, and natural ability. They simply chose to ignore society's expectations for women of their generation. Their coaches met the challenge to convert raw talent to medal-winning potential.

2 | Pathbreakers In Track And Field

★

The athletes who sought places on the 1932 Olympic track and field team reveled in competing, and they arrived in Chicago for the trials that July determined to win. All had survived the filter of local or regional qualifying meets and some held national titles, but most were oblivious to the political infighting and philosophical hair-splitting that had surrounded track and field. They had no idea that echoes of past controversy might reach them and affect such basic decisions as who competed in which events.

When the AAU assumed control of women's track and field, one motive had been to meet the need for sports for women outside the schools and colleges. Such sports opportunities increased with the growth of industrial recreation programs. The first national champions in 1923 had come from schools, athletic associations, and industrial and commercial clubs—sponsors as diverse as the Robinson Female Seminary, Philadelphia's Meadowbrook Club, the Prudential Insurance Athletic Association, the German-American Turnverein, and the City Bank Club of New York.[1] The same sorts of sponsors backed 1932 Olympians.

Following the 1928 Olympic Games, track and field drew more and more women to both indoor and outdoor competitive circuits. In New England, the Boston Swimming Association was joined by such clubs as the Medford Girls Club and Malden's Onteora Club. They all sent teams across the border to compete with the Toronto Ladies

Athletic Club and to Mid-Atlantic meets with New Jersey's Prudential, Philadelphia's Meadowbrook, New York's Millrose, and more.

Further west were Cleveland's New York Central [Railroad] Athletic Club, the Headlight Athletic Club of St. Louis, and the dominant
Illinois Women's Athletic Club in Chicago. By 1930 Dallas had a major industrial recreation league with teams representing the likes of
the Dr. Pepper Bottling Company, Employers' Casualty Insurance, and
Bowen Air Lines.

Southern California boasted a cluster of private clubs familiar to
national meets—the Los Angeles Athletic Club, Hollywood Athletic
Club, and Pasadena Athletic Club. The Northern California Athletic
Club had fielded teams for some time, and in 1932 San Francisco's
Western Women's Club sponsored several Olympic athletes.

Even with continued growth and popularity, the general state of
track and field athletics remained rather primitive in 1932. Starting
blocks for sprinters belonged to the future, and each woman's equipment included a trowel to dig "starting holes" in the cinder track surface. High jumpers landed in sawdust or rock-solid sand pits, not on
poly-foam cushions. Timing and judging could be erratic. Coaching
and practice facilities varied widely from place to place. Track and field
still had something akin to second-class status, and its female athletes
still challenged an idealized vision of the American woman.

Three members of the 1928 track and field team returned to
claim second Olympic berths four years later. Each took a unique
route to the Olympics, but all three had experiences fairly typical for
the woman athlete of the late twenties.

Jean Shiley was a sixteen-year-old student at Haverford Township High
School in Pennsylvania when she qualified for the '28 Olympic team
as a high jumper. Sister of three younger brothers, she was born in
Harrisburg on November 18, 1912. By her sixth birthday the family
had settled in what is now Havertown, twenty-six miles west of Philadelphia. In this rural setting, she grew up a country girl and a tomboy.
What her brothers did, she did—from tree climbing to football. She
spent hours jumping and doing handstands and cartwheels.[2]

She attended Haverford Township High School, which offered a
richly varied sports program for girls as well as boys. From her fresh-
man year on, Jean enjoyed tennis, hockey, basketball, and track and

field. Standing just under five feet nine inches, she excelled in basket-ball, which showcased her phenomenal jumping ability and opened the door to the Olympics.[3]

Haverford's games received good press coverage. During the 1927–28 basketball season, serendipity brought a sports reporter with a special perspective to cover the Haverford girls' basketball team.

The Inquirer's Dora Lurie was one of a trio of women sports writers in Philadelphia in the twenties who wrote under their own bylines. A high jumper herself in her student days at Temple University, Lurie recognized true potential when she saw Jean in action. She sold the teenager on the idea of trying her skill at the high jump bar, but when Lurie asked Jean if she would like to compete in the Olympics she had to explain the Games to her. Jean thought, "Well, it's just another track meet. Sure. Anything in sports is great."[4]

Dora Lurie resolved to get Jean the best coaching on the Eastern Seaboard. She arranged a tryout for her at Franklin Field with the University of Pennsylvania's Lawson Robertson. The dean of college coaches, he had coached men's Olympic track teams since 1920 and would again in '28 and '32. Lurie took Jean to talk with Robertson and demonstrate her ability. He had intimidated more than a few men who sought his coaching, and Jean recalled that when she talked to him she was petrified. "He had a very gruff, Scottish burr in his voice and he didn't smile." Lurie was ecstatic when Robertson agreed to coach her discovery, but Jean still "didn't realize then how big a thing this was."[5]

She went into the city to work with Robertson every Wednesday morning and practiced daily at home, jumping over a cast-off fishing pole delicately balanced between two clothesline supports. Robertson taught her the basics and the "little tricks that one does to concentrate." She always said, "Everything I learned, I learned from Lawson Robertson."[6] And she learned it well.

Jean had little backing at home. Her father, an automobile mechanic, ruled a traditional home and held traditional, restrictive views of a woman's role. He was not comfortable having a daughter with a strong athletic bent. He never saw her compete. He thought it worthless, and she later guessed, "I gave him a few gray hairs," adding they remained "two trains going down separate tracks."[7]

It was an uncle and aunt, her mother's sister and brother-in-law, who really encouraged her. They took her to Newark for the 1928

Olympic trials on July 4. Jean still had only a faint idea of what the Olympic Games were all about and she did not realize exactly what she was in for. She just loved to jump.[8]

City Field in Newark resembled a steam bath that day. A monumental electrical storm blew in midway in the competition, putting the jumping on hold for an hour. The novice jumper, competing unattached, wore her brother's shirt and a pair of short pants her mother had made. She tied for first place with Mildred Wiley, national champion from the Boston Swimming Association. In the jump-off, Jean placed second—sufficient to win a spot on the Olympic team.[9]

Jean's family was in an uproar in the week before the team sailed. Her distraught Pennsylvania Dutch Grandmother Shiley insisted she should not be allowed to go to Europe alone. On the other hand, her maternal grandmother was delighted and bought her new clothes for the trip. A week later most of the family went to New York to see her off aboard the SS President Roosevelt on an adventure she felt literally changed her life.[10]

In Amsterdam her jump of 4 feet 11½ inches put Jean fourth behind Canadian Ethel Catherwood's gold medal height of 5 feet 3 inches. The wonder and awe of her introduction to a wider world minimized any disappointment over her finish. Mingling with the international athletes lifted her sights beyond Haverford Township, and she would never see anything quite the same way again. At a post-Games international meet in Brussels she took second in both high jump and running broad jump. Jean returned with the team to a New York ticker-tape parade and the customary official greeting from ebullient Mayor Jimmy Walker.[11]

She then began her athletic career in earnest with a search for a club sponsor. She literally begged Philadelphia's Meadowbrook Club to accept a female high jumper. Wanamaker's department store sponsored Meadowbrook. Generations of Philadelphians customarily rendezvoused near the Wanamaker eagle, but few saw the facilities the store provided for its track team. They had an outdoor track on the roof and a makeshift space indoors. Jean described that spot as a "dingy old place on the top floor" where she practiced surrounded by stored mannequins and rolling racks full of returns and mark-downs. She would spread out a thin mat, put up two standards and a bar, and take off. Landing on that mat made the hard outdoor sand pits feel good by comparison.[12]

In the autumn of 1929, just before the stock market crash, Jean enrolled at Temple University. She received a small academic scholarship stemming in part, she was sure, from her Olympic experience, but she also had to earn her own way. To be eligible for the Meadowbrook team she had to be a Wanamaker's employee, so during her years at Temple she spent many evenings, weekends, and vacations on the selling floor.[13]

With Meadowbrook supporting her at competitions, paying per diem expenses of $2.50, she became the nation's most consistent high jumper. Her championship records rose each of the next four years, until the Indoor Nationals in 1932. There Jean dropped from 5 feet 3 inches to 5 feet 1¼ inches in a meet that took place four months after an appendectomy threatened to completely derail her 1932 Olympic plans.[14]

Her strong suit in high school was biology, and for a time she hoped for a career in medicine. Aside from the fact that medical schools did not admit women gladly in the early thirties, it was financially impossible for her. As many able women with an interest in science did at that time, and especially those gifted athletically as Jean was, she majored in physical education. The Temple department hewed to the NAAF Women's Division's line of no competition for women; this came as a distinct shock to Jean after the program at Haverford Township High. She and the faculty never reached accommodation on this point, and she recalled that "every time I met a professor in the hallways they asked me when I was going to quit," but jumping "was such a sheer joy that they couldn't stop me from doing it."[15]

On the other side of the continent, a similar scenario played out on the campus of San Jose State College in California. Two graduates of the University of Wisconsin's prestigious Women's Physical Education Department headed the program at San Jose, and they kept it free of the taint of competition. Margaret Jenkins, a competitive athlete and spirited student iconoclast, hated their restrictions. She gave thanks the day Laura Heron joined the faculty, never dreaming that Heron would point her toward the Olympic Games.[16]

The faculty newcomer thought women should be allowed to compete and she relished a free spirit. She knew Margaret could "throw the basketball and baseball a city block and asked [her to] throw the javelin in a telegraphic meet." Margaret had never held a javelin. She practiced briefly with one Heron borrowed from the men's gym and entered the national telegraphic meet. After her second-place finish Heron learned there were lighter javelins for women.[17]

Perhaps Margaret Jenkins was born to nonconformity. Her grandfather, Emmett Jenkins, arrived in California a year ahead of the Forty-niners. After he "discovered gold up in the valley, he never told a soul" and bought land in Mountain View. Margaret's father was born there on the Jenkins tract, later the site of the Navy's Moffet Field. Her mother, however, is likely the main source of Margaret's love of sports and freedom. Mala Etta Helm Jenkins had happily taken to the bicycle and joined the Garden City Cyclers in 1896. She also sported bloomers, the fashion that had shocked society.[18]

When Margaret was born, July 2, 1903, Frank and Mala Jenkins lived in Saratoga. Their orchards in Saratoga and Cupertino supported a successful fruit business. Their two daughters entered the Saratoga Grammar School where Margaret's ability made her a recruit for the boys' baseball team. In high school she played on the Santa Clara girls' team. She graduated in 1921, went on to San Jose State, and soon made her mark there in sports. She was an exceptionally talented all-around athlete. She later remembered her competitive years as a time when entering athletics "placed a woman in the category of 'oddball,' a curiosity or worse." She played socially acceptable tennis with the San Jose Tennis Club and held Santa Clara County singles, doubles, and mixed doubles championships from 1924 to 1926.[19]

Armed with a new bachelor's degree, in 1925 Margaret launched a thirty-year career with the Santa Clara schools, teaching sixth, seventh, and eighth grades. She returned to the javelin in her spare time, and spent long practice hours after school on shot put and the basketball throw as well. She trained for local and regional meets staged by the Northern California Athletic Club and the Pacific Association of the AAU. In the spring of 1927, her javelin throw of 121 feet 3¼ inches set a women's world record and sent her in search of a coach.[20]

She said, "I just plain screwed up courage enough to go see Dink Templeton at Stanford" one afternoon that spring. Robert (Dink) Templeton, known as "the boy coach," and himself a maverick who upset traditions, was one of the first coaches to approach athletics analytically. He said he had never coached a woman but would give it a try. He told Margaret, though, that she would first have to go see Dr.

Mosher—Clelia Duel Mosher, M.D., from Johns Hopkins, longtime medical adviser to women students, and Professor of Hygiene at Stanford. Dr. Mosher was a staunch advocate of exercise for women, but securing her approval of competitive athletics and a male coach might prove difficult.[21]

Sixty-four years later Margaret Jenkins wrote of that crucial meeting: "I can still see that dear person—that mannish tailored suit—and her cravat—and ground gripper oxfords." Margaret had known she would be talking to a "stiff, proper person—but [recalled] I had a little gift of gab and could use it." Dr. Mosher "didn't know" about Jenkins' working with Templeton; she "hemmed and hawed." Finally Margaret told her that anything she or one of her Stanford students might accomplish would reflect glory and publicity on the doctor and her department. Permission was granted.[22]

Margaret asked no quarter and Templeton gave none. She received the same coaching and salty language he dished out to the men while they polished her javelin skills for the Olympics. They learned early in 1928 that javelin was not on the program for Amsterdam. Templeton thought she should be content with her javelin title, but, as she recalled, "I bet [him] . . . I could learn to throw that D___ discus enough to make the team—I won—but he told me NOT to broadcast it—he never liked losing." Not even a bet with Margaret.[23]

On that oppressively hot and sultry Fourth of July in Newark, Margaret did Dink Templeton proud by qualifying for the Olympic team in the discus. Marion Holley, one of Dr. Mosher's Stanford students, reflected a little more glory back to Palo Alto as the fourth high jumper to make the team. San Jose's Laura Heron, who had started it all, sailed with them on the *President Roosevelt*.[24]

Neither Jenkins nor Holley placed at Amsterdam, but four years later, Margaret took aim at a place on the 1932 team. A reporter spotted her practicing with the discus and wrote an article advising her to forget about the Olympics because she was too old. Reading that made her more determined. When she qualified for the '32 team, the *San Jose Mercury Herald* ran a front page apology, complete with photo.[25]

The Pasadena Athletic Club sponsored the third member of both the 1928 and '32 Olympic teams—Lillian Copeland, a javelin and discus thrower who also put the shot. The Pasadena club's teams for women were coached and supervised by Aileen Allen, 1920 Olympic diver at Antwerp. Those two, along with Margaret Jenkins, were fixtures at AAU Pacific Association meets. Jenkins and Copeland became and remained good friends in spite of an incident at the spring meet in 1927—the year Margaret replaced Lillian as national javelin champion.

Margaret went to that meet in Eureka armed with her personal javelin, handmade for her by Jonni Myra, two-time Olympic gold medalist from Finland. Aileen Allen protested its use because it lacked an authorized AAU stamp. This led to questioning of Copeland's personal javelin as well. After a long wrangle Allen relented, but by then Lillian had become so angry and indignant that she eventually fouled out of the meet. Allen took a position in the middle of the field, and Margaret came close to impaling her with the record throw, far longer than anyone expected. Reporters from Bay Area newspapers, who regularly covered the women's meets, had their own field day with this. Copeland easily put it all behind her and went on to win Olympic gold and silver.[26]

Lillian Copeland was born in New York City on November 25, 1904. When Los Angeles appeared to have solved its water supply problems early in the century, its boosters invited the rest of the country to come west and enjoy the good life. The Copelands moved in the vanguard of a mass migration that would see two million Americans move to California during the twenties.[27]

Los Angeles High School provided the first opportunity for Lillian in athletics. She went on to the University of Southern California to major in sociology and political science. While there she competed in tennis, basketball, and track and field, winning every track event she entered. Her greatest strength lay in the field events and she won her first national AAU championship in 1925—the first of four consecutive shot put titles. In 1926, in addition to the shot, she won national championships in discus and javelin with record-breaking throws for each. Since the program for the '28 Games in Amsterdam did not include either shot put or javelin, Lillian concentrated on the discus. She returned home with the silver medal.[28]

Copeland was somewhat stoic—a big, strong, stocky woman, not exceptionally tall. A brisk manner accompanied an air of complete self-sufficiency. Teammates in 1932 saw her as an elder statesman, older and something of a pioneer. While appearing remote and disinterested at times, she could also be a good person to talk to, on the order of a mother-confessor. In addition to those characteristics, she possessed a formidable intellect.[29]

The University of Southern California's successful sports teams—especially football—helped lure financial resources to improve the professional schools and build buildings to house them. The School of Law's new building went up in 1925. Two years after her medal-winning performance in Amsterdam, Copeland joined the ranks of students in a law school rapidly gaining in quality and prestige. Not abandoning track and field, she won her last national titles in 1931, in shot put and javelin.[30]

This left Lillian in good position to return to Olympic competition the next year. The burden of law school delayed full-time training, but she managed to fit Sunday practices in Pasadena into a busy schedule. Dropping out completely would have been unthinkable for the woman who inscribed a photograph she gave to friend and rival Jenkins: "Competition is the spice of life."[31]

Track and field flourished in California. By the time serious training began for the '32 Games, Jenkins and Copeland had been joined by a growing cadre of competitive and talented young women.

The Pasadena Athletic Club occupied a large building complete with meeting and banquet rooms and a swimming pool. It stood on Green Street, one block south of Colorado Boulevard near the heart of downtown. The club held its Sunday track and field practices a few blocks away at Paddock Field on the Cal Tech campus. The field bore the name of Charlie Paddock, the great Olympic sprinter who won gold in 1920 at Antwerp and silver both that year and in 1924 at the *Chariots of Fire* Games in Paris.

California had fielded few women nationally in track and field. Most major competition was in the East, and an athlete had to qualify in one of the larger West Coast meets to be in line for financial backing to go East. The Californians never lost sight of the Olympic trials, however, and the Sunday training sessions assumed greater importance as the Olympics approached.

Aileen Allen left the Pasadena club to coach at the Los Angeles Athletic Club. The two organizations cooperated closely and she continued to go to the Paddock Field sessions. The coaching available on Sundays would barely qualify as such by 1990s standards. Since Allen's background was in swimming, her husband Arthur, with few apparent credentials, took over track.[32] Always on the lookout for talented newcomers, she arranged for an aspiring hurdler from Monrovia to come for a tryout on Easter Sunday, 1932.[33]

Simone Schaller was born in Manchester, Connecticut, on August 22, 1912, the daughter of immigrant parents—a Swiss father and an Italian mother. For decades, ailing Americans had sought relief from ill health in the California sun. Simone's father suffered badly from asthma, so just after World War I he left his job in a silk factory and moved the young family to Monrovia and a healthy outdoor job. He managed the orange groves on the celebrated Loretta Turnbull Ranch and a five-acre grove of his own, where his son and three daughters thrived on the country life.[34]

Simone had learned to hurdle by watching the boys on the Monrovia High School track team. Her natural athletic ability made up for a lack of coaching. She became part of the Sunday workout group that trained for the Olympic trials, driving the family's Model A Ford the eight miles each way on the "more or less paved" road to Pasadena.[35]

The girls' program at Monrovia High hewed to the noncompetitive line, but Simone did play intramural sports. She excelled in volleyball, basketball, and softball. After graduating she worked in an office and played basketball and softball in night leagues. At the end of the 1932 basketball season she had gone in search of a track team.[36] Within four months she rated odds-on chances of being an Olympic hurdler.

Another talent had come to Aileen Allen's attention when Vincent Humeston wrote to her in May 1931. The high school history teacher and boys' track coach in Tustin was looking for training and sponsorship for seventeen-year-old Evelyn Furtsch. Allen sent him the Pasadena club's schedule; their first meet was set for Sunday, May 17. She said they would be glad for Evelyn to come "and see what she can do . . . [with] official timers, etc." Humeston and his wife drove Evelyn and her parents up to Paddock Field the morning of the seventeenth. She ran away from a 100-meter field that included Anne O'Brien, a member of the 1928 Olympic team in Amsterdam.[37]

Evelyn won next at the 1931 national qualifying meet held in the Los Angeles Coliseum to dedicate the lights installed for the upcoming Olympics. Her constantly improving times at the Paddock Field sessions moved the Los Angeles Athletic Club not only to sponsor her, but, with five hundred dollars in expense money, to underwrite her trip to the 1931 national championships in Jersey City, New Jersey.[38]

Evelyn Furtsch was born in San Diego on April 12, 1914, the daughter of transplants from Traverse City, Michigan. They moved to Santa Ana and then four miles south to Tustin, which in 1930 numbered only 926 people. Her trip to the Nationals in New Jersey marked her first venture beyond California's borders.[39]

The science teacher at Tustin Township Union High School doubled in physical education. She introduced Coach Humeston to the competitive young woman who by her own admission just *had* to be first in every race. He said Evelyn "just seemed to float effortlessly as she ran away from the rest. Anyone could see she had great potential." Humeston did not change her running style, but taught her the starts when she began practicing with his track team. The boys happily accepted her, and soon she was "just one of the gang."[40]

Evelyn had strong encouragement from her family. Her father, who was an order clerk with the Santa Ana wholesale grocery firm of Smart and Final, loved having a daughter in sports. Her older brother enthusiastically supported all of her athletic pursuits, and her mother went to all her practices and meets. She even made the long trip to the 1931 Nationals.[41]

In Humeston's four-door sedan they drove the by now familiar forty-five miles to Pasadena and turned east onto Route 66. They climbed up over Cajon Summit, and rolled on to Needles to begin the 2,900-mile trek to the East Coast. The trio sweltered across Arizona and New Mexico on unpaved, corduroy roads. They stayed in what Evelyn later called "crummy auto camps and dumpy little cabins"— standard for early thirties motor travel on a tight budget. By the time they reached New Jersey, they had coped with a boiling radiator, multiple flat tires, a broken axle, and an empty gas tank. Somehow on that eleven-day grind they kept to a schedule that allowed time for her to train. She ran on the school track wherever they stopped each evening.[42]

A crowd of 15,000 saw the championship meet at Jersey City's

Pershing Field. Track judging lacked a great deal in consistency, and place judges occasionally picked the wrong finishers or none altogether. This appears to have been the case in the 50-yard dash when Evelyn failed to place. Humeston had her picked no less than second, and total strangers said she came in either first or second. She went on to make a good showing at 100 yards, placing a strong second to veteran Eleanor Egg of Paterson, New Jersey. More important, Evelyn finished ahead of Cleveland's virtually unbeatable Stella Walsh. The unknown Californian did well enough in her first meet of any consequence to convince Humeston they should go back and start to work toward the coming year's Olympics.[43]

The Sunday trips to Paddock Field continued for another year. With the Pasadena Freeway still eight years in the future, the drive could be nearly two hours each way. On Sunday, June 12, 1932, Evelyn set a new mark of 11.8 seconds for the 100 meters, below the accepted world record of 12 seconds flat. But hard luck continued for "pretty little Evelyn Furtsch," as the Los Angeles sports press often labeled her. Although three timers had clocked her at 11.8, they were not sanctioned AAU timers, so her outstanding time was not official. In a widely promoted try for a sanctioned repeat the next week, she ran the 100 meters at only 12.2 but did a more than respectable 220 meters in 26.1 seconds. There remained no question that the Olympic trials came next.[44]

The road to the Olympic trials wound through the 1931 Nationals for many more future Olympians. In addition to the entries from California—others had made the trip by train—athletes came to Jersey City from the Midwest and Southwest as well. By far the largest percentage were from the Eastern Seaboard's extensive network of clubs and associations. Two of Boston's streetcar suburbs sent sprinters. Though they did not win championships, both would represent their clubs the following year at the Olympic trials.

Medford, Massachusetts, north of Boston and Cambridge and bisected by the Mystic River, was home to the Medford Girls Club. Any girl could join the club. Members paid small dues and the club regularly held dances as fund-raisers. Sports days in Medford featured swimming races in the morning and track events in the afternoon. The club had no swimming program as such, and since neither the club nor the city had a pool, any swimming had to be in the river.[45]

The club's track program was outstanding. The young women felt themselves lucky to have their dedicated and talented coach, Eddie Pidgeon. Pidgeon taught physics and chemistry at Medford High School and coached its boys' track team. He donated time to the Girls Club and gave generously to develop promising young talent. They practiced wherever they could find space or where Pidgeon could get them in. In winter, training for the indoor season, they might practice in the school lunchroom or occasionally use the facilities at Tufts College. In spring they trained in the Medford High stadium, running with Pidgeon's boys.[46]

Around 1926, when the Medford Girls Club had just started, Marion McDonald, a junior high physical education teacher, steered a true talent into its program. McDonald and a director at the YWCA in neighboring Malden had spotted ability in a little freckle-faced red-head named Mary Carew. The two women urged her to join the Girls Club and more or less sponsored her. They underwrote her expenses until, with Eddie Pidgeon's coaching, she became a defending champion sprinter; then the AAU took over.[47]

Mary Carew was born in Medford on September 8, 1913. Both parents died in the disastrous influenza epidemic of 1918, leaving four small children to be distributed among relatives. Mary went to her mother's sister in Greenwich, Connecticut, but she soon proved too heavy a burden for the mother of five other children. Her father's brother, Larry Carew, took her back to Medford where she joined a household that already included his mother-in-law, Mary's baby sister, and his own daughter and four sons. She later said, "he took me in temporarily, and I never left."[48]

She grew up in that very happy home with four boys—all athletes. Mary herself started in athletics at an early age, and the whole family took great pride in her success. Although money was tight, her Uncle Larry tried to see that she had good running shoes and whatever else she needed along the way.[49]

Any successful athlete focuses fully on training and the competition at hand. Mary Carew focused on little else. She burned with a competitive drive and the determination to win. She said, "I wasn't serious about anything but competing. You find that you live, eat, sleep, drink it. It's an obsession if you want to succeed at it; it becomes your whole life. . . . You give up a lot, but it's worth it."[50] The Medford Girls Club took her on the annual winter circuit. They went from meets in the Boston Garden to the Millrose Games in New York, on to New Jersey and Philadelphia, and back to New York and Boston. Summer meets included a few in Canada.

By 1928 she had won the national indoor 40-yard championship, the first of four consecutive titles. At the outdoor Nationals in 1930 she won the 50-yard championship and had the distinction of having beaten Stella Walsh at that distance. She was exceptionally quick on the starts and stood to repeat at Jersey City in 1931. But she lost her title to Alice Monk of the Newark Athletic Club and failed even to place. She had been sick for two weeks and her doctor had ordered her out of the competition; he might as well have told her to stop breathing. The indoor season that followed was highly successful, however, and when the Olympic trials began she was ready.[51]

In neighboring Malden, the Onteora Club delighted in the accomplishments of another sprinter—immensely talented Louise Stokes. Onteora Club membership also was open to all. Operating under the sponsorship of park commissioners, it, too, took teams on the New England and Eastern track circuits. Malden, just north of Boston and Everett and between Medford on the west and Revere on the east, embraced a population of 58,000 in 1930. Mr. and Mrs. William Stokes and their six children numbered among Malden's 632 African American citizens that year.[52]

Once again basketball figured in an Olympic opportunity for a talented track athlete. Louise Stokes was playing basketball and running track at Malden's Beebe Junior High School when a basketball teammate persuaded her to join the Onteora Club. She soon ranked as one of New England's leading sprinters and broad jumpers. In 1931, her sophomore year at Malden High, she won the James Michael Curley Cup at the Boston Mayor's Day Races. She set a New England record for 100 meters that day and placed second in the 50-yard dash and third in broad jump. Later that same year at an indoor meet in Roxbury, Louise equaled the world's standing broad jump record with a leap of 8 feet 5¾ inches.[53]

The Boston Swimming Association still fielded a track team. Its sprinter Olive Hasenfus, Medford Girls Club's Mary Carew, and

Onteora's Louise Stokes usually finished ahead of all others in New England. Carew and Stokes more often competed head-to-head, and they developed a friendly rivalry.[54]

At the 1931 national championship meet in Jersey City, the ailing Carew did not place at 50 yards and Stokes came in fourth. The following December Carew barely nipped Stokes for first at the indoor Roxbury meet, and at Lynn, in July 1932, Louise returned the favor by besting Mary over 100 yards. All three New Englanders went to the 1932 Olympic trials. Although Louise Stokes later described herself as "just a cute little girl that hardly [knew] anything" that summer, she more than held her own in the company of champions at the trials in July.[55]

The Midwest's largest contingent at the 1931 Nationals came from the Illinois Women's Athletic Club. A perennial power, the Chicago club had sent 1928 gold medal sprinter Elizabeth Robinson to Amsterdam. Its relay teams always challenged the rest of the country for first place. A reminder of the IWAC stands just off Lake Shore Drive, near Chicago Avenue on the downtown campus of Loyola University. In the twenties and thirties, what became the university's Lewis Hall was the imposing home of the exclusive, private IWAC—a social, athletic, and residential club. The club's athletic facilities, complete with swimming pool, occupied floors fourteen through sixteen. Because the building lacked an adequate indoor track, its teams trained in the nearby National Guard Armory during indoor seasons, and the rest of the year they practiced at adjacent Lake Shore Playground.[56]

For the most part, the club's athletes remained separate from its social activities—the "beautiful parties and dances." Rather, they would check in at the club, get their uniforms, walk to playground or armory, practice, go back, shower, and go home. Practices might run from midafternoon well into the evening in summer, three days a week. The IWAC had no coaching staff as such, but DePaul University's track team also practiced at Lake Shore Playground, and its coaches gave a willing assist to the young women. An IWAC team member recalled, "[W]e worked out with the [DePaul] guys and the coaches would help us—tell us what we were doing wrong."[57]

From such training came the 1931 national champion 440-yard relay team. At Jersey City, Illinois women also placed in individual events—50-yard dash, 80-meter hurdles, shot put, high jump, discus, and javelin.[58]

Ethel Harrington took second place behind Alice Monk at 50 yards that July, and she carried the baton in the third leg for the victorious 440-yard relay team. Harrington had moved to Chicago from her native Winnipeg, Manitoba. She began competing seriously in 1927 at the IWAC, whose swimmers had by then set national, world, and Olympic records. The slender brunette, rather shy and retiring, belied the masculine stereotype that critics would impute to a highly competitive sprinter. Teammates used such words as "sweet" and "frail" to describe her. At twenty-four she was the IWAC team's oldest member. While less than hardy and robust, she was tenacious, and the Olympic trials the following year found her anxious to make her mark.[59]

The IWAC team's best throwing arm belonged to Nan Gindele. Chicago born, on June 3, 1910, Nan excelled in javelin and the basketball throw. She began competing in 1930 and became a standout at Central AAU meets. From 1933 through 1936 she held the national title for the basketball throw, a non-Olympic event. At the 1931 Nationals in New Jersey, she placed third in the javelin behind California's Lillian Copeland and Elsie Sherman of the Newark Athletic Club. The following June, with a throw of 153 feet 4½ inches, Nan set the javelin world record that stood until 1938.[60]

Gindele stood a compact five feet six inches. She was fun to be with. Possessed of an irrepressible grin and sparkling eyes, she infected the IWAC team with a sense of joy and amusement. She graduated from the Chicago Normal School of Physical Education and had begun teaching in the Chicago schools by the time she qualified in javelin for the games at Los Angeles.[61]

The youngest member of the IWAC team, Annette Rogers, finished her junior year at Chicago's Senn High School just weeks before going to the Nationals in July 1931. Having already gained regional prominence in sprints and high jump, she anchored the national champion relay team at Jersey City. She placed second going over the bar.[62]

Her parents, John and Mary Rogers, had immigrated from Ireland to Boston, where Annette was born on October 22, 1914. When she was three years old, the family moved to Chicago and her father became a streetcar motorman. When Annette was ten, she began athletic pursuits at the Chicago Board of Education's Hayt Playground. From that point on she enjoyed the wholehearted backing and support of her parents, brother, and two sisters.[63]

She took part in everything, year-round, but excelled in running and high jump. In 1930 she reached the point where she needed more coaching than Hayt Playground offered. The teacher in charge, Margaret Leimer, understood and appreciated Annette's exceptional talent and arranged for her to join the Illinois Women's Athletic Club. Leimer made early and lasting impressions on the future Olympian, who said "she instilled the importance of Good Sportsmanship in all of us." Her insistence that "it's nice to win, but the important thing is to participate" stayed with Rogers and posed no contradictions for her in her highly successful, decidedly competitive career.[64]

The DePaul coaches who helped the IWAC team at Lake Shore Playground often had an assist themselves from a man who worked as a chauffeur for a family who lived nearby. His tutoring, in a heavy German accent, further polished the young high jumper's skill. He taught Annette to turn and get her hips away from the bar as she went over, adding height to her scissors jump while ensuring that her feet would cross first. His coaching may be what kept her from harm's way in 1932 disputes surrounding the scissors jump and the legality of the Western Roll.[65]

In her second place finish at Jersey City, Rogers jumped just shy of the mark of defending champion Jean Shiley, who set a record in retaining her title that day. Annette went on to win the Central AAU 100-meter title in 1932 and a month later she entered the Olympic trials with winning momentum.[66]

Evelyne Ruth Hall went to Jersey City as a member of the IWAC team in 1931 to defend her national 80-meter hurdles title. Using her defending champion's travel money, she and husband Leonard drove east in their battered Studebaker. They returned to Chicago to retool her hurdling form and prepare for the Olympic trials.[67]

When Evelyne was born in Minneapolis, September 10, 1909, no prospect could have been more remote than a career in athletics. Her premature birth made survival doubtful, and she endured bouts with pneumonia and scarlet fever before she was ten years old. Her parents' divorce further complicated childhood. After her mother moved to Chicago, Evelyne lived for a few years in a Windy City orphanage until her mother remarried and brought Evelyne home.[68]

An only child in a neighborhood of large families, she learned to run as a survival skill. She said, "All the kids would sit on these high front steps on the tenement houses" in summer, and they divided into teams for games such as run-sheep-run. In winter they hitched sleds to passing cars. A favorite pastime was hopping onto ladders on in-coming boxcars to ride into nearby railroad switching yards. She be-came a real daredevil.[69]

For many Americans the Depression began long before the Wall Street crash, and parks and playgrounds were a godsend for their chil-dren. Evelyne made her start in athletics at the parks, and as a child, with a nickel for bus fare, she spent winter Saturdays at the Jewish People's Institute. The JPI welcomed everyone. Its exceptional facili-ties included a pool, and its athletes occasionally reached national com-petition. In summer she regularly entered dashes and cartwheel races at the many picnics sponsored by neighboring churches and syna-gogues. Chicago parks proved a magnet for her as a teenager. She recalled, "We used to just go over there and hang out, really," but she tried everything they offered. In 1926, a park instructor put her into her first true race, and, wearing a long-sleeved middy blouse and black bloomers, she won her first medal. She has always said, "[T]hat's what started me on the road."[70]

For Evelyne, 1927 was a milestone year in more than one respect. She left her first post–high school job in a Walgreen's Drug Store for work in an office, and on October 1 she married Leonard Hall. Hall was a pole-vaulter and broad jumper who worked for the telephone company. Later that winter, office coworker Nellie Todd, former na-tional broad jump champion, took her to the Illinois Women's Athletic Club.[71]

There she became a hurdler as well as a sprinter. When the woman in charge saw Evelyne go over IWAC's one hurdle in its small indoor gym, she entered her in the 50-yard hurdles at the Central AAU's track meet set for the following week. With no hurdling expe-rience, Evelyne placed second behind Helen Filkey, national outdoor 60-yard hurdle champion since 1925. Evelyne now had an event and a sponsor but no coach. Leonard took over the coaching role; from their very modest apartment on Chicago's South Side, the nearly penniless couple could not always make the long trip to Lake Shore Playground for team training sessions.[72]

When the AAU hurdle event changed from 60 yards to 80 meters in 1929, she and Leonard changed her style to accommodate the greater distance between hurdles. Rather than lengthening stride to the usual three between hurdles, their solution was to stay with four and alternate her lead foot going over the barriers. Evelyne would sail high over one and barely skim the next—ungainly to say the least. She used this approach for two years. Awkward or not, it took her to the national title in 1930, on a hot Fourth of July in Dallas, and to the national indoor 50-yard championship in 1931.[73]

At the Nationals in Jersey City that summer of 1931, she led off for IWAC's champion relay team with her incredibly fast start. In the preliminaries of the 80-meter hurdles she found herself in the same heat with Mildred Didrikson from Dallas, who was in her first national competition as a hurdler. They ran in adjacent lanes. Deciding to try three steps between hurdles, Evelyne matched the taller Didrikson stride for stride, but she lost a few inches each time. She hit the sixth hurdle, and in the finals, running on a swollen foot, she placed third behind Didrikson and Nellie Sharka of Newark. Although she lost her title, she discovered how much easier it was to bring the same foot over each time.[74]

She and Leonard spent the next year perfecting three-step form and working to get her lead foot down as soon as possible after clearing the hurdle. With a lot of hard work and customary determination, Evelyne was ready for the Olympic trials the following summer.

In Texas, where almost by definition everything is larger than life, athletes had sponsors of similar dimensions. In the early thirties, what has become the Dallas–Fort Worth "Metroplex" boasted thriving commercial and industrial recreation leagues. The Employers' Casualty Company of Dallas ran one of the best financed and most successful programs. Its women's teams, the Golden Cyclones, always challenged for championships. Employers' Casualty had a stellar publicity vehicle in its winning teams. To assure their successes the company provided its women athletes with "first-class equipment, excellent coaching, flamboyant uniforms of bright yellow or orange and plenty of time to practice."[75]

Additional ingredients of success came with their coach, "Colonel" Melvin J. McCombs. For thirty years he had coached both school and independent teams in Texas, Oklahoma, and Louisiana—football, baseball, basketball, and track. In 1924 he went to work for Employers' Casualty, and his job was specifically to develop Golden Cyclone teams. In the winter of 1930, on a basketball scouting trip in Houston, he made the discovery of the half century—a Beaumont High School junior named Mildred Didrikson.[76]

McCombs knew talent when he saw it, but could he possibly have imagined how far his discovery would go? Could he have known the extent of his protégé's ability? He would soon know how coachable she was, how willing to learn, and that she lived only for sports and loved and excelled in them all. He could hardly have guessed the number of records she would set. He surely did not foresee that she would virtually revolutionize golf for women, nor that a 1950 Associated Press poll would, by an overwhelming margin, name her woman athlete of the first half of the twentieth century.[77]

Mildred Ella Didrikson was born June 26, 1911, in Port Arthur, Texas, the sixth of seven children of Norwegian immigrants. The family moved to Beaumont when she was three, and she grew up in the shadow of the Magnolia Refinery in the oily grit of the city's south end. A tough, impoverished neighborhood spawned a combative, boasting, uncompromising, yet funny and entertaining young woman. With her enormous natural physical talent, honed in the rough-and-tumble of playing with the neighborhood boys on equal terms, she found sports her only way to get ahead. She never saw herself as anything but an athlete. In high school she kept grades just high enough to be eligible for the teams, and she played on them all—volleyball, tennis, golf, baseball, basketball, swimming.[78]

The family called her "Baby" when she was a child, but along the way she became "Babe." It was *Babe* Didrikson who finally gained her parents' permission to go to Dallas, work for Employers' Casualty for $75 a month, and play basketball for "the Colonel." She made her first appearance as a Golden Cyclone on February 18, 1930, the day after she left Beaumont High. Playing forward on a national champion team, she scored 195 points in six games one season and was twice named All-American.[79]

Her job classification was stenographer; in reality she was an Employers' Casualty athlete. In the spring of 1930, to keep her occupied when basketball season ended, Coach McCombs introduced her to track and field—javelin, baseball throw, shot put, high jump, and long jump. She practiced late into the night at Dallas's Lakeside Park to get ready for her first track meet, and she won the four events she entered. The AAU held its 1930 Nationals in Dallas. In her own backyard she won baseball throw and javelin titles and charged onto a path leading to track and field history and controversy.[80]

She reaped a golden harvest of publicity as a basketball player. By the summer of 1931, Babe had the admiring eye of the entire sports press at the Nationals in Jersey City. Even the *New York Times*'s Arthur Daley, not at all inclined to praise women athletes, waxed enthusiastic. He began by saying, "A new feminine athletic marvel catapulted herself to the forefront as an American Olympic possibility at Pershing Field." He called her "this remarkably versatile girl" and noted her newly set records in the baseball throw and broad jump, saying the "crowd of 15,000 looked on in amazement." Of her new world's record for the 80-meter hurdles, Daley said, "Her timber-topping effort was far and away her finest performance. She streaked over the sticks with the utmost finesse. . . . [T]he crowd fairly gasped as she flew over the barriers."[81]

The young Texan caused immense excitement that day. Evelyne Hall, who lost her 80-meter hurdles title to Babe that afternoon, remembered the "spectators got out of hand" and "it was just bedlam." The crowd poured out of the stands to get closer to the phenomenal new star, and mounted police moved in to clear the field.[82]

Legend and myth tend to assume lives of their own. The sports press was present at the dawn of the Didrikson legend and, in reporting it, allowed more than a little myth to creep in. The sports press had held the country in thrall for a decade. Half a century later its hyperbole and occasional fabrication sound dated and more than a bit quaint, but it still had tremendous appeal in 1932. Readers devoured columns written by such giants of journalism as Grantland Rice, Damon Runyan, and Paul Gallico. In the case of "The Babe," embellishments were hardly necessary—her unprecedented accomplishments spoke for themselves.

Shrewd promoters in Dallas exploited the power of the press to publicize their superstar. The promotion and ballyhoo had begun al-

most with her first national titles in 1930; she soon became an enter-
tainer familiar to Dallas radio fans. Other athletes at the Jersey City
Nationals who had known her before felt Babe had changed since the
1930 meet. She appeared to have managers or handlers who catered
to her every need and want. She was cockier and "not nearly as
friendly" as the year before.[83]

By the time of the AAU national meet in 1932, which coincided
with the Olympic trials, "she had become a prima donna: petulant,
unreasonable."[84] Colonel McCombs decided that she would be Employers' Casualty's sole entrant in that meet; the rest of the team would
stay behind. The company was willing to underwrite all her expenses
for the six weeks up to and including the Games in Los Angeles. What
better vehicle than a victorious one-woman track team could a sponsor desire? McCombs devised a strenuous training program for her,
and she worked at it full-time through the spring and into the summer. She repeated again and again that she intended to enter nine
events and win them all.[85]

Acclaim mounted in the press. Some writers, for instance those
who would have deplored 1928's 800-meter event in Amsterdam, may
have had mixed feelings about the phenomenal athlete whose persona
did not come close to the ideal of womanhood. Many may have
agreed with Paul Gallico that she was a "muscle moll," and with his description of her as "a hard-bitten, hawk-nosed, thin-mouthed little
hoyden from Texas."[86] All probably appreciated the feminine emphasis in the reports of her chaperoned departure for Chicago and the
Olympic trials.

> Chic-looking in pink raiment, including her first hat and also
> her first purse, one of white leather, the Babe was sent away to the
> tune of cheers from her Cyclone teammates, her coach, Col.
> Melvin J. McCombs, and other office associates. She radiated
> confidence.[87]

A battery of cameramen met her and her chaperone, Mrs. Henry
Wood, at the station in Chicago. At their hotel the next morning more
photographers caught them before their visit to the national AAU
offices.[88] The twenty-one-year-old Texan probably was the only competitor to receive a personal welcome to Chicago from Avery
Brundage.

★ ★ ★

With or without the personal greeting of the new president of the American Olympic Committee, as it was then known, competitors arrived in Chicago from the West Coast throughout the week of July 11. A Southern California delegation of Lillian Copeland, Anne O'Brien, and Simone Schaller left Los Angeles by train on the tenth. Evelyn Furtsch, her mother, and Coach Humeston retraced their 1931 crossing of the Mojave Desert, heading for Chicago along Route 66 in his un-airconditioned sedan. On this trip they turned north through Iowa for a stop in Ames, so Evelyn could run on the track at Iowa State College.[89]

Three San Francisco Bay–area athletes arrived in Chicago on Monday, the eleventh. Besides discus thrower Margaret Jenkins, the others sponsored by the Western Women's Club were Gloria Russell and Wilhelmina von Bremen.[90]

The Western Women's Club, a posh social and residential club, would seem an unlikely sponsor for track athletes in 1932. Its handsome building at Sutter and Mason in the heart of downtown San Francisco housed a swimming pool, but the club had no athletic programs. One 1932 Olympian, swimmer Eleanor Garatti Saville, belonged to the club as a social member. When it appeared the track and field women from the area would remain "unattached," the club was persuaded to stand as sponsor for them for the Olympic trials. It assumed no responsibility, however, financial or otherwise. Sometime in the late 1930s the Western Women's Club vacated its splendid home for smaller quarters. It finally vanished entirely, perhaps a victim of the Depression or World War II.[91]

Gloria Russell arrived in Chicago to throw the javelin. She was born January 24, 1912, in Eureka, California, but her adoptive family had long lived in Oakland. She was a regular in Bay Area track and field competitions, and under the banner of the Northern California Athletic Club she had won the baseball throw national championship in 1929. Gloria's parents supported her wholeheartedly in athletics and thrilled to her success. Her father owned an upholstery business, and he endeared himself to her California teammates by making canvas equipment bags for the discus and other gear—no small thing in the days before nylon tote bags with corporate logos or designer signatures.[92]

Prankish and gamine-like, with straight blond hair, Gloria had a great sense of humor. She was forever playing tricks, full of fun and always laughing. Teammates remembered that even when something went wrong, Gloria would laugh it off. When the train pulled into Chicago on July 11, she was ready for the trials—javelin, pranks, jokes, and all.[93]

Another promising athlete on the train from San Francisco was tall, blonde, blue-eyed Wilhelmina von Bremen, also sponsored by the Western Women's Club. The twenty-two-year-old native San Franciscan, a graduate of its High School of Commerce, worked six days a week as an accountant for the Emporium department store. At 5 feet 10½ inches, she was a standout on the store's basketball team and a winner in track.[94]

Billie, as everyone called her, delighted in athletics, and said, "If I never had taken a trophy in my life, I would still feel that playing on the company basketball team and going out for track were worthwhile, because of the added joy they have been." She further revealed her priorities when she said in 1932, "I enjoy every minute of my life, because there is so much to do, but right now winning a place in the Olympics is the all important thing."[95]

She spent most Sundays on the track, and the Emporium allowed her two afternoons a week to train for the upcoming Games. Her performance improved day by day. Primarily a sprinter, she ran beautifully with long, fluid strides. She held no national track and field titles until that summer of 1932, when she won the 100 meters in 12.3 seconds. Happy, friendly von Bremen became a team favorite, a tenacious competitor in Chicago, and the gold medal hope at Los Angeles that summer.[96]

The city of Chicago had always maintained outstanding park and recreation facilities and programs. Its famed South Park District served as a national model. During the twenties and into the thirties its Board of Education Playgrounds offered sports programs and competition for neighborhood youngsters. Chicago was one focal point of the great northward migration of African Americans from the South that began in the 1890s. One sociologist wrote in the mid-twenties that some of those Chicago playgrounds were "the only facilities offered the colored youth in the black belt."[97] In 1932 one young African

American from the playgrounds represented her hometown in the Olympic trials.

Tidye Pickett was a seventeen-year-old student at Englewood High School that year. Englewood, south and west of the black belt, had at the turn of the century become home to upper- and middle-class African American families.[98]

The Picketts lived just across from Washington Park, and Tidye started running there. She entered races at picnics sponsored by the *Chicago Daily News* and soon began taking home all the prizes. Then she caught the eye of gym teacher Pearl Greene at the Carter School Playground. Miss Greene added her to the track team. Tidye, at barely five feet three and a hundred pounds, could outrun everyone. At an invitational meet in the Armory on Cottage Grove Avenue, she met John Brooks, who went on to qualify for the 1936 Olympic team himself as a long jumper. Tidye was on her way in track and field after Brooks sought and got her mother's permission to be her trainer. She later said he outfitted her with proper running shoes and sweats, adding, "And that was it—I'm gone!"[99]

Working with Brooks, Tidye became an outstanding hurdler and broad jumper as well as a sprinter. She soon began running in citywide meets and traveling to competitions across the country, winning everything she entered.[100] By July 17, 1932, she had reached peak condition to try for a spot on the Olympic team.

Chicago's energetic tumult, the cool sophistication of San Francisco, and the glitter and flash of Los Angeles seemed light-years away from small-town, rural mid-America in 1932. Farms in the heartland did not yet enjoy the benefits of electrification, and few paved roads linked them with market towns. Dusty crossroads hamlets still claimed their identities with post office, general store, and a gasoline pump.

Shelbyville, Missouri, population 704, was the county seat, but by 1932 neighboring Shelbina was the largest town in Shelby County. Those two communities, about 50 miles west of Mark Twain's Hannibal, had a spirited sports rivalry. Fred Schwengel, history teacher and all-purpose coach at Shelbina High School, had to admit that the rival girls' basketball team was by far the better. He attributed this to their center, "one of the world's best athletes—Ruth Osburn."[101]

Known throughout Shelby County as "Casey," the dark-haired, five-foot-eleven-inch high school junior was a standout athlete in all sports. Coach Schwengel, a college discus and 220 man in track, appreciated her great talent. In the spring of 1932 he told Shelbyville boosters that Ruth Osburn was good enough for the upcoming Olympic Games in Los Angeles; all she needed was a coach. Civic pride responded and every evening someone drove Ruth the seven miles to Shelbina so she could train with Schwengel's track team.[102]

Ruth Osburn was born and raised on her family's farm west of Shelbyville. She had three older brothers and three sisters. She helped her father on the farm, and the two of them became close companions. When he died suddenly in January 1932, the family moved into town. Ruth was at loose ends, even with basketball in the after-school hours. Her brother Morris, who was then Shelby County Prosecutor, virtually insisted that she take up track and field to fill the void in her life.[103]

Ruth proved unbelievably coachable when Schwengel began to work with her. He handed her a discus for the first time on April 5. A month later she threw it 108 feet 2¼ inches to win the title at the Missouri Valley AAU championship meet, which also served as preliminary Olympic trials. She took first in the baseball throw, shot put, and javelin that day as well.[104]

She sprained an ankle playing baseball soon after that and had to put Olympic training on hold. That was only the first setback. Remembering 1932, Ruth said, "I just about killed myself that summer." Riding with a friend in his small, open, Indy-type race car, she received facial cuts, broken ribs, a wrenched shoulder, and assorted bruises when the car flipped into a triple roll-over in loose gravel. A very worried Coach Schwengel immediately took his protégé to the osteopathic school in Kirksville for an assessment of her damaged arm.[105]

She could not even throw a baseball, but her sprained ankle had healed by then and she could run. Every morning and evening she bundled her arm in alternating hot and cold packs, and she ran. Twenty-five days before the Olympic trials, she went to live with the Schwengels and resumed serious training. They concentrated on throwing the discus and she showed remarkable improvement. Within two weeks she could hurl it beyond 130 feet, and the entire county followed her progress through reports in the *Shelby County Herald*.[106]

Calling herself "just a green kid who had been raised on a farm," Ruth later said she had not realized fully that spring what the Olympic Games meant, but she had fun working with Coach Schwengel to prepare for the trials. In a little over three weeks after the auto mishap, Casey Osburn's cuts, bruises, and fractures had improved considerably. While her arm had not reached pre-crash condition, she still planned to enter javelin, shot put, and discus at the Olympic trials. She made the trip to Chicago with Fred and Ethel Schwengel, riding in the rumbleseat of their Model A Ford.[107]

As the drama of injury and recovery unfolded in Shelby County, on the other side of the state, in Kansas City, another promising athlete prepared for the Olympic trials. She, too, had won at the Missouri Valley Track and Field Championships on May 14. She, too, returned home to work hard with her coach for the next two months.

Elizabeth Wilde had just graduated from Loretto Academy, a secondary school operated in Kansas City by the Sisters of Loretto. The Academy's physical education teacher, Virginia Oliver, certainly did not have the "no competition for girls" mentality. She encouraged Elizabeth in all sports. Basketball was almost a given for the five-foot-eight-inch Elizabeth, as it had been for so many others, and when track season arrived Elizabeth really came into her own.[108]

Virginia Oliver had determined that Elizabeth should go as far as possible with track. Her husband, a math teacher in the city's public schools, became a willing aide, and they took Elizabeth to all the meets. She competed in a variety of events—high jump, standing and running broad jump among them—and held the Kansas City high jump record for several years. But she made her mark as a sprinter.[109]

She won the 100-meter race at the Missouri Valley meet in Columbia with a time of 12.3 seconds. Coach Oliver took her newly qualified runner back to Kansas City, and they set to work preparing for the trials. For the next two months Elizabeth practiced at the high school tracks, running against the boys' teams. She spent a lot of time perfecting her starts, and to get her to extend herself Oliver would start her off 50 yards behind the boys. She soon could overtake them.[110]

Elizabeth Wilde was born October 18, 1913, in Kansas City. Her father, a furrier, had followed his brother from Germany a few years earlier and they established a family fur business. They did not use

English at home, and German-speaking Elizabeth found her early years in school difficult. The language barrier finally melted, and the years at Loretto Academy prepared her well for college.[111] The Academy also sponsored her Olympic bid, sending her and the Olivers to the trials in Chicago.

By the time the Missourians drove up to Chicago with their coaches, most of the young women had arrived from across the country. The majority came by train, but rail fare was beyond the reach of some. Four representatives of the Medford Girls Club drove from New England, pooling Mary Carew's AAU defending champion's travel money with funds raised at dances and raffles. To save money, Jean Shiley drove with a high school classmate, a reporter for the *Philadelphia Record*, rather than taking the train with the Newark team as she usually did.[112]

They had come to Chicago by way of the 1928 Olympics in Amsterdam, the 1931 Nationals in Jersey City, the Missouri Valley Championships, and other regional qualifying meets held earlier in the year. Those who had been on the circuit for a while knew many of their rivals before the trials. Some had never before ventured into national competition. Their backing ranged from the likes of the prestigious Illinois Women's Athletic Club to the civic boosters of Shelbyville, Missouri. Some came as unheralded as a Simone Schaller or a Tidye Pickett, while Babe Didrikson arrived with publicity, promotion, and hype such as no woman athlete before her had received.

Before two hundred contenders had been winnowed to seventeen, they would provide athletic exploits, drama, and controversy. Records would come and go in the process of selecting the second women's Olympic track and field team in the nation's history.

3 | Track
And
Field
Trials

★

Chicago played host to a good many famous guests in the summer of 1932. New York Gov. Franklin D. Roosevelt broke with tradition and set a travel precedent on July 2 when he flew from Albany to accept the Democratic Party's presidential nomination in person at Chicago Stadium. The nine-hour flight was the first ever by a potential president. He broke more new ground in announcing a campaign that would rely extensively on the comparatively new medium of radio.[1]

On that same July weekend the Central AAU held its men's track and field championships on the Northwestern University campus in Evanston. Sprinters Frank Metcalfe and Eddie Tolan commanded the sports pages, as they would in Los Angeles. The meet, billed as Olympic semifinal trials, used the same Dyche Stadium cinder track that the women would use on July 16.[2]

The upcoming International Golden Gloves tournament crowded other topics from the *Tribune*'s sports section. The paper predicted a turnout of 40,000 at Soldier Field on July 26 for bouts between American and German amateur boxers. Some of the Germans were members of their Olympic boxing team and would go on to Los Angeles.[3]

Fabled racehorse Equipoise received more press in Chicago than the Olympic hopefuls in the weeks preceding the women's trials. The one big story in women's track in early July centered on Stella Walsh, cornerstone of the New York Central Railroad's Cleveland track team.[4]

Stella, the first woman to run 100 yards in under eleven seconds, wore sweats with "Twentieth Century Limited" printed across the back of the shirt. She turned in record times more often than the crack streamliner did between New York and Chicago. Born in Poland on April 11, 1911, Stella had just announced her intention to become a United States citizen. She was set to try for a spot on the U.S. Olympic team when the railroad terminated her job, and suddenly her future in running became secondary to earning a living. On July 12, the day before she was to take out naturalization papers, she accepted a job in the Polish Consulate in New York and made plans to run for Poland in Los Angeles. She took a heavy barrage of criticism in the press for that decision.[5]

The city of Cleveland had offered Stella a job in its Recreation Department but she rejected it. Fred Steers, chairman of the AAU women's track and field committee, had warned her that taking a job related to physical education would render her a professional and thus ineligible for Olympic competition. She did not intend to become a professional, saying "there's no fun in it."[6] There was also no money in it in 1932.

Press coverage of the women's Olympic trials began the Tuesday Babe Didrikson arrived in Chicago. She came to enter eight events and brashly said she expected to win them all, win the AAU team title, and qualify for several Olympic events. The *New York Times,* usually not much interested in women's athletics, announced: "Miss Mildred Didrikson, the sensational young lady from Dallas, Texas, is expected to be the standout of the meet." It went on to herald all the athletes as "the pick of the [nation's] talent with the exception of . . . [Stella] Walsh of Cleveland."[7] Stella's absence cleared the way on the field and in the news for Babe's ascent to stardom.

The visiting athletes stayed in hotels or with friends and relatives throughout the Greater Chicago area. California's entire delegation stayed in a dormitory on Northwestern's campus, just a block from the stadium. Temperatures ranged over 100 degrees, and the humidity of a Chicago summer made sleep all but impossible before the early morning hours.

Workouts at Dyche Stadium were light in the few days leading up to the meet. The Illinois Women's Athletic Club team practiced under Frank Loomis, 400-meter hurdle gold medalist at Antwerp in 1920. He rated their chances very good and said, "if effort means anything, they are bound to win." He had caught the out-of-towners appraising the team's workouts, and few of them disputed that IWAC was the team to beat.[8]

Individual Illinois women played down their prospects. Nan Gindele modestly vowed to try to beat her own javelin world record, adding, "I am glad to hold the javelin record as much as I was surprised to win it." Ethel Harrington hoped to qualify for the Olympic sprint relay. With considerable reserve she said she enjoyed train travel and "would like to go to California." Sprinter and high jumper Annette Rogers, quietly confident, aimed to jump 5 feet 4 inches in the trials and said she expected six IWAC athletes to be on the Olympic team.[9]

Babe Didrikson, anything but modest, confined her training to "long walks and one gymnasium workout." Colonel McCombs had originally intended for her to compete in all ten events. At the last minute he held Babe out of the 200 meters and the 50-yard dash because she was still slow on starts. Neither was an Olympic event, and to run them would only sap her strength.[10] Texas-sized boasts and claims did not allow for finishing second.

Had people been paying much attention to details, they might have wondered how competing in eight events that day squared with the AAU rules of competition.

> No woman shall be allowed to compete in more than three events in one day, of which three events not more than two shall be track events. . . . The relay shall count as one track event.
>
> —Rules of the Amateur Athletic Union
> in force January 1, 1932[11]

The battles to control women's track and field undoubtedly had left the AAU looking over its collective shoulder. They saw the "three event rule" as helping to ease doubts over health and safety and to disarm critics of competition. The 800-meter debacle in Amsterdam in 1928 ensured that the rule would stand. Fred Steers, now Olympic team manager as well as chairman of the women's track and field committee of the AAU, had been on that committee since 1922. Always mindful of the pitfalls, he had effectively enforced regulations on competition and amateur standing. Why he did not do so in 1932 is not known. Earlier in July, the Dallas press had reported that at the coming trials and national championships "competition will be thrown wide open, contestants being allowed to enter as many events as they desire."[12] Texans perhaps knew something the others did not.

After the trials, Babe charged Steers with harassing and hampering her in Evanston, and continued the accusation during and after the Games themselves. According to a letter Babe wrote to McCombs from Evanston, Steers apparently did not acquiesce easily in the matter of the three-event limit.

> Gosh but Steers was mad. He wasn't going to let me enter eight events and he said that I would just have to scratch so I told him that I was supposed to enter eight and . . . when they called the events I just went on over and got into them.[13]

No one claims anyone could have matched Babe Didrikson's versatility, but wider knowledge of any rule waiver could have allowed others to prepare for more than three events. The rule suspension propelled Didrikson further to the forefront as the "one woman track team" from Texas.

Saturday, July 16, brought a hot and humid morning to Greater Chicago, and by afternoon it would be sweltering in Evanston. Sleep patterns had more or less adjusted, but butterflies of anxiety made it difficult to rest completely. Having claimed victory before the fact, Babe Didrikson was ripe for a large share of anxiety. She recalled that she did not get to sleep until daybreak and then overslept. On a frantic taxi ride between her hotel and Dyche Stadium, she changed into her track suit in the back seat while chaperone Wood held a blanket around her.[14]

A crowd of 5,000 was on hand when the Evanston American Legion Post's drum and bugle corps led an Olympic-style parade of athletes into the stadium. Two hundred women from twenty-two states shared parade honors with the Hungarian swimming team and Finnish track and field athletes. Both teams were in Chicago en route to Los Angeles.[15]

At two o'clock the meet began. When the Employers' Casualty

team was introduced, the crowd roared a greeting to the Texan whose
fame and confident predictions had preceded her. She rushed from
heat to heat and event to event, and the crowd had little chance to pay
much attention to anyone else. Babe's eight-event afternoon created a
logistical nightmare. Events were held up to accommodate her, and
other athletes frequently had to sit for long stretches between heats.[16]

Even though they had to wait for Babe to finish and for photographers to record her exploits, all the athletes made dynamic and com-
pelling contributions to the competition. To the sports reporter of the
Northwestern University student newspaper, their good humor and
obvious enjoyment in competing "seemed to take the audience in its
grasp and make this meet one of human as well as physical interest."[17]

With the running of the 80-meter hurdles, the second act opened
in a drama begun the year before in Jersey City. Evelyne Hall had perfected her hurdling technique after losing her title to Babe at the 1931
Nationals. In the preliminaries in Dyche Stadium she did 11.8 seconds
to Babe's 11.9. Both were below Didrikson's national mark of 12 seconds flat. In the finals, Babe barely nipped Evelyne at the tape. In a
show reminiscent of the 100-meters judging in Jersey City, the place
judges may have inadvertently allowed promotional hype to become
self-fulfilling prophecy. Evelyne recalled hearing the first-place judges
announcing her as the winner and the second-place judges naming
her for second as well; in the confusion, the clerk of the course said of
Didrikson, "Well, she must have been first." Babe took the title again
in 12.1 seconds.[18]

The by now old adversaries claimed two of the three hurdle spots
on the Olympic team. The third went to Pasadena's Simone Schaller.
Of the trials in Evanston she said, "I ran my darnedest—I wanted to
make that team so badly—of course everybody did—it was quite an
experience. Actually, that was the first big meet I had been in." For
Schaller, as for many of the others, this was also her first encounter
with Babe, and she soon got the impression that Babe "was pretty sure
of herself."[19]

Developments at the high jump bar also built tension and suspense.
Babe had only recently added high jump to her phenomenal list of
skills, and she used the Western Roll—a jumping style popular then

with male jumpers. (The "Fosbury Flop" was beyond imagination.) She told a reporter after the trials in Evanston, "I'm the only girl, as far as I know, that jumped western style, like the boys. I lie flat over the stick instead of sitting up."[20] This fairly well describes the Western Roll, which, with the jumper rolling across the bar horizontally, could come close to diving.

It allowed greater height over the bar, but it also allowed a greater chance for the head to cross the bar first. And in 1932 the rules for women explicitly stated:

> A fair jump is one where the head of the contestant does not go
> over the bar before the feet. . . . Neither diving nor somersaulting
> over the bar shall be permitted.

Coach Lawson Robertson advised Jean Shiley to forget the Western Roll and stick with the conventional, upright, foot-first scissors jump to avoid any chance of fouling. The coaching Annette Rogers received at the Lake Shore Playground also stressed the proper form of scissors jump.[21]

The high jumpers knew Babe Didrikson only by headline reputation and newspaper quote. Annette Rogers recalled having to wait at the high jump for Babe to finish other events, but she said, "I don't think I said two words to Babe—she took off from the right side, I took off from the left." Jean Shiley had gone to meets in Texas but had not competed against Babe before the trials in Evanston.[22] This first meeting between the two began a competition that culminated in one of Olympic history's more enduring controversies.

On that hot afternoon in Evanston, tension mounted as jumpers were slowly eliminated. One who went out at 4 feet 8 inches protested Babe's style, insisting it was diving. At the end of the day, Rogers had clinched the third high jump spot on the Olympic team. Babe tied with defending champion Shiley at 5 feet 3 $\frac{13}{16}$ inches as they broke the world record set by Carolina Gisolf of the Netherlands.[23] The high jump drama reached a climax when they all met three weeks later in Los Angeles.

The javelin event, added to Olympic competition in 1932 to replace the 800 meters, calls for the excellent all-around athlete with good running speed, coordination, excellent timing, and strength. The contestants who gathered at the javelin runway in Dyche Stadium met the criteria. Californian Gloria Russell placed third to qualify for the Olympic team. Nan Gindele of the Illinois Women's Athletic Club did not equal her world record throw that afternoon and she placed second. Babe took the title and qualified for a third Olympic event with a throw of 139 feet 3 inches.[24]

The trials produced some surprises, including the discus outcome. Margaret Jenkins and Lillian Copeland, both former national javelin champions, lost their bids to qualify in the javelin. They gained places on their second Olympic team, however, by placing second and third respectively in the discus. Copeland had won the discus silver medal in Amsterdam, but she could not match Ruth Osburn's record-breaking throw in Evanston that day. Babe Didrikson placed fourth and did not qualify for the Olympic discus.[25]

Ruth had concentrated on the discus while recovering from her injuries, so Coach Fred Schwengel decided just before the trials that she should drop all except discus to save the arm that had not regained full strength. That afternoon he told her, "Give it all you've got on the first throw, you may not have a second." The athlete who said she "trained out in the cow pasture" made the most of it, sending the discus 133 feet 3¾ inches. This bettered the world record held since 1929 by Poland's Halina Konopacka and placed Ruth on the Olympic team.[26]

The memory of searing heat stayed with all the athletes. As the afternoon wore on, the mercury climbed past 100. Jean Shiley remembered, "[I]t was so hot that one of the girls ordered a 100-pound block of ice and we all took turns sitting on it."[27]

The temperature was brutal on the cinder track, where it took seven preliminary heats, quarter- and semifinal heats, and finals to qualify sprinters for the 100 meters and the 4 × 100-meter relay. Judging and decisions as controversial as waiving the three-event rule marked the sprint trials.

In the first preliminary heat, Elizabeth Wilde came in first and Mary Carew second. Billie von Bremen and Louise Stokes placed first and second in the third, and Evelyn Furtsch and Tidye Pickett won the fourth and fifth heats. Pasadena's Anne O'Brien ran ahead of Babe

Didrikson to win the seventh. Annette Rogers entered the 100 meters as well as high jump, but, wearing new shoes, she lost the left one in the preliminary and finished out of the running.[28]

Hot, humid air and the long delays sapped energy. To save Elizabeth Wilde's stamina and leg strength for the following heat, Coach Oliver's husband carried her from the finish line each time.[29]

In a puzzling development, IWAC's Ethel Harrington, running well ahead, stopped 10 yards short of the wire in her preliminary heat. She did not move on to the quarter-finals, so sprinters who reached the finals and had already run three times under the unrelenting sun were surprised to find Harrington at the starting line as a seventh entrant. It probably came as no surprise that she won the final heat after having run only about 80 meters so far that afternoon.[30]

Harrington's appearance in the 100-meter final was due to the most baffling decision of the day. She apparently thought she had crossed the finish line in her heat and simply stopped. Officials huddled and decided to let her enter the finals and try for a place on the Olympic team, but not for the AAU title, which went to second-place finisher von Bremen. Elizabeth Wilde placed third after posting the day's fastest time, 12.4, in her preliminary heat. Three other Olympic qualifiers were Mary Carew and Louise Stokes, tied for fourth, and Tidye Pickett.[31]

Missing at the wire was Evelyn Furtsch, who had run the 100 meters earlier that summer in 11.8. Running hard and challenging for the lead, she fell barely short of the finish line and lost a sure place on the team. The Dyche Stadium track was as good as any around Chicago, but late in the day the cinder surface had begun to show wear. One sprinter had complained that "holes were all chopped up and the track was terrible." Coach Humeston thought she stumbled over a clinker on the track. Evelyn said, "The track was pretty well chopped up—other than that I have no excuses."[32]

In theory, the six finalists automatically qualified for the Olympics. The addition of Harrington in a seventh lane created a dilemma that was more than logistical. Some drama attended this, as the *Chicago Defender* reported. One of the city's leading, influential African American institutions, the *Defender* heralded Tidye Pickett and Louise Stokes for having won places on the Olympic team. There was no question about Stokes's placing, but the *Defender* said, "Miss Pickett will have to thank George T. Donoghue, member of the South Park commission and one of the judges, for her success." In sixth place, she had qualified for an Olympic berth. When officials allowed Harrington to compete in the finals and win, the *Defender* continued:

> Miss Pickett became seventh and was thus automatically out of it. Then Mr. Donoghue stepped up and fought for Tidye's place in the finals in view of the charity being shown the other girl. Mr. Donoghue, white, is to be congratulated for his fairness in the Race girl's behalf.

Not using the term "Negro," with which virtually every newspaper in the country prefaced all references to either Pickett or Stokes, the *Chicago Defender* held to its policy of referring to "Race men," or, as in this case, "Race girl."[33]

By the end of the day, Babe Didrikson had completely captivated the nation's sports press and stood ready to assume a legend's mantle. She now owned five individual national championships—80-meter hurdles, javelin, shot put, baseball throw, broad jump—a tie for first in the high jump, and three newly established world records. She reaped the greatest harvest in both press and legend by piling up enough total points to win the national team championship as well. The one-woman-track-team label stuck, to be picked up and amplified by sports columnists in Los Angeles.

The notoriety of the solo performance may have extracted a price. The Golden Cyclones left behind in Dallas had been denied an Olympic opportunity. Many of them had come to resent Babe and to detest "her swaggering, me-first attitude." A Cyclones teammate told Babe's biographer, "She was built up by this man McCombs . . . she was out for Babe, honey, just Babe. . . . She was not a team player. . . . Babe was out for fame."[34]

Her new Olympic teammates readily acknowledged her extraordinary ability and versatility. However, they hardly could have enjoyed an Associated Press article that appeared in newspapers from coast to coast. The AP proclaimed:

> Miss Mildred (Babe) Didrikson of Dallas, Texas, will lead the American women's Olympic track and field team, and such assis-

tance as she may need against the foreign invasion will be provided by fourteen other young women.[35]

After that day in Evanston some began to wonder why she had been allowed to enter so many events. No one openly challenged it— not at a time when few young women questioned authority. But the bending of rules and schedules to accommodate her while inconveniencing all the others sowed the seeds for resentment of Babe and her relentless promotion.

Several possible explanations exist for waiving the three-event rule for the Texas Babe. One might assume it was because she alone *was* the team, but not when Employers' Casualty purposely kept its other athletes in Dallas. Track and field for women was still a fairly new province for the AAU, and the advantages of a genuine superstar to generate publicity would be very appealing. Dallas and North Texas, with strong amateur programs, apparently wanted a greater voice in AAU affairs. According to George White, columnist and champion of Babe's claims against Fred Steers, an AAU official had gone to Dallas early in 1932 to study the situation and try "to pacify the rebellious local leaders." White said they feared North Texas might pull out of the AAU after the Olympics, taking with them substantial contributions to the AAU's treasury.[36] Suspending the three-event rule could seem a simple way to placate them.

AAU politics made for strange compromises, and once the rules were breached it was difficult to deny other claimants. Special dispensation for Babe and unusual consideration for Chicago's Ethel Harrington surely figured in another instance.

When the newly chosen Olympic team's train left Chicago, a deeply disappointed Evelyn Furtsch was not on board. She and her mother were on their way back to California, driving Route 66 again with Coach Humeston. Before they left, in view of all that had happened, Humeston put in a call to Aileen Allen in Evelyn's behalf.[37]

Aileen Allen had long experience with AAU and Olympic officials and politics, dating back to 1916. The AAU charged her with professionalism that year in the first such case involving a woman swimmer. But the Board of Governors deemed hers an honest mistake and allowed her to continue in good standing.[38]

As 1932 Team Chaperone, with three Olympiads already to her

credit, Allen had some influence. She knew full well what Evelyn Furtsch could do in the 100 meters. In all likelihood Allen called in a few political debts for the sake of Evelyn's potential contribution to the team. At any rate, when the trio arrived at the Furtsch home in Tustin, Evelyn's father greeted them with the news that she had made the team after all and they wanted her in Los Angeles immediately. She said, "We turned right around and headed for the Chapman Park," the team's headquarters hotel.[39]

The track and field women left Chicago's Union Station Monday morning, July 18. They traveled in their own Pullman car that displayed a banner announcing "The U.S. Olympic Team." They all relished the trip, but still having heard so little about the Olympics, some visualized just another track meet ahead.[40]

Few of them had ever traveled on a "sleeper," and some of the younger ones had never been away from home for so long a time. Elizabeth Wilde had left Kansas City with only an overnight bag and few expectations. She left Chicago with the same overnight bag; it had to suffice until her mother met her in Los Angeles later with more clothes.[41]

When she learned that no athlete's coach could go with the team, Ruth Osburn refused to go without Fred Schwengel. She went back to Shelbyville, where her brother Morris convinced her to make the trip. He saw to it that she met the train and got aboard at Ames, Iowa.[42]

Funding for the Games in that deepest year of the Depression presented an enormous problem for the Olympic Committee. Chicago area team members had to provide $500 toward their travel expenses. Family, friends, and Alderman Frank Keenan of Chicago's 49th Ward pitched in to help Annette Rogers raise her share.[43]

The team stopped in Denver for a break in the long trip to the coast. The Mile-High City welcomed them for an overnight stay in the elegant Brown Palace Hotel. They worked out at Denver University's stadium on Wednesday morning, and later made guest appearances on a radio broadcast. At the stadium, team manager Fred Steers predicted they would win the Olympic title, break some records, and take at least three gold medals. The Texas phenomenon seized the limelight at the radio station, making predictions, and playing the harmonica; she even managed to gain the microphone during interviews with other athletes. By now the team knew Babe had to have center stage. Jean Shiley later said, "If you weren't paying any attention to her she would reach in her pocket and get out her harmonica and start to play—and she played it *very well*."[44]

The Brown Palace saluted the team with a banquet, but the occasion left two of the young women with the taste of ashes. Louise Stokes and Tidye Pickett, far from being honored in the ballroom, had dinner that night in their room. The reality and true pain of discrimination first hit them when they were separated from the rest of the team and assigned a room near a service area on an upper floor. Recalling the humiliating indignity, Pickett said, "All the other girls had private rooms, went to the banquet, were interviewed by the reporters. Louise and I shared a room in the attic and ate our dinners upstairs on trays."[45]

Back on the train, more of the country flashed past and enthusiastic crowds hailed the team at every stop. It was a trip to remember. Babe made sure that all the passengers knew who she was—to the extreme embarrassment of some teammates. She and the fun-loving Gloria Russell kept the other athletes on their toes. Pillow fights filled the air with feathers, and lower berth curtains provided perfect cover for frequent ice showers on the unsuspecting. The Californians were going home, but most of the others had never been so far west. Evelyne Hall, among them, cherished the whole experience. Remembering that the stop in San Bernardino gave the first true "feel" of California, she said, "That was marvelous. That's where we really saw the orange trees. You can imagine Midwestern people seeing orange trees—and palm trees —they were just glorious. We were just lifted into a completely new world."[46]

One order of business remained for the team before they reached Los Angeles—electing a team captain. They nominated Jean Shiley, Lillian Copeland, and Babe Didrikson. Some maintain Babe would never have been chosen; nonetheless, with an eye toward future team harmony, Copeland withdrew to avoid siphoning votes from Shiley, who subsequently won the election.[47]

Their train pulled into the Union Pacific's Los Angeles station at 8:30 in the morning of July 23. They debarked in high spirits, singing "Hail, Hail, the Gang's All Here," and other standard songs of celebration. Jean Shiley met the press to speak officially for the team. She modestly said they "were by no means overconfident," and intended to train seriously and do their very best. In their interview with the one-woman–track-team, reporters immediately asked Babe how many events she would enter. She said, "As many as they'll let me. How about four, coach?" Team coach George Vreeland replied that three would do it.[48] Olympic rules would prove inflexible.

After posing for a group photograph in front of the station, they boarded buses to the Chapman Park Hotel, their home for the next three weeks. There the young Americans shared with counterparts from abroad, most meeting foreign nationals for the first time. Olympic enthusiasm escalated in Los Angeles and the magic of Hollywood added to the excitement. What some had thought just another trip to just another track meet had become the trip of a lifetime.

4 | Swimming And Diving Glamour Athletes

★

The Olympic swimming and diving trials drew a large field and attracted throngs of spectators to Jones Beach on the south shore of New York's Long Island. Socially acceptable women's swimming had become a popular spectator sport early in the twenties as well as an established event in the Olympic Games. Almost a year to the day before the 1932 trials, the annual water derby sponsored by the *New York Daily News* drew a crowd of 50,000 to the lake near the Mall in Central Park.[1]

The Amateur Athletic Union took control of women's swimming in 1914 only after a long debate about modesty and proper attire. Ever alert to decorum and responsibility, in 1917 the AAU began funding travel expenses of women chaperones for swimmers under the age of twenty-one. By 1923 it had ruled that *no* woman swimmer could take overnight trips without a female chaperone.[2]

Swimsuit styles remained something of a controversy in the United States—one that came back to haunt the Olympic divers in 1932. Many earlier reservations had been fairly well overcome, however, thanks in large part to the growing acceptability of the female form and the sportswoman for use in advertising.

With AAU approval, a team of swimmers and their chaperones sailed to Bermuda for the opening of a new hotel in 1922, and the sanctioning of women's international participation soon followed.[3] This first trip to Bermuda set a precedent for promotional exhibitions and swimmers' travel. It put women's swimming on the road, and set its tone as a mixture of sport and show business.

Throughout the twenties, swimmers swung regularly around the competitive circuit in the East. They touched base in all the large swim centers and gave exhibitions in resorts and hotels. As the sport grew, the annual route through Florida attracted more and more swimmers nationwide, and Hawaii became an irresistible draw after Honolulu's Mariechen Wehselau swam on the 1924 Olympic team. Exhibitions that pulled large crowds always followed national championship meets. Women's swimming was popular entertainment and, somehow, not so at odds with the public's conception of woman's proper place.

The swimming sorority was closely knit. Widely diverse personalities from a variety of backgrounds came together in a true bond of sisterhood. As with siblings, competition could be fierce, but out of the pool it was one for all and all for one.

The first national swimming championships for women took place in 1916. From then on the AAU staged two national meets each year—outdoor (long course) in summer and indoor (short course) in winter. Events at long course meets were measured in meters, at short course meets in yards. Claire Galligan, swimming for the National Women's Life Saving League, won three of four outdoor freestyle championships and two indoor titles in 1916.[4]

The National Women's Life Saving League developed as a separate unit from the larger national league around 1910 and became New York's main organizing group for women's swimming. When it disbanded in 1917, its members and leaders continued as the Women's Swimming Association, which produced teams that dominated swimming in the United States throughout the twenties. The power behind the WSA was Charlotte Epstein, its guiding genius, who remained a force in women's swimming for two more decades.[5]

American teams competing in the Olympics from Antwerp through Amsterdam had a definite WSA flavor, with such great freestylers as Ethelda Bleibtrey, Gertrude Ederle, and Martha Norelius, and diver Helen Meany. In both 1920 and 1924, WSA coach L. DeB. Handley coached the Olympic teams.

Coaching in the United States made remarkable progress during the 1920s, and in many respects reflected Handley's approach as it became more professional, systematic, analytical, and scientific. Swimming facilities had multiplied many times over by 1932 and, both

Right: Ruth Osburn, phenomenal basketball player as well as track and field athlete, stands beside her high school in Shelbyville, Missouri, ca. 1931. (Courtesy the Osburn family) *Below:* Athletes at the Illinois Women's Athletic Club in Chicago. Front row: Ethel Harrington, Evelyne Hall, Doris Anderson; back row: Annette Rogers, Mary Terwilliger, Nan Gindele. Rogers ran on the gold medal–winning relay team; Hall won silver in the 80-meter hurdles; Gindele held the national javelin championship from 1932 to 1938. (Courtesy Evelyne Hall Adams)

Charlotte Epstein, guiding force in women's swimming for two decades and assistant Olympic team manager in 1932. Rarely photographed, "Eppy" is seen here at the 1935 national meet at New York's Manhattan Beach. (Courtesy Mary Lou Petty Skok)

Some 1932 Olympians at the 1930 national championship meet. Left to right: Georgia Coleman, Lenore Kight, Josephine McKim, Helene Madison, Agnes Geraghty (1928 Olympian), unidentified, Lisa Lindstrom (1928 Olympian), Dorothea Dickinson, Eleanor Holm. (Courtesy Helene McIver Ware)

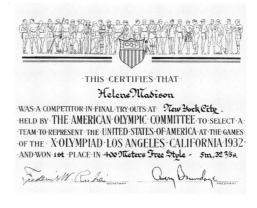

Top: Renegade swimmers from the Los Angeles Athletic Club who "bolted" the team when funding did not materialize. They may have been the first airborne Olympians when they flew cross-country to the 1932 trials at Jones Beach on Long Island. Left to right: Georgia Coleman, Josephine McKim, Jennie Cramer, Noreen Forbes, Marjorie Lowe. (Courtesy Mary Lou Petty Skok). *Bottom left:* Helene Madison, Katherine Rawls, and Margaret Hoffman at the 1932 Olympic trials at Jones Beach. Press photographers invariably posed 14-year-old Rawls between taller and older teammates. (Courtesy Helene McIver Ware). *Bottom right:* Competitor's certificate from the 1932 Olympic Games. (Courtesy Museum of History and Industry, Seattle)

Top: During the week before the Games began, Hollywood celebrities entertained the Olympians royally. Frederick March and two of the Marx Brothers hosted this group. Standing: Katherine Rawls, March, Georgia Coleman, Josephine McKim, Mickey Riley; kneeling: Groucho Marx, Eleanor Holm, Chico Marx. (Courtesy Helene McIver Ware). *Bottom:* Sportswriter Grantland Rice boosted the career and legend of Babe Didrikson. Here, he and two other journalists pose with Babe, Helene Madison, and Georgia Coleman. Left to right: Madison, Rice, Didrikson, humorist and syndicated columnist Will Rogers, Coleman, and *Los Angeles Times* sports editor Braven Dyer. (Courtesy Mary Lou Petty Skok)

The Fox studios hosted a luncheon for all the women athletes before the Games began. Actress Janet Gaynor is shown here with Babe Didrikson at the star-studded affair. (Courtesy Mary Lou Petty Skok)

Track athletes pose in the garden of the Chapman Park Hotel, team headquarters for the Games. Front row, left to right: Evelyne Hall, Evelyn Furtsch, Mary Carew, Margaret Jenkins, Billie von Bremen; back row: Babe Didrikson, Nan Gindele, Gloria Russell, Elizabeth Wilde, Annette Rogers. (Courtesy Evelyne Hall Adams)

Top: The 1932 Olympic track team beside the Chapman Park Hotel. Arranged by height, right to left: Mary Carew, Evelyn Furtsch, Tidye Pickett, Evelyne Hall, Ethel Harrington, Louise Stokes, Simone Schaller, Gloria Russell, Babe Didrikson, Nan Gindele, Elizabeth Wilde, Margaret Jenkins, Annette Rogers, Jean Shiley, Wilhelmina von Bremen, Ruth Osburn. (Courtesy Evelyne Hall Adams). *Bottom:* Track and field team members at a practice session. Left to right: Babe Didrickson, Annette Rogers, Jean Shiley, Gloria Russell, Evelyn Furtsch, Mary Carew, Coach George Vreeland, and a friend of Evelyne Hall's from Chicago. Seated: Anne O'Brien, a 1928 and 1936 Olympian from Los Angeles. (Courtesy Evelyne Hall Adams)

Top: Sprinters Mary Carew, Evelyn Furtsch, and Annette Rogers in a relaxing moment in the hotel garden. (Courtesy Evelyne Hall Adams). *Bottom:* The gold medal–winning 4 × 100 sprint relay team at a practice session. Left to right: Annette Rogers, Evelyn Furtsch, Coach George Vreeland, Mary Carew, Wilhelmina von Bremen. (Courtesy Evelyne Hall Adams)

The 1932 United States Women's Olympic Track and Field Team. Standing, left to right: Evelyne Hall, Simone Schaller, Gloria Russell, Wilhelmina von Bremen, Ruth Osburn, Babe Didrikson, Evelyn Furtsch, Mary Carew, Jean Shiley, Louise Stokes. Seated: Tidye Pickett, Ethel Harrington, Elizabeth Wilde, Nan Gindele, Lillian Copeland, Annette Rogers, Margaret Jenkins.

The 1932 United States Women's Olympic Swimming Team. Seated, left to right: Katherine Rawls, Noreen Forbes, Lenore Kight, Dorothea Dickinson, Georgia Coleman, Marion Dale Roper, Jane Fauntz, Dorothy Poynton, Helene Madison. Middle row, standing: Eleanor Garatti Saville and Anna Mae Gorman. Back row: Helen Johns, Margaret Hoffman, Jane Cadwell, Ann Govednik, Joan McSheehy, Eleanor Holm, Edna McKibben, Josephine McKim.

Top: Olympic divers Mickey Riley and Georgia Coleman. She constantly denied engagement and marriage rumors throughout the trials and the Games; it was a golden match the press could not resist. (Courtesy Mary Lou Petty Skok). *Bottom:* Opening ceremony of the Xth Olympiad, Los Angeles, California, July 30, 1932. (Courtesy Mary Lou Petty Skok)

Top: Swimmers, dressed in their official uniforms, marched smartly in the opening ceremony's parade of athletes. Left to right, front rank: Dorothy Poynton, Jane Cadwell, Edna McKibben, Jane Fauntz; second rank: Katherine Rawls, Dorothea Dickinson, Georgia Coleman, Helen Johns; third rank: Eleanor Holm, Lenore Kight (obscured by Rawls' hat), Eleanor Garatti Saville, Joan McSheehy. (Courtesy Mary Lou Petty Skok). *Bottom:* The controversial finish of the 80-meter hurdles final. Evelyne Hall and Babe Didrikson hit the wire in an apparent dead heat. Simone Schaller, number 79 on far left, appears to have finished for the bronze, which went instead to South Africa's Marjorie Clark, number 376. (Courtesy Evelyne Hall Adams)

Helene Madison and Clarence (Buster) Crabbe, 400-meter freestyle gold medalists who remained lifelong friends. Crabbe's medal was the one bright spot in the 1932 Olympics for the American men. (Courtesy Mary Lou Petty Skok)

The gold medal–winning 400-meter freestyle relay team. Left to right: Josephine McKim, Helen Johns, Eleanor Garatti Saville, Helene Madison.

Top: Medalists in the 400-meter freestyle: Helene Madison (gold), Lenore Kight (silver), and South Africa's Jennie Makaal (bronze). *Left:* Lenore Kight, 1932 silver medalist in the 400-meter freestyle. Swimming for the Carnegie Library of Homestead, Pennsylvania, she won 17 individual national freestyle titles, ranging from 100 yards to 1,500 meters, and anchored the club's national champion relay teams. (Courtesy Lenore Kight Wingard)

United States Olympic divers who won every medal in the 1932 Games. Left to right:
Jane Fauntz, Marion Dale Roper, Georgia Coleman, Dorothy Poynton, and Katherine
Rawls. (Courtesy Mary Lou Petty Skok)

Top: Helene Madison showered with confetti in a victory parade through downtown Seattle following her three-medal triumph in the 1932 Games. (Courtesy Museum of History and Industry, Seattle) *Right:* Helene Madison teaches her three-year-old namesake daughter the basic start technique at the Washington Athletic Club pool in Seattle, ca. 1940. (Courtesy Helene McIver Ware)

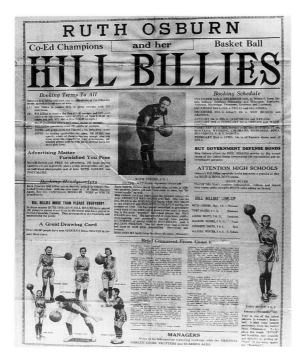

Promotional flyer for the Ozark Hill Billies, the barnstorming basketball team that Ruth Osburn managed after five years as starring center for the original All-American Red Heads, ca. 1940. (Courtesy Ruth Osburn)

The Chicago press covered Annette Rogers' 1936 preparations for Berlin and her second Olympiad. The high jumper–sprinter won her second gold medal that year in the 400-meter relay. It would be forty-eight years before her back-to-back medal feat would be repeated. (Courtesy Annette Rogers Kelly)

indoor and out, pools now presented splendid training opportunities. Some organizations still had no pool, but many small towns and school districts across the country had built them and instituted competitive programs for girls as well as boys.

Jones Beach opened to the public in August 1929. Developed by visionary master planner Robert Moses, the immense park had risen from what he described as "a mosquito-infested tidal swamp full of stagnant pools flanked by shifting dunes." Dedication ceremonies took place during a sandstorm amid predictions that nobody would ever go there again.[6] Four years later, however, at its Zach's Bay, Jones Beach hosted the country's fourth Olympic swimming trials for women.

One newspaper account described the Jones Beach facility as "the ideal course laid out in the beautiful lagoon known as Zach's Bay." The women who competed there on July 16, 1932, had a slightly different perspective. They managed to set more than a few records that day even as a stiff breeze kicked up the rough water of the tidewater bay course. A backstroker accustomed to an indoor pool in Seattle thought they had done marvelously in "just about as rough water as anybody ever swam a sprint race in." A veteran freestyler recalled, "In the course of the day, particularly in the afternoon, the wind would sweep in and bring in these waves that would sort of shift us from one lane to the other—it was really rugged."[7]

Regardless of the water and wind conditions, seven young women who had gone to Amsterdam in 1928 came to compete for a trip to Los Angeles. Two freestylers, one backstroker, one breaststroker, two divers, and one breaststroker-turned-diver sought second Olympic berths at Jones Beach.

If swimming was the glamorous entertainment sport, Eleanor Holm was its exemplar. She captured title after title with verve and gusto, radiating vitality and sex appeal. In 1932, captions under photographs displaying her dazzling smile regularly heralded her as the swimmer who turned down a Follies offer from Ziegfeld to train for the Olympics.[8]

Her greatest notoriety as an Olympian came later, in 1936, when she was expelled from her third Olympic team. That penalty, for drinking aboard ship on the crossing to Berlin, kept headlines ablaze.

Eleanor was born December 6, 1913, daughter of a Swedish father and an Irish mother—Charlotte and Franklin Holm. She had six older siblings. Her father was a fire department chief in Brooklyn, and when she later reflected on her childhood in Brooklyn she said, "It was a big kick to go out with my father and ring the bell on his shiny red car."[9]

The self-described "water rat" spent her early summers at the family's cottage on Long Island's Long Beach. Totally fearless, she made repeated forays out into the waves well beyond her depth. The lifeguard who retrieved her each time taught her the rudiments of swimming on the way back to safety. Eleanor took to competitive swimming after watching Women's Swimming Association meets and exhibitions at the Long Beach pool.[10]

At the age of twelve, over her father's objections, she joined the WSA. Versatile Eleanor became a medley swimmer, and at age thirteen won her first national AAU title in 1927 in the 300-meter individual medley. Because the medley was not an Olympic event she concentrated on backstroke, even though freestyle and breaststroke came more naturally to her. She credited Coach L. DeB. Handley for her successful mastery of backstroke. She later said, "He worked me like a washerwoman six days a week, and on the seventh let me relax." Swimming was fun, though, and she did not remember ever feeling any real pressure.[11]

In 1928 Eleanor made the Atlantic crossing aboard the *SS President Roosevelt,* bound for Amsterdam as a fourteen-year-old backstroker from the Women's Swimming Association of New York. She thought that as a very young competitor she had lacked a strong will to win at the 1928 Olympics. She placed fifth after winning her preliminary heat. However, Eleanor said that when the American flag went up at Amsterdam she "got the spirit" and told herself, "Next time that's going to be for me."[12]

For four years she pointed toward an Olympic gold medal. She repeated as national 300-meter individual medley champion in both 1929 and 1930. She won the 200-meter backstroke championship in 1929 and held it until 1934. She first captured the 100-yard backstroke title in 1930 and, in defending it at the 1932 Indoor Nationals, shattered the world mark with a time of 1:11.6. The 300-yard individual medley crown was hers from 1928 through 1932. Excepting 1933, she swam the backstroke leg of the 300-yard medley relay for WSA teams from 1930 through 1936. In all, the petite, charismatic backstroker won twenty-nine American titles and set seven world records. No one came near her in backstroke. Katherine Rawls took Eleanor's 300-meter medley title in 1931, but as she later said, "I could never beat Eleanor in backstroke—and neither could anybody else."[13]

When the women gathered at Jones Beach in 1932, it was not unlike a family reunion. Always popular and a team player, Eleanor Holm came to the reunion a true family favorite, both in and out of the water. Her powerful yet graceful stroke would put her on the train to Los Angeles, while her brilliant, glamour-girl smile would put her in the newsreels and help make her a celebrity.

Homestead, Pennsylvania, site of the bloody 1892 steel strike massacre in the sooty shadow of Pittsburgh's smokestacks, might seem an unlikely home for swimming champions. A Carnegie Library would seem an even more unlikely sponsor, but Homestead's was no run-of-the-mill Carnegie Library.

The library itself was typical brick "Carnegie traditional," with front steps leading to reading rooms and charge desk. Two companion buildings flanked it; one was a meeting and concert hall and the other housed a gymnasium and swimming pool. One dollar entitled a Homestead youngster to three months of swimming or sports instruction in the gym, or both. With trained teaching and coaching, the library turned out its fair share of titleholders.[14]

Josephine McKim was one of its champion freestyle swimmers in 1928. That summer she won the national 1,500-meter championship, and at the Olympic trials held at New York's Rockaway Playland Pool, she placed fourth in both 100- and 400-meter freestyle. When the *President Roosevelt* pulled away from Pier 86 on July 11 to steam down the Hudson and out of New York Harbor, Jo McKim stood at the rail, bound for Europe with the women's Olympic team.[15]

She returned from Amsterdam with the 400-meter freestyle bronze medal. Not long after, her family moved to the Canal Zone. In 1929, as an unattached swimmer out of the Canal Zone, Jo took three more AAU national championships—400-, 800-, and 1,500-meter freestyle.[16]

Josephine had begun her competitive career swimming against two superlative freestylers—Martha Norelius and Albina Osipowich, American gold medalists in Amsterdam. Another immovable object blocked Jo's championship path at the 1930 indoor nationals in Miami.

Helene Madison came out of the Pacific Northwest that winter to dominate freestyle for the next two years.

By then a student at the University of Southern California and swimming for the Los Angeles Athletic Club, McKim was destined to place second to Madison at 100, 220, and 500 yards in Miami. Later that year she swam in the outdoor nationals in Long Beach, California, still recovering from an illness suffered on a trip home to the Canal Zone. She lost her 1,500-meter title to Madison and placed second to her at 400 meters. With McKim in the anchor spot, the Los Angeles Athletic Club team won the 800-meter relay championship in both 1930 and 1931.[17]

Much-traveled Josephine McKim was born January 4, 1910, in Oil City, Pennsylvania. In keeping with swimming's image as the glamour sport, she fit the role of beauty queen, and Los Angeles proved an ideal location for her. After the 1932 Olympics she appeared in more than a few motion pictures, swimming in difficult underwater scenes. The press labeled her petite or dainty, and photographed a small, short-haired pixie with a shy smile. A true beauty, she attracted a lot of attention, much of it from sportswriters. At the time of the trials at Jones Beach she was dating columnist Paul Gallico. In one article, Gallico listed her among the beautiful swimmers—a "slim girl with a soft mouth and eyes like a doe." Jo McKim projected a naivete in contrast to Eleanor Holm's growing sophistication. Friendly to everyone, she was both popular and respected among the swimming sisterhood, who welcomed her to Jones Beach to try for a spot on her second Olympic team.[18]

Further east in Pennsylvania, Scranton marked another stop on the swimming circuit. The United States surged ahead of the rest of the world in freestyle in the twenties and thirties, but breaststroke records and titles stayed in Europe. With good timing and good fortune, the Scranton Swimming Association's Margaret Hoffman emerged as America's hope in breaststroke.

In the winter of 1927, Scranton coaches Wright Jones and Hoadley Hagen took a water polo team to a match with the YWCA in the Wilkes-Barre suburb of Kingston. Peg Hoffman, the Y's standout swimmer, caught their eye. After the game they approached her parents about letting her swim with the Scranton club. This would mean she could swim in meets throughout the state. The Hoffmans agreed, as long as it did not interfere with her schoolwork, and her mother gladly drove the twenty-six miles to Scranton for weekly two-hour workouts.[19]

Because crawl was her mainstay stroke for water polo, Hagen had Margaret swimming freestyle. She soon could hold her own with the best and before season's end defeated them all. While observing a training session one day, her mother suggested that the coach try her on the breaststroke. He did, and the first time she swam 100 yards breaststroke she did it in record time. At the 1928 Middle Atlantic indoor championships in Philadelphia, she surprised everyone by setting a new meet record in her 100-yard breaststroke heat. Margaret still swam freestyle events, too, and the long day took its toll in the breaststroke final. She lost by a slight margin, but her heat time stood as the record.[20]

The Scranton coaches took several swimmers to the 1928 Olympic tryouts at the Rockaway Pool. Hagen had this to say about Margaret's performance:

> The stars didn't pay any attention to us as they were too busy watching each other. But while they were doing this Margaret stepped in for third place although it was the first time she ever covered the Olympic distance. She didn't know anything about judging pace, but just followed the leader and was coming strong at the finish.

In view of European breaststroke dominance, American Olympic officials debated taking just two breaststrokers and an extra diver to the Games. They finally decided in favor of a third swimmer. Margaret went on to be the only United States point winner in the 200-meter event, placing fifth at Amsterdam.[21]

The seventeen-year-old returned from the Games to her senior year at Kingston's Wyoming Seminary. An exceptional student, Margaret never found swimming a burden, as her parents had once worried. She continued to drive to Scranton workouts with younger sister Elizabeth now frequently her companion in the family's sedan. The following year she entered Mount Holyoke College.[22]

Margaret and Elizabeth were the only children of Edwin Albert and Louise Witherow Hoffman. Their father, a civil engineer, headed the Wilkes-Barre transit system. Neither parent swam. Elizabeth recalled, "My mother could not swim a stroke. Father swam under protest." He had no interest in sports, but Louise Hoffman, influenced by her daughters, became a fan. (A charter subscriber to *Sports Illustrated,* as she neared her ninety-ninth birthday "she was busy reading a book on how to be a TV quarterback.")[23]

Raised to value nature, music, and good literature, Margaret went to South Hadley with the idea that there was more to college than studying. The New England sports press labeled her the ideal student athlete when she was at Mount Holyoke and, considering her the region's own, regularly reported her swimming achievements. While maintaining top grades, she took the national 200-meter breaststroke title from New York Olympian Agnes Geraghty in 1930 as well as winning the indoor 100-yard crown. Tall (five feet seven inches), slender, blue-eyed, blonde Peg Hoffman relished the camaraderie of the swimming circuit and the challenge of the sport. She remained close to New York's WSA swimmers, in particular 1928 Olympic teammates Eleanor Holm and Agnes Geraghty.[24]

Mount Holyoke had no swimming pool. Smith College in nearby Northampton had built Scott Gymnasium with a magnificent pool in 1929, but, even with access to it, Margaret had no transportation. So training during the school year was not easy, although she did not have opposition from faculty members as other 1932 collegiate Olympians did.[25]

Electing to study for exams in the spring of 1932, Margaret skipped the indoor nationals, which were held in the new Olympic pool in Los Angeles. Hence she surrendered her title to Jane Cadwell of Detroit. When school ended in June, she had a month to train for the Olympic trials. She regained competitive form at the Irem Temple Country Club pool back home in Kingston.[26] After missing the gathering in Los Angeles earlier that spring, Margaret Hoffman looked forward with enthusiasm to the reunion at Jones Beach.

Jane Fauntz arrived at the Jones Beach trials as an Olympic breaststroker, determined to leave as an Olympic diver. Swimming for the Illinois Women's Athletic Club, Jane had finished ahead of Peg Hoffman at the Playland Pool four years before. She went to Amsterdam as the country's number two breaststroker, but even then, she had harbored thoughts of trying for the team as a diver.[27]

Midwesterner Fauntz was born in New Orleans, December 19, 1910. Her father worked for the Illinois Central Railroad, which ran its famed "Panama Limited" between Chicago and the Crescent City.

She said her mother"just happened to be in New Orleans" at the time she was born.[28]

She did not take to the water early. At age fourteen, and a self-described "skinny little kid in high school," she nearly drowned in Lake Michigan. Shaken and embarrassed, she decided to learn to swim. She went to a local swim school, learned to swim correctly, and swam in the school races. Then the diving board beckoned and she soon became good enough to enter competition. Her first meet as a diver pitted her against eighteen-year-olds. She never forgot it, saying, "When I stepped up on the diving board everybody laughed at me because I was so tiny and so skinny. That made me mad." Diving well subsequently proved the best revenge. She completed her dives, finished first, and upset the local champion.[29]

That meet also netted her a coach and a sponsor. Mrs. Lillian Winter Riley asked her to represent the Illinois Women's Athletic Club. Training twice a week in the pool on the club's sixteenth floor, Jane continued diving and developed 100-meter breaststroke as her main event. She swam in AAU meets in the area, and dreamed of the Olympic team. As the 1928 trials neared she increased her stamina for a try at 200 meters, the only women's breaststroke event in the Games. And she held on to thoughts of competing in diving as well.[30]

Sometime in late January she met with near disaster when a car hit her in a crosswalk on Chicago's Michigan Avenue. Regular swimming rehabilitated her damaged right arm, but she had to put diving on hold. Her father shared her Olympic determination and pushed her to gain strength for the 200 meters. Calling him "the great trainer," she said, "He'd get me up early in the morning and make me run around the block before school every day, rain or shine, snow or sleet or hail—I had to go."[31]

En route to Amsterdam she shared the team's shipboard training routine—five minutes, twice a day, swimming in place while tethered in a makeshift pool. The wooden pool, about eight feet square and lined with canvas, was filled daily with fresh sea water. She did not place in her event, but at seventeen, no longer a skinny little kid, Jane Fauntz enjoyed all the social aspects of the trip to Europe.[32]

When it was time to leave Amsterdam, she and Josephine McKim decided at the last minute to spend all their guilders before embarking for home. They were still shopping when the *President Roosevelt* signaled its departure. A ship's tender had to be sent back to bring them out. Gen. Douglas MacArthur himself, President of the American Olympic Committee, welcomed them on board. He was not amused.[33]

In 1928 Jane visited her brother, a Navy officer stationed in Southern California. She spent fall semester at San Pedro High School and trained with an assistant to diving coach Fred Cady of the Los Angeles Athletic Club. Fauntz returned to Chicago as a new and serious challenger for diving honors. She won the indoor titles in both 100-yard breaststroke and 1-meter springboard diving at the national meet in Chicago in 1929. She was determined to keep the crown and prove to the Californians that 1929 had not been a fluke, so at the 1930 indoor nationals in Miami she executed a perfect running full twist to stay in first place.[34]

By the summer of 1932, Jane was an art education major at the University of Illinois. The women's physical education faculty at the university opposed competition and allowed only intramurals and telegraphic meets. Their pool was inadequate for diving, and Jane could not get permission to dive in the men's pool. Training for Olympic 3-meter springboard competition had to wait for summer vacation, giving her only the month of June to get ready for Jones Beach.[35]

Perhaps Gertrude Ederle was looking past the 1925 championships to her future English Channel swim when she lost her 50-yard freestyle title to Eleanor Garatti that February. The completely unheralded fifteen-year-old from San Rafael, California, scored the upset of the year at the championships in St. Augustine, Florida, when she defeated the 1924 Olympic medalist. Not even the staunchest supporters of the self-taught swimmer had predicted her victory over the likes of Ederle and other luminaries from New York's Women's Swimming Association.[36]

California moved convincingly onto the national scene in women's swimming with Eleanor Garatti. After the usual round of exhibitions following her sensational debut in Florida, she headed home. When she reached the Bay Area, enthusiastic crowds met her train in Oakland and later the ferry boat on its arrival at the slip in San Francisco. A final throng, complete with brass band, waited for her across the Golden Gate up in San Rafael. Eleanor Garatti returned home, modest and self-effacing as ever, and she assured supporters that she would continue to swim for San Rafael, the city that financed her trip to Florida and made her victory possible.[37]

The following year she successfully defended the 50-yard title, but a prime example of officials' ineptitude and inconsistency denied her the record for the distance. All records set at the nationals, again held in St. Augustine, were discarded when the course proved to be four inches short. Showing its sympathetic bias, the San Francisco press said, "What excuse the Florida promoters can offer for such gross negligence is hard to imagine." For the next three years Eleanor remained virtually unbeatable at 50 yards on the West Coast, and she won the national 100-meter freestyle championship as well in 1928.[38]

At the Olympic trials that year she more than rewarded the confidence of such San Rafael boosters as The Redwood Empire and Marvelous Marin, two local groups that had long given her financial backing and moral support. By placing first in 100-meter freestyle she secured her spot on the Olympic team. In Amsterdam, she came in second in the 100 meters behind Albina Osipowich of Worcester, Massachusetts. In spite of the poor training facilities available to the swimmers, the victorious American 400-meter freestyle relay team, with Eleanor swimming the second leg, set a new world record of 4 minutes 47.6 seconds. Eleanor again returned to a San Rafael welcome, brass bands and all, but this time she came with Olympic medals—one gold, one silver.[39]

After repeating as national 100-meter freestyle champion, in world record time, at the 1929 nationals in Honolulu, Eleanor retired from competition. For the next three years she swam only for exercise and recreation. On June 2, 1930, she married Laurence Saville of San Francisco. Saville, an engineer, was a noted swimmer himself, a perennial standout in the era's famed Golden Gate swims. After a honeymoon in the Pacific Northwest they established their home in San Francisco.[40]

Eleanor's competitive instincts surfaced as another Olympiad approached. With the 1932 Games coming virtually to her doorstep, she decided to seek another Olympic berth and began training in the winter of 1931. Now a member of San Francisco's Western Women's Club, Eleanor started serious practice in the club's pool. To prepare for the open water trials at Jones Beach, however, she resorted to the city's longer, outdoor Fleishacker Pool. She also trained at the grand and historic Sutro Pool where she and her husband had met in 1927.[41] The Sutro Baths (destroyed by fire during dismantling in the mid-1960s) stood out at the Sea Cliff near Point Lobos.

Seven years after her teenage triumph in Florida, Eleanor Garatti Saville boarded the train in Oakland for another cross-country trip. After a three-year absence from competition, she looked forward to returning. She later said the swimmers always enjoyed having the glamour-girl label and, laughing, added, "I was not a beauty, but I got by. I could include myself in their group." She relished a reunion with old friends and a chance to meet new ones while trying for her second Olympic team.[42]

The Los Angeles Athletic Club's Aileen Allen had pointed the way to greatness as a 1920 Olympic diver. She had won the AAU's first 3-meter springboard championship in 1916 and the platform diving title in 1917.[43] Beginning with performances in Amsterdam, two young Southern California divers followed in the path she had marked. Dorothy Poynton and Georgia Coleman became the cornerstone of a diving dynasty centered in the LAAC and its companion clubs in Pasadena and Hollywood.

As a young child in Portland, Oregon, Dorothy Poynton had more interest in dancing than diving. When the Portland School Board required her parents to hire a tutor if Dorothy were to dance in stage shows at the city's Orpheum Theater, the Poyntons packed up their family and moved to Los Angeles.[44]

The Ambassador Hotel opened on Wilshire Boulevard in 1921. Like many luxury hotels in the twenties, the Ambassador staged swimming and diving exhibitions in its pool. Dorothy's father worked for the hotel, and she appeared in its dancing and diving shows. It did not take the Hollywood Athletic Club long to bring her into the fold after its coach saw her in action. Three times a week her father took her to work with coach Clyde Swenson at the club on Sunset Boulevard. When Dorothy was only twelve years old she made her national debut at the junior championships in Detroit.[45]

At the Olympic trials the following summer, then representing the Pasadena Athletic Club, Dorothy placed third on the 3-meter springboard behind fellow Californian Georgia Coleman and preeminent Olympian Helen Meany from the Women's Swimming Association. Barely aware of what the Olympic Games were all about, Dorothy celebrated her thirteenth birthday on board the *President Roosevelt*. When she won the springboard bronze medal in Amsterdam, the tiny, smiling blonde became the youngest person ever to win an Olympic medal.[46]

By 1932, five-foot-one-inch Dorothy was a student at Fairfax High School in Los Angeles, still dancing, and continuing to work with diving coach Clyde Swenson. All the area clubs were now competing under one banner, so she had the Los Angeles Athletic Club as official sponsor.[47]

Two divergent philosophies developed in California diving circles. One school of thought concentrated on attaining perfection in simpler, straightforward dives. The other went for dives with the highest degree of difficulty, putting flawless precision second. A perfectionist, Dorothy chose the first option.[48] When she left for New York in July 1932 she took her impeccable diving form to challenge on both platform and springboard.

The Los Angeles Athletic Club was a glamorous sponsor for athletes in the twenties and thirties. Its magnificent building at Seventh and Olive in downtown Los Angeles opened in 1912, with meeting, dining, residential, and athletic facilities unequaled at the time. It was the club of the business and social establishment and the site of more than a little planning for the Xth Olympiad. Denizens of the film colony favored the club—Chaplin, Valentino, Pickford, Jolson, and the Gish sisters, to name a few. In 1913 the club launched into competitive athletics, providing coaching that continually improved as time went on.[49]

In the mid-twenties LAAC lured swimming and diving coach Fred Cady from the Philadelphia Turngemeinde where he had taught such notables as Olympic diver Betty Becker Pinkston and Margaret Kelly, mother of Jack and Princess Grace. Cady set out to build a strong diving team in Los Angeles. In 1927 he rejoiced to find a young woman who he said was "able to do the same difficult dives the men do." He had discovered refreshing, exuberant, vibrant and spirited, ever-smiling Georgia Coleman.[50]

Georgia was born in St. Mary's, Idaho, January 23, 1912, but her family soon left Idaho for Los Angeles. Georgia spent her summers on Catalina Island, wearing overalls when not in a swimsuit. Always popular wherever she went, she had a marvelous sense of humor and retained a touch of tomboy deviltry.[51]

She had been diving only six months when Cady took her to

New York and Rockaway Playland Pool for the 1928 Olympic trials. The sixteen-year-old Californian placed second on the 3-meter springboard, behind Helen Meany, and joined the Olympic team on the *President Roosevelt* for the trip to Amsterdam. The ship's miniature, makeshift pool offered divers even less than it did swimmers. They practiced timing and kept legs in shape on a springboard, making their usual approaches and hurdles and landing on a thin mat on the deck. Miraculously there were no serious injuries beyond a few mild ankle sprains.[52]

In those 1928 Games, Georgia won the silver in platform diving, behind repeat gold-medalist Betty Becker Pinkston. On the springboard she took silver to Helen Meany's gold. She went on to win the AAU national titles in both platform and 3-meter springboard for the next three years. Georgia Coleman always delighted in dives that most found too difficult; she had been the first woman to do a two-and-a-half forward somersault in competition.[53]

She graduated from Polytechnic High School in Los Angeles between Olympiads and continued to train year-round. She often said she hoped to go to the University of Southern California. Perhaps one reason she did not lies with the philosophy of the women's physical education department at USC, where "you did not compete, period."[54]

Georgia Coleman was a favorite at the Los Angeles Athletic Club. A team player, she always found time to help the younger divers and stood loyally beside all the divers and swimmers.[55]

Loyalty to teammates resulted in drastic action in early July 1932, when the LAAC announced it would send only two of its team to the Olympic trials. It would fund Georgia and Josephine McKim, but not the three other members of its national champion relay team. McKim and Coleman countered with, "Either we all go or we quit the team." The Club did not budge, and the five walked out, vowing to compete at Jones Beach "unattached," even if they had to hitchhike. The idea of attractive young Olympians joining a small army of Depression migrants caught the fancy of the press. Carefully posed photos of the smiling swimmers "hitting the road," hobo bundles slung over their shoulders, appeared in Rotogravure sections in newspapers coast-to-coast.[56]

Fledgling American Airways stepped in and offered to fly the quintet East at no charge. They immediately accepted the offer of what must have been a first in Olympic travel. They left Los Angeles in the afternoon and—after what sounds like a nightmarish cross-country trip of landing, changing planes, and taking off in a series of short hops and stops—reached Newark Airport late the next night on a Ford trimotor. On landing, Coleman told reporters, "All five of us qualified in our sectional tryouts for the Olympic team. . . . The other girls had been faithful to the club. We are all good friends and we were all angry, so we walked out together."[57]

The AAU paid travel expenses for current national champions Coleman and McKim, and Georgia said, "[W]e are splitting that up five ways. It will keep us while we're here." They checked into Manhattan's Hotel Commodore with minimal funds and little or no idea of what lay in store.[58] But, one for all and all for one, they would be at Jones Beach on July 16.

A third Los Angeles diver made the cross-country trip to the trials that summer, although not courtesy of American Airways. Marion Dale had been diving for some time in a variety of places in Southern California, including the Lake Norconia Club in Riverside County east of Los Angeles. Friends and family described her as a strong-minded and beautiful woman. While a bona fide member of the glamour-girl set, she took a truly regal bearing onto the springboard. She had just married petroleum geologist Bill Roper when she left for the East Coast that summer to compete under the banner of the Los Angeles Athletic Club.[59]

The California contingent came to the Olympic trials confident of victory. They were determined to hold their own with longtime New York rivals from the Women's Swimming Association. Swimming competition had grown enormously since 1928 and expanded far into the hinterland. The sisterhood now had to reckon with talented newcomers, including Florida's Katherine Rawls.

Just fourteen years old, Katherine was the youngest among the women at Jones Beach. The press made much of her age and size that summer, describing her with such observations as "about as big as a minute. She can't weigh much more than 90 pounds soaking wet." Katherine first drew national attention as a competitor in 1930 when, as a twelve-year-old diver, she bypassed the junior category and entered the senior indoor championship meet in Miami because it was near home. She placed a close second to Georgia Coleman on the 3-meter spring- board. She also drew the attention of noted diving coach Willis Cool- ing, who trained Pete Desjardins, springboard and platform gold medalist at Amsterdam. Cooling soon started to work with Rawls.[60]

Florida championship meets frequently looked like Rawls fam- ily affairs. Katherine and younger sisters Evelyn, Dorothy, and Peggy claimed victories in breaststroke and freestyle events and all the med- leys and relays. Younger brother "Sonny" took honors in diving. The sister combination gave exhibitions and became known in Fort Lau- derdale swim circles as the Rawls "Water Babies."[61]

In the summer of 1931 Katherine surprised the swimming world by winning the national 200-meter breaststroke title and upsetting Eleanor Holm in the 300-meter individual medley. This brought a cascade of praise from Holm's coach, the venerable L. DeB. Handley. He called Rawls "the brightest Olympic breast-stroke prospect the United States has harbored since the games of 1924, a fancy diver of international rating and a freestyle and back-stroke swimmer of won- derful promise."[62] The only person coming to the 1932 trials to com- pete in both swimming and diving, she arrived in New York running second only to Georgia Coleman on the springboard.

Another teenage breaststroke prospect appeared at Jones Beach from an unlikely venue. Chisholm, Minnesota, far from Florida's warm beaches and Manhattan's bright lights, lies about halfway between Duluth and International Falls—the nation's coldest reporting weather station. While other regions and towns boomed and grew during the twenties, Chisholm lost population, and the Mesaba Range town of 8,300 suffered badly in the Great Depression. Many jobs in the mines were lost and others cut to half-time, but the school system remained strong. This included the high school swimming program. In 1932, cheering the exploits of one sophomore in that program, young Anne Govednik, provided welcome relief for the entire town.[63]

Daughter of an immigrant iron miner, Anne Govednik was born in Chisholm on June 21, 1916, a year before her father's final natural- ization papers were processed. Martin Govednik, native of Suhar, Aus- tria, arrived in New York on September 15, 1905, and soon sent for his

wife and their infant son. The young family found its way to the upper Midwest and Martin, although a skilled shoemaker, took work in
the mines. He swam a strong breaststroke himself and encouraged his
children to swim.[64]

Anne learned the breaststroke in 1930, after starting with that
typically American stroke—the crawl. She and her sister Mary swam
in a pond known locally as "Weedy Bottom." In all likelihood the pond
was a test pit left south of town by crews exploring for iron in the
1890s. Both Mary and Anne perfected their swimming skill on a team
coached by women; Bernice Adsit, Alice Rudberg, and Lazelle Zieger
had no difficulty with the idea of competition. When Zieger married
in 1930, Helen Manson replaced her. It was Helen Manson who
coached Anne all the way to Jones Beach.[65]

Once settled on the breaststroke, Anne and Coach Manson set
about lowering her time for 100 yards. In the preliminaries at the 1932
state championships held in nearby Virginia, Minnesota, she did 100
yards in 1:18 flat. Meet referee was University of Minnesota swim
coach Niels Thorpe. He knew Anne's time was 1.6 seconds off the
world mark and promptly started a fund to send her to the Olympic
trials in July. He also arranged an official repeat attempt for the record
with AAU timers at another meet upcoming in Virginia. Anne did the
repeat try in 1:18.9, still below 1:21.4, the best from among 1928
Olympians Fauntz, Geraghty, and Hoffman. Helen Manson immediately started her charge's training for the longer 200-meter Olympic
distance.[66]

Slender and fragile looking at five feet four inches and weighing
only 99 pounds, Anne and her flashing smile became an instant rallying
point for the entire region. The *Hibbing Tribune* urged "the people of
the Mesaba Range to loyally support" the public fund-raisers, the exhibitions, and water carnivals. The paper claimed her for all the area's
towns, saying:

> The little swimming marvel does not represent Chisholm alone.
> She belongs to the Arrowhead. The amount of advertising she will
> bring this section of the country cannot be estimated in dollars and
> cents.[67]

Anne had never been farther from home than Duluth when she
and Helen Manson boarded the train early in July for Chicago and an

invitational meet at the Illinois Women's Athletic Club.[68] From there, it was on to New York and another round of exhibitions and water carnivals preceding the main event in Zach's Bay. The trail that began in "Weedy Bottom" led to a meeting with national champions and Olympic medalists.

The Detroit Yacht Club at Belle Isle, a far cry from "Weedy Bottom" and Minnesota's Arrowhead, produced another Olympic breaststroke hopeful. The rise of Jane Cadwell was as meteoric and unexpected as that of Anne Govednik.

R. T. Cadwell, busy and probably preoccupied member of the club, happened by in late spring of 1932 to watch his daughter swim in the club pool. George Van, who kept an eye on the club swimmers, had just timed Jane. With stopwatch still in hand he told her father she could win the national 100-yard breaststroke championship if only she were in Los Angeles that week. No one could have been more surprised than dad. Jane had been swimming on the club team since 1929, in meets with the Illinois Women's Athletic Club and the like, but the family had no hint of her ability. When George Van added that it was too bad there was no chance for her to make it to California in time for the national meet that started in just four days, Cadwell found a way. In a rare move for that era before jet flights, he booked airline tickets, and father and daughter took off for the coast. She lived up to expectations, winning the title with a time of 1:25.6.[69]

Landing back in Detroit a week later, the unassuming seventeen-year-old champion plunged into final exams. She graduated with honors from the city's Northwestern High School that spring. She also found time to set a new record for 200-meter breaststroke at the Canadian Nationals in Windsor, Ontario.[70]

Club members thought the grueling 200-meter Olympic distance would be too much for her. Determined now to make it onto the Olympic team, Jane set herself a demanding schedule. She moved her two-a-day workouts from the club pool to the Detroit River where she swam upstream against a strong three- to four-mile-an-hour current.[71]

Jane and three other young women represented the Detroit Yacht Club at Jones Beach. The club's former swim coach, who had moved east to New York's Downtown Athletic Club of Heisman Trophy fame, told friends in Michigan he had seen no swimmers to compare with their entries.[72] Hopes were high in the Motor City.

The Southeastern AAU Championships held at Darlington Lake in Rome, Georgia, served notice early in July 1932 that the South was ready to rise. In addition to Florida's Katherine Rawls, Georgia's own Louisa Robert of Atlanta emerged from the meet as a strong candidate for the Olympic team. The seventeen-year-old from the Atlanta Athletic Club shattered the regional 100-yard backstroke record in a time of 1:16.[73]

Louisa Robert had been swimming competitively for two years. Undefeated in backstroke, she was Junior National champion at 100 yards. Early in her swimming career she had worked out in the club pool before and after classes at Atlanta's Washington Seminary, with her mother as her only timer and training guide.[74]

Preparing for her triumph in the Rome meet, with the avowed goal of one day beating Eleanor Holm, she steadily bettered her own time. She spent May and June working with a coach at Sea Island Beach and reached peak physical and mental form for the longer 100-meter Olympic distance in perfect time for the trials.[75]

Her parents, Mr. and Mrs. L. W. (Chip) Robert, personally escorted Louisa to New York. They were remembered by a teammate as "a very handsome pair." Chip Robert, a prominent Atlanta businessman, was president of the Atlanta Crackers, the city's minor league baseball team. Following the 1932 presidential election, he served in the Roosevelt administration as an undersecretary at the Treasury.[76]

With regional pride, the *Atlanta Constitution* proclaimed the city the first in Dixie to send north "a girl prodigy . . . ready to challenge the nation's best." The paper, whose sports editor at the time was its great and courageous future editor Ralph McGill, strove for balance, however. It allowed that perhaps Louisa was "not a heroine born," but stressed the "keen competitive instinct with which she is so admirably endowed." Future teammates at the Olympic trials found her totally different from the rest. They recalled her as "an entity unto herself," lovely and dainty, a Southern belle, a beautiful debutante.[77] No matter how she may have been viewed, at Jones Beach she would prove the hometown paper both right and wrong with her formidable and gutsy performance.

★   ★   ★

Another regional favorite daughter sought an Olympic backstroke berth at Zach's Bay. Joan McSheehy at one time held every New England backstroke record and she had never lost a race in her own backyard. A native of the village of Whitinsville, Massachusetts, she began competing on the local swimming association team. In 1932, then a student at New York University, she swam for the Women's Swimming Association.[78]

Her physician father, Dr. Morgan T. McSheehy, started her swimming at an early age and he coached her to one of New England's more memorable accomplishments. In the spring of 1928, the fourteen-year-old astounded even her strongest supporters when she broke six world backstroke records and established a seventh in an exhibition specially staged at the Whitinsville Swimming Club under the auspices of the New England AAU. She shattered marks set by the great Sybil Bauer, 1924 Olympic gold medalist from the Illinois Women's Athletic Club. Resting between events, young Joan rewrote the numbers for 200, 440, 500, 600, 700, and 880 yards. Since there was no recognized record time for 400 yards, her 5:58.2 at that distance that night was considered a new standard.[79]

Her rise in the ranks of leading backstrokers coincided with Eleanor Holm's, and the two became good friends as well as competitors. After her astounding feat in May, Joan was touted as a favorite for the 1928 Olympic team, but she did not appear at the trials in Far Rockaway that summer. The following year she became national 100-yard indoor champion. In 1930 she lost that title to Holm, who held it until McSheehy won it back in 1933.[80]

Witty, irreverent, and fun-loving, Joan McSheehy was a favorite in the swimming sisterhood.[81] Now an attractive standout among the glamour girls, in 1932 she again ranked high on the list of potential Olympians when they gathered in New York for the trials.

Massachusetts sent Worcester's Albina Osipowich to the Amsterdam Games and she returned with the 100-meter freestyle gold medal. Another freestyler appeared on the Bay State scene before the trials in 1932 and rewarded New England's hopes for continued Olympic fame.

Helen Johns, born September 25, 1914, in Boston, broke onto the sports pages in March 1930. When she won the second race she had ever entered, the *Boston Globe* proclaimed, "A Brilliant Future Is Predicted for a Fifteen-Year-Old Girl." In her fourth race a month later, she placed second to Osipowich, who set a regional 100-yard freestyle record that night. In May, Helen went on to take the New England AAU 100-yard junior title, cutting 7.6 seconds from the record in the process.[82]

The short, happy swimming career of Helen Johns began indirectly at the Medford Girls Club. Her father, a friend of track coach Eddie Pidgeon, encouraged her to run at the club. The Girls Club had no swim team but staged water exhibitions and races in the Mystic River. Helen recalled, "I'd sit in the stands with my father and I'd say, 'I know I can beat those kids.'" Never formally taught to swim, she stayed with track and won a few races. She often ran against future Olympian Mary Carew who, she remembers, "could go off like a shot."[83]

Evelyn Johns, Helen's older sister, was a graduate of Boston University and the renowned Sargent School of Physical Education. She taught in Brookline High School's excellent program, which offered every sport. Brookline's conservative faculty women allowed no varsity competition, and at times when Helen was competing Evelyn actually feared for her job. Ironically, it was in Brookline that her sister's great talent came to light.[84]

Strictly a self-taught ocean swimmer, Helen had never been in a pool until the day Evelyn took her to the Brookline municipal pool used by the high school classes. Jay McNamara, coach of the Women's Swimming Association of Brookline, watched Helen swimming, found out who she was, and told Evelyn he wanted to talk to their father. McNamara thought Helen could be good enough for the Olympic team.[85]

Helen recalled, "Of course when my father heard this, all thoughts of running were forgotten." She joined the Brookline association, which was open to the public, and three nights a week her father took her to practice sessions. When women were swimming, men were not allowed in the building. She said, "In the New England winter my father had to drive me over and get lost for three hours. Now that was tough." Saying her parents' lives seemed to revolve around getting her places, Helen added, "I never could have done anything without my father."[86] Most of the 1932 Olympic swimmers

enjoyed great support from their parents, but Edward Johns, a successful contractor in the business of repairing and refitting ocean liners,
may have outdone them all.

Helen gradually became aware of the personalities on the swimming circuit. She remembered her first glimpse of Eleanor Holm,
from the balcony at the Brookline pool: "I looked down and saw this
girl in an off-the-face hat—she was in a fur coat—I never saw such a
beautiful face." When Brookline accepted an invitation to swim exhibitions with the WSA at Newport, Rhode Island, the teenager was
dazzled by the likes of Holm and Joan McSheehy, and totally awestruck
by their very formal and reserved coach—L. DeB. Handley.[87]

Every freestyler contending in 1930 and '31 eventually came up
against Helene Madison. Helen Johns's first encounter with Madison
came at the Indoor Nationals in New York in April of 1931. Just before the meet, Helen was hit with a recurring illness that later proved
to be appendicitis. Determined to compete, she entered the 100 and
220 yards. The press credited her with keeping up fairly well with
Helene, who retained her title in the 100, but Helen only remembers
how weak she was, near drowning, and total embarrassment.[88]

Helen graduated from Medford High School with Latin and
French honors in 1932, just before the Olympic trials. She continued
to train hard even though coach Jay McNamara had left the Brookline
Swimming Association for Phillips Exeter Academy and had not been
replaced. She had again finished behind Madison at the Outdoor Nationals the year before but ahead of Josephine McKim, which boded
well for her at Jones Beach. When Helen boarded an Eastern Steamship Line boat on July 9 for the overnight Boston–to–New York run,
she went to the trials with confidence and expectations—her own and
those of all New England.[89]

The Carnegie Library Club in Homestead, under Coach Jack Scarry,
continued to turn out great Pennsylvania freestylers after Josephine
McKim departed for the Canal Zone. In 1932, Scarry's 800-meter relay team won the first of its three national championships with Lenore
Kight, a relative newcomer on the scene, swimming anchor.[90]

Lenore Kight was born in 1911 in Frostburg, Maryland, second
from the youngest in a family of three boys and two girls. The Kights
moved to Homestead when she was four years old, and at age thirteen,

Lenore took her dollar to the Carnegie Library for three months of instruction and learned to swim.[91]

She won her first novice race in 1927, qualifying to go to all the meets. To give them an unparalleled experience, Scarry took the whole team to the Olympic trials at Rockaway Pool in 1928. Lenore had started swimming twice a day in 1926—a regimen she continued for the next ten years. She was up every morning at 5:00 a.m. and at the pool to work out before school.[92]

A resolute and determined swimmer, she stuck faithfully to training. Journalist Paul Gallico later labeled the five-foot-two-inch, brown-haired, blue-eyed competitor "Miss Lion Heart Kight." She always said, "You have to have dedication. You have to give up a lot. . . . I wanted to do it, I enjoyed it because I was getting better and better."[93]

She was indeed getting better and better. She chose to stay in Homestead and swim after she graduated from high school in 1929, giving up a scholarship arranged for her at Temple University by the school principal. Two teammates had gone to Temple the year before, and she saw that "when they came back their swimming had dropped." She told the principal, "If I go to college I can't swim, so I'm going to take a chance and keep on swimming. . . . I was afraid I'd lose it, and I had just started up and didn't want to stop." The no-competition-for-women philosophy at Temple had plagued high jumper Jean Shiley, so Lenore made the right choice for a tenacious competitor. She later said, "I'm glad I did—I never did go back to school."[94]

The pressure to pursue her goal came from within. Her parents supported her and the whole family was proud of her, but she said, "It was all my doing." The relentless training and resolve should not suggest a stoic with tunnel vision. She truly enjoyed it and said, "It was pleasure, too—it was fun—going on the trips—the summer and winter Nationals. And the trips to Florida."[95]

Lenore Kight, too, had run into Helene Madison's freestyle buzz saw before they met again at the 1932 Olympic trials. However, when they all left Jones Beach and headed for Los Angeles, the press would call Kight "the swimmer to watch."[96]

Blessed with water in abundance, Seattle's citizens took eagerly to swimming before the turn of the century. During the twenties, spurred gently by its progressive woman mayor, Bertha Landes, Seattle's Park

Board added new swimming beaches and revised and improved existing bathhouses and beach facilities. The beaches of Green Lake, a small jewel in the city's north end, produced the nation's most dominating freestyle swimmer of the era—the incomparable Helene Madison.

Helene was born in June 1913, in South Bend, a small lumber town on Willapa Bay in southwest Washington. Her mother's family had come from North Dakota to settle at South Bend. Her father, Charles Madison, migrated from Ludington, Michigan.[97]

Her mother was something of a tomboy. In winter she bundled up her only child for bobsledding, and in summer she put Helene in her carriage and wheeled her out to the baseball field. The Madisons moved to Seattle when Helene was two years old, and her father started a successful dry cleaning business. Hot summer days found mother and daughter at Madrona Beach on Lake Washington, where Helene would splash and pretend she was swimming. When she was six the family moved to a house within a block of Green Lake. West Green Lake Beach became a second home for the grade schooler who was growing by leaps and bounds. She joined the Camp Fire Girls, played all the school sports, and learned to swim.[98]

The Park Department ran an extensive beach swimming program with University of Washington students as teachers, coaches, and lifeguards. Jack Torney, who later became the university's men's swimming coach and an Olympic team adviser, was a student mainstay at West Green Lake Beach in the 1920s. Early beach teams coached by Torney regularly won city championships. After he helped Helene overcome her fear of diving and taught her an effective racing start, she quickly moved beyond summer league competition.[99]

In 1928, at age fifteen and nearing five feet ten inches, Helene Madison left all comers in her wake at West Green Lake. Her powerful and efficient crawl stroke developed along with an iron will to win.[100] Her beach achievements that year caught the eye of Ray Daughters, a teacher and coach at Seattle's Crystal Pool. Daughters and Helene worked together for the next four years and they turned enormous talent into complete mastery of freestyle.

Swimming unattached in 1930, she swept the indoor national championships for 100-, 200-, and 500-yard freestyle, and that summer took the long-course freestyle titles at 100, 200, 400, 800, and 1,500 meters. The Seattle Chamber of Commerce underwrote Helene's long train trip to Miami in March, and the Chamber led the parade, literally, to welcome her home from her smashing national debut. She had gone into the meet virtually unknown and came out hailed as a swimming marvel.[101]

She stopped in Portland, Oregon, on the return trip and, after a banquet in her honor, flew the 175 miles on up to Seattle for the greatest civic homecoming since that given troops returning from World War I. A cheering crowd of 4,000 met the single-winged trimotor when it touched down at Boeing Field, and throngs packed the sidewalks to witness her triumphal tour of downtown Seattle. The thousand or so guests at a civic banquet that evening watched a screening of movie film showing Helene pulling far ahead of Jo McKim to win the 220-yard event at Miami.[102]

Later that same year, downtown Seattle's private Washington Athletic Club opened its doors to members, and Ray Daughters moved into its state-of-the-art pool as swimming coach. He took his star freestyler with him. Swimming under the WAC banner, Helene swept the AAU short course national championships again in 1931 and '32, and triumphed in all events at the 1931 outdoor nationals.[103] In all, in 1931 she broke sixteen world records for distances between 100 yards and 1,500 meters and placed second in balloting for the Sullivan Award as the nation's Amateur Athlete of the year.

Helene Madison took superstar status with her to Jones Beach in 1932. Nearly all the freestyle contenders had finished behind her at one meet or another, and Josephine McKim and Eleanor Garatti had seen her destroy their national records. But no one would concede her a place on the Olympic team. They met to give her the stiffest competition yet in Zach's Bay, and she rose to the challenge.

An expanded swimming sisterhood arrived on Long Island from the four corners of the country. The women came with swimming experience ranging from the Amsterdam Olympic Games in 1928 to only the most recent Minnesota high school meet. Their sponsors varied from municipal booster groups to exclusive private clubs—from the Redwood Empire to the Detroit Yacht Club. Coaching varied from L. DeB. Handley and Fred Cady in New York and Los Angeles to catch-as-catch-can at the Atlanta Country Club. At Jones Beach the glamour girls came face to face with newcomers from the hinterland—Eleanor Holm met Louisa Robert and Georgia Coleman met young Katherine Rawls. They came prepared to have a marvelous time themselves and to entertain. In the sometimes choppy water of Zach's Bay they would provide thrills and surprises and produce a nearly invincible Olympic team.

5 | Aquatic
    Trials
    At
    Jones
    Beach

★

When Jones Beach hosted the two-day Olympic trials in 1932, New York had been the capital of women's swimming for a decade and a half. Its Women's Swimming Association won team and individual championships with monotonous regularity, but the association's hold on aquatics went beyond team victories.

Swimmers from other clubs often envied WSA teams their coach. L. DeB. Handley, a leading innovator, receives credit for changing the leg action for freestyle from a conservative four-beat flutter kick into a powerful one of six or eight beats. In addition to coaching, Handley spread the swimming gospel in columns that appeared simultaneously in three New York newspapers under his byline. *Encyclopedia Britannica* called on Handley to write the entry on swimming for its twelfth edition.[1]

The true secret of New York's success and influence can be traced to a behind-the-scenes administrator—Charlotte Epstein, professionally a legal secretary and court reporter. Never a strong swimmer herself, she became interested in the sport during the Stockholm Olympics in 1912, when women's events were first included. She helped create the Women's Life Saving League and guided it through its transition to the New York Women's Swimming Association. Authoritative and determined, Charlotte Epstein played a sizable role in the Amateur Athletic Union debates in 1914. The decision to include women's swimming under the AAU umbrella owes a great deal to her influence.

She later planned and supervised hotel exhibitions and meets, bringing swimmers to Florida from throughout the East. In 1920, she led in the effort to send American women to the Olympic Games in Antwerp, and her swimmers were on every Olympic team thereafter through 1936.[2] In 1932 "Eppy" herself was named assistant manager of the swimming team.

That nickname, "Eppy," conveyed the respect and affection of women swimmers nationwide. Her ever-present advice radiated integrity and good sense. The younger 1932 Olympians, somewhat in awe, found her "somebody you just knew you weren't going to fool around with." Swimmers who year after year had benefited from her efforts were, as Margaret Hoffman phrased it, "very high on Eppy [and knew] she pushed all the buttons." She truly cared about all the swimmers and was especially fond of Eleanor Holm. Lenore Kight, Holm's 1932 and '36 Olympic teammate, insisted Eleanor would not have been in trouble with the Olympic committee in 1936 "if Eppy had been on that boat" on the way to Berlin.[3]

Her hand clearly showed in details at the Jones Beach trials and in team affairs in Los Angeles, and her efforts did not go unnoticed. In his official report, the 1932 American Olympic Swimming Team manager saluted her, saying, "For her experienced care and management of the women's team the commendation of the committee is due Miss Charlotte Epstein."[4]

Georgia Coleman had been near the protective wing of Charlotte Epstein since 1928. Small wonder that when the renegades from the Los Angeles Athletic Club landed in New York for the trials in 1932, Georgia said they would ask Eppy "just what we're going to do" about sponsorship.[5] No difficulties surfaced, and the Los Angeles contingent joined with all the others in a round of pretrial meets and water carnivals.

No one loafed through these tune-up meets. They brought out the best in even the highest rated swimmers, who treated spectators to dramatic finishes and record-breaking performances. Thursday night, July 8, at a pool in suburban Rye, Eleanor Holm electrified the crowd by swimming the non-Olympic 200-yard backstroke event at the blistering pace of 2 minutes 28 seconds. (Her time stood as the record for twenty years.) The following Sunday, in a swim carnival at the Jerome Cascades pool, Helene Madison finished 75 yards freestyle in

44.6 seconds, a yard ahead of Jo McKim, bettering the record set in 1925 by Olympian Ethel Lackie.[6]

The swimmers stayed at hotels located from mid-Manhattan to Garden City on Long Island. It was not all work. The days leading to the trials offered leisure and entertainment that included an afternoon as guests at Yankee Stadium, where they saw future Hall-of-Famers Babe Ruth and Lou Gehrig play. They gave individual and group press interviews, and the newsreel movie cameras filmed them often. They were celebrities. From hotel to beach or pool and back, their taxis or team buses raced along behind police motorcycle escorts with sirens at full volume.[7]

They enjoyed the popularity, but as Friday the 15th approached, so did the butterflies, and each coped in her own way. Atlanta's deb-utante, Louisa Robert, spent Thursday at the Elizabeth Arden Salon. She went in for the entire Arden treatment that included leg waxing. (This put her decades ahead of later swimmers who sought to lessen water resistance and gain a psychological boost with extensive body-shaving.) Anxiety ran high among first-time Olympic aspirants.[8]

The swimming trials ran for two days, as opposed to just one af-ternoon for track and field, and they had radio coverage, a sure indica-tion of the popularity of women's swimming. Ted Husing, a top CBS sportscaster, aired a resume of morning events each noon hour and returned at three in the afternoon with a live description of the day's finals. Radio allowed hometowns to share the immediacy and excite-ment of their favorite daughters' exploits and to hear their short post-race interviews. Back in Minnesota, all of Chisholm listened intently, rejoicing in Anne Govednik's success, and waited for her brief personal message after the breaststroke final. Unfortunately, the local station pre-empted the end of Husing's broadcast with a stock market report before Anne's turn on the air.[9]

The starter's gun fired at 10 a.m. Friday, sending off the first heat in 100-meter freestyle. A stiff breeze blew over Zach's Bay that morning, and by afternoon waves made it difficult for a swimmer to stay in her own lane. Heat number one went to Lenore Kight (1:10.2) with Helen Johns next to touch the bulkhead. Jo McKim finished first in the sec-ond heat (1:10.75) and Helene Madison coasted home in heat three (1:12.4). On the comeback trail, Eleanor Garatti Saville took heart with her winning time of 1:09.8 in the fourth preliminary heat. That afternoon, the first semifinal ended with McKim coming in first and Garatti Saville next. Madison dropped her time to tie Kight's earlier 1:10.2 and win the second semi, followed by Kight and Johns. In the finals Madison was first (1:09.2), McKim second (1:10.6), Saville third (1:10.8), Johns fourth (1:11), and Kight fifth (1:11.8). The first three would represent the United States in the 100-meter event, and all five qualified for the 4 × 100 relay.[10]

Katherine Rawls came to Jones Beach as both swimmer and diver. A year before, when she took Eleanor Holm's national 300-meter individual medley crown, she also dethroned Margaret Hoffman, 200-meter breaststroke champion. Youngest and smallest of the lot, Rawls now appeared the brightest Olympic breaststroke prospect for the United States since 1924.[11]

Few knew anything about current indoor title holder Jane Cadwell, and Anne Govednik came to the trials virtually unheralded. Hoffman had been training only since the end of Mount Holyoke's spring term, so with the wind kicking up waves that Friday, record breaking seemed out of the question in 200-meter breaststroke.

Hoffman won the first heat, four seconds ahead of Cadwell, and Govednik touched three seconds ahead of Rawls in the second. No semifinal was needed. The final produced one of the great surprises of the trials. Peg Hoffman pushed her way through rough water to set an American record with a time of 3:12.4—seven seconds better than her own Olympic showing in 1928. Anne Govednik touched second and Jane Cadwell came in next, barely nipping Rawls at the finish. This clinched the third spot on the Olympic team for Cadwell and sent Rawls on to diving.[12] Olympic times for the 200-meter breaststroke did not fall below three minutes until after World War II.

Far from unnerved by losing her breaststroke title, Rawls calmly rowed out to the diving platform and joined the other springboard hopefuls. She blended skill acquired in hundreds of hours on the board in Florida with poise that belied her fourteen years. In the upset of the afternoon, Georgia Coleman made one bad dive and Katherine Rawls edged past her to place first. Jane Fauntz followed close behind Coleman, rounding out the springboard trio to represent the United States in Los Angeles. Fred Cady, Coleman's coach, had seen the surprising turn of events coming. For more than a year he had been praising Rawls's diving, especially her consistently superb entry.[13] Cady, who remained on the West Coast, must also have had some concern about distractions his own diver would have as leader of the Los Angeles Athletic Club mutineers.

The weather Saturday afternoon, only slightly better than the day before, affected the platform diving. Because of high wind that morning several divers scratched from competition, including Fauntz and Rawls, who had already qualified for the Olympic team in springboard. Georgia Coleman, again favored, again suffered an upset. Fellow Californian Dorothy Poynton executed four dives from the platform in beautiful, precise fashion to take top honors. Coleman's running swan entry was slightly short of perfect; she failed to meet her own standard and placed second. Marion Dale Roper placed third to secure the final spot on the team.[14]

With Dorothy Poynton yet to turn seventeen, and Katherine Rawls nearly three years younger, a new generation moved toward diving supremacy. Further proof of a youth movement was the failure of the great Helen Meany Balfe, Olympic diver in 1920, '24, and '28, in her comeback try for a fourth Olympic team. Marion Roper bested her running swan from the tower by a fraction of a point.[15]

Training for the 100-meter backstroke, Louisa Robert had swum miles in Atlanta and at Sea Island, propelled by the dream of defeating Eleanor Holm. In a sense, the dream came true in the choppy water of Zach's Bay. Eleanor won her preliminary heat in the morning, with a time of 1:26.2. In the second preliminary, Louisa came in first with a faster 1:25.4.[16] For a short time she could savor the realization of her ambition; though not head-to-head, she had beaten Eleanor Holm.

The lane draw for the afternoon finals put Louisa on the outside in the roughest water. Even so, with waves breaking over her head and slapping in her face, Robert lowered her own morning time by a tenth of a second. Holm met the newcomer's challenge, though, taking the lead at the start and holding it all the way. Her good friend Joan McSheehy, starting fast and maintaining the pace, forced Holm into setting another world record—1:18.2. Robert came on quickly, barely losing to McSheehy, whom she had beaten in the morning. Given the water conditions, the performances of all three qualifiers gave the coaches reason enough to consider backstroke in good hands in Los Angeles.[17]

A crowd of 35,000 was on hand that day. Diving always pleased the crowds, and Holm more than rewarded them in backstroke. Helene Madison reminded everyone of why she was considered essentially in a class by herself in freestyle.

In keeping with upsets and near-misses, the day's 400-meter freestyle event proved to be closer than anyone would have predicted. Lenore Kight won her preliminary heat in the morning. Madison easily took hers, finishing ahead of Kight's Carnegie Library teammate Anna Mae Gorman. Norene Forbes of the Los Angeles Athletic Club won a third heat, with Dorothea Dickinson of New York's Women's Swimming Association close behind her.[18]

In the finals that afternoon, a beautiful start put Madison 2 yards in front. She pounded through the water with her metronome-steady kick and powerful arm stroke but could not shake Lenore Kight. At the 200-meter mark they left the rest of the field far behind. In spite of the taller Madison's advantage on the turns, the distance between the two had closed to no more than a foot at the finish. They set a blistering pace through the rough water and Lenore's stiff challenge pushed Helene to yet another record. Her time of 5:32.4 cut 6.9 seconds from the old mark held since 1927 by the great Martha Norelius. The tempo was so fast that Kight, too, at 5:37, was under Norelius's time. Noreen Forbes placed third to qualify for the other Olympic spot in 400-meter freestyle.[19]

It had been understood from the outset that the first three placing in each event automatically won a place on the Olympic team. The selection committee announced on Friday that they would not make final team choices until after Saturday's events, reserving the right to choose an outstanding swimmer who "might be the victim of an unfortunate contingency, such as a cramp, and not show in her true colors."[20] The committee did not subjectively replace anyone already qualified, but they did name three alternates to go to Los Angeles, all freestylers. By virtue of her strong showing at 400-meters, Anna Mae Gorman filled one alternate spot; Edna McKibben of Seattle's Washington Athletic Club and Dorothea Dickinson were named second and third alternates.

The crowd of spectators included celebrities ranging from Supreme Court Justice Benjamin Cardoza and Lt. Gov. Herbert H. Lehman to Gertrude Ederle. Ederle came to the sisterhood's reunion to support the next generation of Olympians. Smartly dressed in a suit coordinated with hat, gloves, and purse, she cheered them on from along the wooden dock. With swimming events behind them, and corsages pinned to their swimsuit straps, the women were swept up in a festival of picture-taking on dock and diving boards. Governor Lehman beamed with a political glow, Eleanor Holm flashed her huge smile, and Helene Madison grinned broadly as the three posed for a photograph that appeared in most newspapers across the country.[21]

A week later, Lincoln Werden, who wrote "Women in Sports" for the *New York Times,* departed from his usual low-key coverage of golf and tennis to focus on the recent trials. He hailed them as "one of the most spectacular events of its kind ever held," in part because they gave "many thousands an opportunity of seeing the stellar women swimmers of the nation perform." He thought those who saw the two-day competition should "retain the mild satisfaction of having seen swimming of Olympic caliber even though they cannot travel westward to view the Olympic Games."[22]

The swimmers, who *did* travel westward, wrapped up the trials festivities with a banquet Saturday night. They spent Sunday with friends and relatives and left for Los Angeles Monday evening, July 18. Feverish activity and some suspense marked the two days.

Atlanta's Louisa Robert had realized one ambition in bettering Eleanor Holm's time in the trials only to have her parents oppose her continuing on to the Games in Los Angeles. Some teammates felt her parents had "brought her up to New York just to satisfy her whim and to have a good time—and she confounded them by placing third in the backstroke." Tension mounted on the eve of the team's departure, and Louisa pleaded with them in the lobby of the Concourse Plaza Hotel while everyone milled around. Team and Olympic officials huddled nearby to discuss the dilemma, and Charlotte Epstein's touch can be seen in the solution. They promised her mother and father that everyone would look out for Louisa and, on the spot, Eppy picked a roommate for her stay at the Chapman Park. The Detroit Yacht Club's Jane Cadwell was acceptable, and her parents finally agreed to let Louisa go.[23]

Later in the day the entire group moved on to the marble, cathedral-like concourse of Pennsylvania Station where a seventeen-car special train waited to carry them and other Olympians on their 3,600-mile odyssey. The projected running time of three and a half days was a full day faster than the normal schedule. They would stop in North Philadelphia, Lancaster, and Chicago to add about seventy-five more male oarsmen, field hockey players, weight-lifters, and gymnasts. (Men's track and field trials took place in Palo Alto, California.) The train included extra baggage cars for trunks, bags, and rowing shells, and a car converted into a gymnasium complete with showers, rubbing tables, and weight training equipment. Two additional special chefs would keep all the athletes contented in the dining car.[24]

The three-member American fencing team joined the swimmers to complete the train's small female contingent. Just before the Olympic Special pulled out of Penn Station, that trio of impeccably dressed women stood on its observation platform and smiled obligingly for photographers.[25]

All three fencers—Muriel Guggolz, Dorothy Locke, and Marion Lloyd—trained at New York's Salle Vince under fencing master Joseph Vince. Locke and Lloyd had toured Germany the summer before. While Lloyd had some individual success in one meet, as a team they were no match for the stronger Germans.[26] They knew they would face the likes of European champion Helene Mayer in Los Angeles, but optimism rode with them to the coast.

Properly dressed in street clothes, and all but fourteen-year-old Katherine Rawls even wearing hats, the swimmers boarded the train. As they departed for Los Angeles and Hollywood, perhaps the glamour girls dreamed of movie careers—1932 saw the release of Olympic swimmer Johnny Weissmuller's first *Tarzan* film. When Georgia Coleman met the press after the rebellious flight from Los Angeles, she denied being engaged to Olympic diver Mickey Riley, and told reporters, "I intend to turn professional and make some money after the Olympics." She already had one motion picture offer.[27]

The women swimmers and fencers may have been more traveled than their track and field counterparts, but not all had been to the West Coast. Easterners crossing the plains for the first time sensed the vastness of the country, and mountain and desert scenery captivated those who had been no further west than Pittsburgh. Welcoming committees greeted the train at stops along the way. Teammates had ample time to become better acquainted, whether in their own Pullman car or the popular, air-conditioned club car. A genial atmosphere spawned countless bridge games punctuated with only an occasional flare of bad temper. To help pass the time, the male athletes took straw votes to choose the "best" and "most" in various categories. Not surprisingly, among the swimmers they named Eleanor Holm prettiest, hailed Joan McSheehy as the wittiest, and labeled Georgia Coleman "the girl with the most dominant personality."[28]

The Olympic Special pulled into Los Angeles in the early morning hours of July 22, well ahead of the train carrying the women's track and field team from Chicago. Their rather untimely arrival did not lessen press coverage. When reporters asked her about Katherine Rawls, who had just defeated her at Jones Beach, Coleman said, "She is absolutely unbeatable," and predicted the team would win all the diving events. Eleanor Holm was again the woman "who turned down a role in Ziegfeld's Follies in order to continue her swimming career." When asked about the rumored Japanese threat in backstroke, she discounted it, saying, with remarkable prescience, "We swam against the Japanese at Honolulu, and I really do not think we have anything to fear from them."[29]

Shortly after they arrived, the men boarded buses for the trip to their Baldwin Hills billets in the Olympic Village. Separate vehicles deposited the women at the Chapman Park Hotel, and they soon met swimmers and fencers from abroad who had been arriving in Los Angeles for the past several days. In the week ahead, between scheduled social events, swimmers tested the pool at the new, state-of-the-art swimming stadium. They found it a welcome change from the rough water and arduous conditions at Zach's Bay.

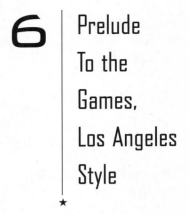

6 | Prelude To the Games, Los Angeles Style

★

In 1932, Los Angeles had no freeways and no smothering blanket of smog. The arriving Olympians found mostly undeveloped country west of Inglewood, open space in Hollywood, and orange trees and minimal congestion elsewhere. Nevertheless, the city was on its way toward its modern image. The 1920s had brought mushrooming suburban real estate development, an oil boom, an influx of tourists, and identification worldwide with Hollywood's movie industry. Population had doubled to 1,470,516 during the decade. Automobiles had begun to replace Pacific Electric's Big Red Cars between city and suburbs. Automobiles and buses were also replacing streetcars within the city itself, but visiting Olympians could and did make use of those still in service, riding free when they wore their Olympic uniforms. Growing traffic had forced the widening of Wilshire Boulevard, and by 1932 it was rapidly becoming the city's main artery. Its "Miracle Mile" glowed with art deco promise—the magnificent Ambassador Hotel on the east, and sparse development west beyond Fairfax to the ocean.[1]

Before the advent of Los Angeles International Airport, California's Southland welcomed travelers on the Union Pacific, Santa Fe, and Southern Pacific at their bustling railroad stations. A sparkling coliseum and new swimming stadium in Exposition Park stood ready for the Games. City officials greeted national Olympic teams on the steps of a new city hall with its now familiar gleaming white tower.

After a decade of development, a vibrant downtown Los Angeles rang with civic energy.

In early July 1932, the Olympic Organizing Committee played its Hollywood trump card. William May Garland had exploited the movie capital's worldwide celebrity at the IOC's 1923 meeting in Rome. (In the quest for delegate votes on site selection for the '32 Games, he identified Los Angeles as a "suburb of Hollywood.") Mary Pickford, "America's Sweetheart," took the lead among Hollywood supporters of the Olympics that summer when she invited the world to the Games on a radio broadcast that reached around the globe by shortwave. Pickford said the athletes would do their part, so everyone else must provide support and cheer them on—"the important thing is to be here." She listed the women's sports and added, "While their records have not yet equalled the men's—notice, I say 'not yet'—they have accomplished wonders in the short time in which they have been competing . . . our cheers will be their inspiration."[2]

Even though the country remained locked in the Depression, people did flock to Los Angeles. The California Highway Department opened new, shorter routes for auto travel from the Bay Area and points north just in time for the Games. Local pride in Helene Madison increased the flow of traffic south from Seattle. The Automobile Club of Chicago recommended routes for the 2,300-mile drive west, and Chicago society pages announced travel plans for the likes of the Chauncy McCormicks and the Potter Palmers. A week after the Olympic Special left Penn Station, a large tour group entrained to follow its route west. A party of more than 700 Texans leased an entire downtown hotel, and organizers anticipated the arrival of a thousand visitors from Japan.[3] The city slowly filled with out-of-state license plates. Trains daily brought swarms of Olympic visitors, and an occasional party landed at Mines field, the small municipal airport southwest of Inglewood that would become LAX. A spruced-up Los Angeles stood ready to welcome everyone.

The Ambassador Hotel had opened on Wilshire in 1921. The Ambassador and the imposing Biltmore, built downtown on Olive at Fifth in 1923, reigned as the city's two grand hotels. Their elegant ballrooms and banquet halls provided sites for gala Olympic functions. During the second week of the Games, the Ball of All Nations honored athletes as special guests at the Ambassador. A few days later Junior Olympic Hostesses entertained the athletes at another ball in the Biltmore's Sala de Oro.[4] The Ambassador's nightclub, the Coconut Grove, regularly attracted athletes, movie moguls and stars, Olympic dignitaries, and civic leaders.

A stone's throw west of the Ambassador and a short block off Wilshire on Alexandria Avenue stood the Chapman Park Hotel. In order to sell his Olympic Village plan, Zack Farmer had made it clear that women would be excluded. The Los Angeles Organizing Committee contracted with the Chapman Park to reserve the entire five-story brick hotel for the exclusive use of Olympic women's delegations. The rates were reasonable, with each nation paying two dollars a day per team member and the Organizing Committee covering the difference.[5]

Grace Walker, on leave from her position as head of the news bureau at the University of Southern California, served as manager of women's housing. At the Chapman Park she combined the roles of concierge, impresario, chaperone, ombudsman, nutritionist, and media consultant. Walker had spent several years overseas with the American Red Cross during World War I and knew Europe well. For help in translation and interpretation, she relied on her multilingual assistant, Linnes Bjorkman, who was fluent in Swedish, German, French, and Italian.[6]

The hotel's lobby and adjoining lounges provided places for teams to mingle and meet the press and public. The athletes occupied double or triple rooms. No repeat of the humiliating hotel experience in Denver befell Tidye Pickett and Louise Stokes at the Chapman Park. Everyone had the same accommodations, rooms, and meals. Gracious living prevailed. During the week before the Opening Ceremony, afternoon tea was served daily in the garden. A profusion of Olympic and national flags, banners, pennants, and bunting graced the dining room where meals were served American style. The kitchen provided special dishes on request, but most would probably echo Jean Shiley's recollection of Depression era austerity—"I was just glad there was something on the table. I didn't care *what* it was."[7]

The Chapman Park's first Olympic guest arrived early in July. New Zealand sprinter Thelma Kench and her chaperone had been at the mercy of limited sailings,[8] and would be among the last to leave in

August for the same reason. With Prince Ferdinand von Lichtenstein in the lead, Austrian athletes and dignitaries arrived in New York aboard the *Europa* and, after sightseeing there, headed to Los Angeles with stops at Niagara Falls, Chicago, and the Grand Canyon. The Danes followed a similar itinerary. A large crowd greeted Denmark's eight women athletes with flowers when they arrived at Chicago's Dearborn Street Station.[9]

On Sunday, July 17, ten thousand members of the Italian community in Los Angeles, many dressed in ethnic costume, greeted Italy's team at the Union Pacific depot. France's sixty-three-member team, including its lone woman, swimmer Yvonne Godard, had docked in New York on Bastille Day. When they arrived in Los Angeles on Tuesday, July 19, "La Marseillaise" rang through the Union Pacific station, again the site of a wild welcome.[10] Freestyler Godard, considered a match for Helene Madison, checked in at the Chapman Park.

A sizable welcoming party of Japanese Americans greeted Japan's delegation, the largest at the Games. It included women track and field athletes and a seven-member women's swim team with its woman coach/chaperone. Their ship docked at 9 a.m., Monday, July 18, and after a full round of welcoming, they finally reached the hotel just before two in the afternoon.[11]

No foreign team had a more enthusiastic reception in Los Angeles than Germany's. The city's German colony turned out in force Thursday morning, July 21. Two bands and hundreds of voices broke into "Deutschland Über Alles" at every opportunity, serenading an overflow crowd at the Santa Fe Station. A parade several blocks long took the athletes to City Hall for a greeting from the mayor, then it was on to the Turnverein for lunch, and finally to the Olympic Village and the Chapman Park.[12]

With considerable Olympic experience, the German women stood to claim a high percentage of medals. Helene Mayer, twenty-one-year-old European fencing champion, had won the gold medal for individual foil in 1928, and was favored to repeat. Greta Heublein placed fifth in discus in 1928, and Marie Dollinger had run in the ill-fated 800-meter race at Amsterdam.[13] Some feared the long, hot trip might have taken its toll; high jumper Helma Notte could scarcely believe that when their train stopped in Kansas City they had come only halfway across the country.

Canada's teams arrived earlier that morning to much less acclaim than Germany's received, but they created their own excitement. The men and women boarded buses at the Southern Pacific station, headed for the Olympic Village with a stop at the Chapman Park, where chivalry proved more than its own reward. The men escorted the women inside, spotted the dining room, and consumed all the food in sight. An astonished hotel staff restored order and replenished breakfast supplies in time for the early arrival of Australia's Bonnie Mealing, always the first into the dining room in the morning.[14]

The Australian women had checked in close behind the New Zealanders. They came early to allow ample time for training, shopping, and touring. Mrs. Chambers, their very proper chaperone, appeared the equal of Charlotte Epstein, having guided the New South Wales Swimming Association for twenty-five years. Bonnie Mealing, Australian backstroke champion, had gone to Amsterdam as a sixteen-year-old and failed to place. She stayed in training while working as a secretary, and was now ready to challenge Eleanor Holm. Claire Dennis, sixteen-year-old breaststroke medal hopeful, continued to nurse a broken toe that hampered training. Frances Bult, a five-foot-four-and-a-half-inch freestyle sprinter, held the favorite's role among the swimmers headed for the 100 meters against a much taller Helene Madison.[15] The Australians had logged many hours in the pool by the time other swimmers began drifting into the Chapman Park.

More teams arrived throughout the week. A small group from Sweden reached Los Angeles the same day as the French. Ingeborg Sjoquist, highly touted Swedish diver, met France's Yvonne Godard in an episode that validated the Olympic bond and vindicated sports competition. It might even have warmed hearts in the anti-competitive Women's Division of the NAAF.

On Sjoquist's first day at the Chapman Park, neither she nor Godard had met any of the other women. Sitting stiffly and formally in the lobby, they were waiting for Grace Walker to take them to dinner when Muriel Babcock, star sports feature writer for the *Los Angeles Times,* happened on the scene. With a bit of sign language and pencil and paper, Babcock managed introductions. The language barrier gave way when they found they were both swimmers. Socializing yielded to business, though, when Godard spotted a picture of Helene Madison in the *Times* sports section. She scanned the pages looking for the American's latest times.[16] Godard and Madison had each tried that spring to have her time accepted first by the International Swimming Federation as the 400-meter freestyle record.

The Poles also arrived in Los Angeles on the 19th. In addition to discus thrower Jadwiga Wajs, the group included Stella Walsh, the Cleveland sprinter who had received severe criticism when she joined the Polish team. On Monday morning, July 25, the Hungarians arrived on the Southern Pacific, and that afternoon the Santa Fe delivered the Austrians. Both brought fencers of medal-winning potential —Hungarian Erna Bogen and Austria's Ellen Preis. The British swimmers, among the last of the women's teams to arrive, docked in New York on Monday, July 25.[17]

Britain's aquatic challengers included freestyler Joyce Cooper and backstrokers Phyllis Harding and Elizabeth Valerie Davies. The versatile Cooper and Davies entered both freestyle and backstroke. Swimmers from the Netherlands were the strongest freestyle challengers; Willemijntje (Willie) den Ouden held gold medal promise—both individually and on the Dutch relay team.

The week in which so many Olympians arrived ended with a Water Festival in the Olympic Swimming Stadium on Friday night. Before the advent of television, people flocked to live entertainment, and large crowds turned out for all the exhibitions. On Sunday, July 24, more than two thousand gathered in Pasadena's Brookside Park for a swimming and diving exhibition that set the swimming world abuzz.

A mild upset occurred that afternoon when Anne Govednick bested Margaret Hoffman in the 100-yard breaststroke, but news flashed around the world, literally, of Helene Madison's loss to Eleanor Saville in the 50-yard freestyle sprint. It was her first defeat in a very long time. Most people, including Madison, probably forgot that Garatti Saville had virtually owned the 50-yard event for five years before retiring in 1929. The two swam in lanes at opposite sides of the pool, and at the short 50-yard distance, Eleanor had too long a lead for Helene to overcome when she realized what was happening three lanes away.[18] Garatti Saville's upset lent some welcome suspense to upcoming freestyle events.

Life at the Chapman Park settled down for a week of training mixed with socializing. Women from the various national teams became friends readily and the language barrier mattered little. "It's great. It's splendid," said Grace Walker. "It seems to be youth calling to youth over the barriers of language, custom, and rivalry."[19] Baron de Coubertin himself could not have expressed Olympic spirit any better.

Rather than a language problem, something akin to culture shock attended the American swimmers' first meeting with Babe Didrikson.[20] Her track and field teammates had weathered her antics and bragging, enduring them for the length of the trip from Chicago. Muriel Babcock, faithful observer of events at the Chapman Park, wrote that Babe "loves to bait the other Americans" around the hotel and reported her accosting Helene Madison to ask about her time for 50-yard freestyle. Whatever figure Madison gave, Babe said, "I did it in three seconds less one day and I wasn't even tryin'." Georgia Coleman showed some surprise when Babe said, "Say, you're a pretty good diver, aren't you? . . . You haven't seen me get going yet, have you? Nope, they won't let me enter the swimming events, but I can show you all."[21] This was not the language of the swimming sisterhood.

The assignments of hotel roommates posed no problem for the swimmers; Eppy made them. She had deftly solved one problem by pairing Louisa Robert with Jane Cadwell before leaving New York, and she forestalled another potential difficulty during the long train trip when she diplomatically recruited Peg Hoffman to room with Helene Madison. Madison was considered something of a "loner" among the swimmers, but, no prima donna herself, Hoffman later said, "It worked out pretty well."[22]

Lacking a Charlotte Epstein, track and field team assignments appear to have been less well considered. Some of the athletes made perfectly clear whom they did *not* want as a roommate. If team chaperone Aileen Allen made the assignment of a three-person room to Mary Carew, Babe Didrikson, and Ruth Osburn, she was astute to include Carew in the trio. Mary had the opportunity to see a different, more benevolent Babe than most did. She later said:

> I think they might have put me in with her because I was so shy and so mousy . . . I was afraid of anything. Here I was in with [Babe] who gave me courage. . . . She was awfully good to me—she considered me a kid—she would use that word—she would say, "Hey, kid, get out there, you're as good they are." . . . She thought I should be more forward. I know she was good for me. I didn't dislike her.[23]

On the other hand, Allen must have forgotten details of the discus qualifying in Evanston, where Ruth Osburn's record-breaking throw pushed Babe into fourth place and out of an Olympic berth. The Texan did not take kindly to that defeat, and she did not give Osburn a chance to see her charitable side. Ruth later recalled that they had not had much use for each other and said:

> There was something there—I think it was because I defeated her—everybody seemed to think that was it, even my coach. . . . It was just one of those things—you see people you dislike—but you try to stay away from them.

Sharing a room made it impossible to stay away, and enmity spilled over onto the training field as Babe continued her push to enter more than three Olympic events.[24]

No team, men's or women's, was allowed to train on the Coliseum track. Each morning during the week of July 25, buses took the women to any of several practice locations—high school fields, playgrounds, the facilities at USC, or the field on Vermont Avenue abandoned by UCLA in its recent move to Westwood.

George Vreeland, United States team coach, set rules and supervised the training sessions, and team manager Fred Steers came to most of them. No one from Vreeland's own Prudential Insurance squad in Newark had qualified for the Olympic team. Most of the women found him impartial and easy to get along with, and they liked him.[25] He monitored performances with an analytical eye but made no attempt to change an athlete's style. Vreeland played a crucial or even controversial role, though, when he selected four sprinters for the 4 × 100-meter relay.

Early on arrival in Los Angeles, team captain Jean Shiley received a telegram from the National Association for the Advancement of Colored People. Given the "elasticity" of rules in Evanston, the NAACP sought to ensure fair treatment for Louise Stokes and Tidye Pickett in the selection of the relay team. Shiley never did understand why the telegram had come to her, thinking it should have gone to the coach or even to the Olympic Committee. She gave the wire to Vreeland, whose primary goal was a relay team that could win the gold medal. Knowing the times each runner was capable of and that on any given day any one could beat the others, he concentrated on passing the baton. He made skill in this critical aspect of the relay the ultimate criterion and all eight had a chance to show their ability.[26]

Both Vreeland and Steers had Babe Didrikson and the one-woman-track-team ballyhoo to handle. The AAU gave ground on the three-event rule in Evanston but had no power to alter the following Olympic rule:

> The maximum number of entries from each nation in each event is fixed by the International Federation.
>
> However, the following numbers cannot be exceeded:
> (a) For individual events, three competitors from each nation (without reserves)
> (b) For team events, one team per nation. . . .[27]

Babe had qualified in three Olympic events—javelin, 80-meter hurdles, and high jump. She did not qualify for the 100 meters and placed fourth in discus behind Osburn, Copeland, and Jenkins. Legend has it that officials unjustly prevented her from entering more than three events. In truth, she had not qualified for more. The United States had three women qualified in the discus and eight sprinters were vying for the relay team. Determined to enter more events, during the week of training Babe focused on the discus and on Ruth Osburn and her still sore ribs and arm.

Babe had written to her coach that in the discus trials she "could not get a good throw. But I'll get this gal who won it and beat her before the Olympics." To stay in shape, Osburn continued to run but did little or no throwing. Typically, at training, Babe would walk beside her and ask if she was "hurting." Ruth later recalled one morning: "[Babe] said, 'You know, I can beat any discus thrower there is.' She said it 'til she knew she was going to make me mad." Osburn finally did get mad and defiantly decided to throw and prove to Babe she could beat her again. Vreeland, who had been walking behind them, intervened and sent Ruth off on the track before she could pick up a discus and damage her arm further.[28] This incident added to the growing animosity between them but did not eliminate Osburn from the discus or get Babe into a fourth Olympic event.

All swim teams trained in the Olympic Swimming Stadium, but with so many teams and so little time they also used both private and public pools at various sites throughout the city. With their events not scheduled to begin until Saturday, August 6, swimmers had two weeks to reach a competitive peak and to become comfortable with the stadium pool. A round of exhibition meets made training fun and entertaining as well as productive.

As in track, the selection of the freestyle relay team rested with the coach. Three relay spots were assured—Madison, McKim, and Saville. L. DeB. Handley, coach of the women's team, worked with the other eligible freestylers and kept them competing for the fourth spot. Only in a rare situation would an Olympic coach make major changes in a swimmer's stroke at that stage. Helen Johns had received little coaching in the short time she had been swimming, but consistently turned in the best times in the training competition. Handley was not satisfied with her stroke, so in this instance he worked to change and improve it.[29]

The Olympians devoted mornings to training but they had afternoons and evenings free for shopping, sightseeing, Hollywood "stargazing," dating, or whatever appealed. The memory of actor Joel McCrea's arriving at the Chapman Park throughout their stay for dates with Josephine McKim remained vivid for everyone. Los Angeles boasted nearly fifty "state societies" made up of transplants from the East or Midwest, and members frequently called to meet and offer hospitality to athletes from their home states.[30]

They could fashion their schedules from a daily list of social events on the hotel bulletin board. One "command" appearance required the entire team's attendance at a broadcast of radio's "The Breakfast Club," and the whole group attended the Mayor's luncheon for women athletes at the Ambassador Hotel. With the Chapman Park so close to the Ambassador, they often walked over to catch their favorite movie stars arriving at the Coconut Grove. In theory, 10 p.m. was curfew time, but in practice it seldom held.[31]

Three celebrities stood out of the crowd for many of the 1932 team— Mary Pickford, Douglas Fairbanks, and Amelia Earhart. This trio, spotted at many sessions of the Games, acknowledged individuals with personal waves of recognition and words of encouragement.[32] In the budding air age, Amelia Earhart's record-setting feats struck a responsive chord with the athletes whose own achievements surpassed the usual expectations for women.

Fairbanks and Pickford, who enjoyed limitless popularity, had supported the Olympic Games since as early as 1924, when they cheered their friend Charlie Paddock to a silver medal in Paris. Pickford had recently broadcast the worldwide invitation for women to come to the Games in Los Angeles, and Fairbanks had aired a companion message for men. Both of them made appearances at the Chapman Park. Mary Pickford had meant it when she told her radio audience, "I'm looking forward to meeting you all at the Olympic Games."[33]

"Pickfair," their English Regency mansion (dubbed the Buckingham Palace of Hollywood by historian Kevin Starr), was something of a mecca for Olympians captivated by the movies. Everyone wanted to go to Pickfair, but by the time the popular pair hosted a reception there for Olympians late in the Games, many from track and field had already left Los Angeles. The swimmers attended in force and mingled with stars and "star journalists" such as Louella Parsons.[34]

Parsons, well known as a Hollywood gossip columnist, wrote a nationally syndicated column. Attracted to the swimming team with its glamour-girl label, she regularly dropped by their practice sessions. She labeled the swimmers potential candidates for the screen and wrote, "Almost any one of [them] could get a job in a studio tomorrow. Are they interested? They certainly are. . . . I wanted to talk swimming, they wanted to ask about motion pictures." She tabbed Eleanor Holm as a likely movie prospect and called Helene Madison "the Juno of the girls . . . [who] has a great admiration for Johnny Weissmuller and, well, who knows, she may do his feminine counterpart on the screen." Parsons linked some of the others with screen favorites of the day. She described Louisa Robert as "a real Southern beauty [with] something of the Lily Damita look, [who] ought to screen well"; she called Jane Fauntz "the Ann Dvorak of the team," and said Anne Mae Gorham had "the look of a young Ruth Chatterton."[35]

It is virtually impossible to overstate the importance of the movies in the life of the nation during the 1930s. Any connection between motion pictures and Olympians, however slight, found its way into print. Everyone relished social activities with a Hollywood link. Some toured the Max Factor cosmetic factory and became loyal converts to its products. Small groups went to gatherings at stars' homes, such as the party at the oceanfront home of Conrad Nagel, where the cast of the "Our Gang" comedies and a young Jackie Cooper mingled with track and swimming stars. A star-studded luncheon and tour of the Fox Studios was an event missed by few if any athletes, domestic or foreign.[36]

Twentieth Century–Fox built its studios on the far west side of Los Angeles. In 1932, before development encroached and swallowed it, the Fox property occupied a spacious open area between Pico and Santa Monica Boulevards that was later to become Century City. On Wednesday of the week before the Games, a host of stars assembled to greet 117 athletes for lunch and a memorable afternoon of entertainment, with humorist Will Rogers as master of ceremonies.[37]

Harry Levette, Los Angeles–based entertainment columnist for the *Chicago Defender*, reported the affair for his readers in Illinois. He wrote:

> Feminine athletes were the guests of Fox Studios, all leaving the Chapman Park hotel where they are housed, and escorted there in a body. Included were the two wonderful Colored girl sprinters, Tidye Pickett of Chicago and Louise Stokes of Boston, Mass. No distinction was made in their entertainment, as they were shown about the lot and stages and honored at lunch with such famous hostesses and hosts as Janet Gaynor, Charles Farrell, Arlene Judge . . . [et al.].[38]

Will Rogers posed for pictures with most of the athletes. In the course of shaking hands with everyone, he quizzed Georgia Coleman about rumors of marriage to diver Mickey Riley, and she again denied it as she had in New York. Never missing a chance, when Babe Didrikson shook hands with Rogers she challenged him to "any kind of sport." Saying he had heard all about her, he replied, "Not me . . . I'll take someone easy." Sitting next to Rogers at lunch was the highlight of Olympic social affairs for Lenore Kight.[39]

One aspect of the Olympic experience did not sit well with many of the Americans—housing the men's and women's teams in separate locations. Jane Fauntz, for one, would have preferred arrangements similar to those in Amsterdam. Decades later she still said, "I really missed the boys. I think we had more fun in Europe when we all lived on the ship together."[40]

The Olympic Village was something of an experiment. To defend and strengthen the Village concept, the Los Angeles Organizing Committee stressed security. Taking great pains to avoid the possibility of distraction or impropriety, they emphasized that women would not be allowed inside. The barrier came down only once; the Village held a reception for the women athletes following the Opening Ceremony.[41]

In one of the true ironies of the Xth Olympiad, the Women's Division of the National Amateur Athletic Federation met in convention at the Los Angeles Biltmore on Friday, July 22. Without mentioning the Olympic Games in her statement, executive committee chair Agnes R. Wayman of Barnard College renewed the Division's stand against competition:

> What the women's division disapproves of is the intense highly specialized type of competition which generally prevails in interscholastic competitive open track-and-field meets, certain kinds of tournaments and other situations where the interest is motivated largely by the championship. Too often in this situation the few have been developed and exploited at not only their own expense but at the expense of the many. The women's division feels that for the school or college girl or girl of like age, the intense, inter-competitive [sic] program is not productive of better girls or better women.

After convention delegates saw an exhibit of athletic clothes, they went on record favoring "the bloomer and blouse type of costumes" and condemned "the track type of gym suit, with low back and abbreviated trunks."[42] Olympians wore the latter.

The Olympic women did not respond directly, but statements from the Women's Division may have brought forth a rare public statement from Lillian Copeland. The veteran discus thrower supported the three-event rule on competition and criticized the AAU for ignoring it in Evanston. She said:

> Competitive athletics for women take the brunt of considerable criticism as it is . . . they are said to be detrimental to a woman's health, . . . They really are not unhealthful, if taken in the right spirit and the right proportion. Women stand no more chance of

suffering physically from athletics than men. The same things that wear out men, wear out women—poor supervision, poor preparation and over-indulgence.

Reasoning thus, she maintained the three-event rule was a sound one, adding, "To set it aside, even for an athletic prodigy such as Babe Didrikson—is unwise in my mind. The rule should be enforced."[43] For the two-time Olympian to take a public swipe at Babe was highly unusual.

No official ground rules covered dealings with the ever-present press. For the most part reporters were considerate and the athletes felt no pressure. An occasional radio interview put women on the air. While most of the women were cooperative, few of them searched for publicity.[44]

Babe Didrikson, who had her own spot on Dallas radio, relished the give-and-take with reporters. She had quickly become their favorite, and after the trials in Evanston her every action and ploy found its way into a column or a news report. Columnist Grantland Rice became an unabashed booster of the Babe. In his nationally syndicated column "The Sportlight," he nurtured the Didrikson legend. His lack of total accuracy helped create some myths that have been perpetuated and embellished along the way.

Rice caught the feeling of the Olympic men, perhaps of the working sports press also, and their attitude toward women's events. On the eve of the Games he wrote:

> Male athletes and most male coaches won't take the feminine side of the Olympic Games any too seriously, but you will find the girls will have a continued appeal to the crowds in the stands. They will provide a refreshing variety, even if they don't come close to male marks.[45]

Those reporters who routinely covered women's sports continued to assess women's team prospects in a professional manner right up to the Opening Ceremony. Edward Bulger of the *Boston Transcript* thought the outlook bright for the freestylers, rated backstroke and breaststroke as uncertain, and said, "The American track competitors are likely to face a harder task, . . . [but] it is the best this country has ever mustered."[46] It remained for the women to win over all the others with outstanding performances.

Crowds surged into town during that week leading up to the Games. Late Thursday evening, residents and visitors alike packed downtown near the civic center for the decorative Olympic lighting of City Hall. A cheering throng greeted Vice President Charles Curtis's train the next morning when he arrived to open the Games as a stand-in for Herbert Hoover.[47] The president had declined the invitation, breaking the tradition of heads of state presiding at the Opening Ceremony that dated back to 1896, King George of Greece, and the first Olympiad of the modern era.

Hoover remained in Washington to cope with such mounting problems as the disastrous ouster of the veterans' Bonus Army from its monthlong encampment at the edge of the nation's capitol. Although California had abundant evidence of hard times and its own symbols of the Depression, nothing could quash the spirit in Los Angeles. As the city had made ready for the approaching Games, Olympic enthusiasm had mounted. Hotels were crowded and every train, ship, and plane that arrived added to the crush. A feeling of Mardi Gras hung in the pristine air at the end of July 1932.

7 | The Games Begin, Track And Field

★

By 9:00 Saturday morning, July 30, Los Angeles was on the move. Downtown crowds already milled in the vicinity of the Biltmore and traffic approached gridlock. Everything focused on the Olympic Opening Ceremony, set for 2:30 that afternoon. At the coliseum, concessionaires and vendors hawking souvenirs already lined sidewalks for blocks in every direction. By noon their business was booming and restaurants overflowed. Small planes droned overhead, towing advertising banners, and a lone dirigible toured the same route above a throng of nearly 20,000 that had filtered into the coliseum two hours early. Several thousand more people continued with picnics on the grass outside the giant concrete structure.[1]

A capacity crowd of more than 100,000 paid two dollars each that day for admission to the coliseum and 50,000 more swarmed outside for a glimpse of the ceremony. The blazing California sun beat down on the mass of colorfully dressed women and white-shirted men. Hundreds of flags flew above the rim of the coliseum and the peristyle at the east end was flanked by the five-ringed Olympic standard. The peristyle itself carried a Coubertin message on the Olympic spirit: "The important thing in the Olympic Games is not winning, but taking part. The essential thing is not conquering, but fighting well."[2]

At precisely 2:30, Vice President Curtis made his way to the presidential box and the Opening Ceremony was underway. The 250-piece band and massed choir of 1,200 voices joined in a rendition of the national anthem that even blasé New York columnist Damon Runyan termed "magnificently impressive."[3]

The athletes' parade began with, traditionally, the delegation from Greece and ended with the host Americans coming last. The women's team waited its turn in the main tunnel leading to the field and then emerged from darkness into blinding sunlight for their first look at the immense crowd. They wore uniforms of white skirts and blouses, red vests, and stiff, new white shoes that rubbed a few blisters in the course of the afternoon. Their red cloche hats had triangles of red and blue stripes over the left ear. The teams all circled the track, marching crisply in formation, and formed into columns the width of the field.[4]

They stood during a program that included more from the band, an artillery salute, the Olympic flag-raising followed by the release to freedom of two thousand pigeons (in lieu of doves), the Olympic hymn, and a dedication address. Finally, the athletes repeated the Olympic Oath and marched out of the stadium to the band's recessional. As the last American disappeared back into the tunnel no one left the stands. The enormous crowd was deeply moved by this most impressive Olympic Opening to date, and they remained, in Runyan's words, "absolutely awed by the majesty of the spectacle, the like of which we shall not see again."[5]

For that one time only, the entire complement of Olympians assembled in one place. From there they dispersed to widely scattered venues—from men's cycling in Pasadena's Rose Bowl in the north to rowing at Long Beach to the south. Fencers would meet in the nearby armory, track and field athletes would return to the coliseum itself, and swimmers would descend on the new swim stadium. Saturday saw a landmark beginning; a new wave of excitement and expectation started building the next day.

More than 50,000 spectators were on hand Sunday when the first events began at 2:30—men's high jump, shot put, and 400-meter hurdle preliminaries. Women's javelin and men's 10,000 meters went at 5:30.[6]

Women's javelin made its Olympic debut in Los Angeles, substituting for the ill-fated 800 meters of 1928. Columnist Westbrook Pegler noted that the presence of women in field events had caused complaining among men of the sports press. Many of them, he said, still insist "women's place in the Olympic meets is in the water and not on land, and [so] urge that they be . . . prevented from cluttering up the lot with delicate parodies of the mighty feats that males perform."[7]

The initial competition should have changed some minds. Babe Didrikson's first toss of the javelin in the opening event for women added to a legend that had been building since Evanston. It could hardly have been more dramatic.

Germany's Ellen Braumuller and Tillie Fleischer came into the competition heavily favored. Babe threw first. Pausing briefly, left hand on her hip, javelin about ear level over her shoulder, she rose slightly on her toes and started down the runway. As she neared the foul line, she pulled her arm back, rotated to the right, and with a hopstep let fly. The javelin sang through the air to be marked at 143 feet 4 inches. The crowd roared appreciatively when the distance was announced; it was more than 11 feet beyond Braumuller's earlier record printed in the official program. Given Babe's record of boasting and challenging everyone in everything, Westbrook Pegler may have been closer than he knew when he wrote that the javelin "stuck in the grass and twitched angrily as though taunting the other girls to throw that far."[8]

The United States had its first woman's gold medal of the Games. Ellen Braumuller won silver for Germany, and Tillie Fleischer took the bronze. Masako Shimpo of Japan placed fourth, followed by Nan Gindele and Gloria Russell. Gindele's best effort that day was only 124 feet 6 inches, but she still held the javelin world record (153 feet 4½ inches) and would until 1938.[9]

When everyone returned to the Chapman Park, *Los Angeles Times* reporter Muriel Babcock was waiting for more of the story. Still wearing sweats, Babe bounced into the hotel to find everyone waiting to applaud and cheer her entrance. She headed through the lobby, grinning and signing fans' autograph books as she went. Babcock asked about the phenomenal throw. Babe told her it was something of a mistake, adding, "My hand slipped when I picked up the pole. It slid along about six inches and then I got a good grip again. And then I threw and it just went." Team manager Fred Steers interrupted to say it would have gone 155 or 160 feet if her hand had not slipped.[10]

Before Babe left the coliseum, she had made what may have been the first post-event radio appearance of an Olympic medal winner.

Radio was still so new a medium that, even in Los Angeles, the thought of tapping it as a source of Olympic funding occurred late in the day. Efforts to sell radio rights for $100,000 did not start until July. CBS radio had aired minimal coverage of the women's trials from Jones Beach, and the day before the Games opened, the network announced that it would carry fifteen-minute summaries beginning Monday. No live coverage was permitted from any of the venues, but Ted Husing would broadcast daily reports at 11:15 p.m., Eastern Daylight Time. Babe's comments on Sunday probably went out over Los Angeles's station KHJ, which had its own nightly summaries.[11]

With Babe more than living up to pre-Olympic billing on Sunday, women's track and field attracted great interest for the rest of the week. Monday afternoon, August 1, another tremendous crowd was on hand to cheer the entrants in the 100 meters when trial heats began at 3:45.

Coach George Vreeland predicted a fast time for the United States in the 100 meters even though they would miss Betty Robinson, who had won gold in Amsterdam. In fact, no place winners from 1928 were present, and their world and Olympic records soon vanished as well. Stella Walsh, running for Poland, bettered both marks in the first trial heat. Finishing in 11.9, she broke the world record of 12 seconds and Robinson's Olympic record of 12.2.[12]

Billie von Bremen, considered this country's leading hope in the 100 meters, found herself in a preliminary heat with Germany's Marie Dollinger and Hilda Strike of Montreal. All three survived into the finals. Elizabeth Wilde astonished longtime observers by finishing her initial heat 10 yards ahead of a field that included Thelma Kench of New Zealand. Kench had recently run the distance in 11.2 on grass.[13]

In the semifinals at 5:00 that afternoon, Wilde ran against Hilda Strike, Dollinger, and Tolina Schuurman, former world record holder from the Netherlands. In the closest women's race of the day, they were so tightly bunched at the finish that it took judges almost half an hour to decide the winner. After checking the so-called "electric and motion-picture timing device," they announced Canada's Strike as first, in 12.4 seconds, followed by Wilde and Dollinger.[14]

For close finishes that day, the women's semifinal took second place to the finals of the men's 100 meters. The men's finish and its judging set the tone for several controversies to follow during the next two weeks.

United States sprinters Eddie Tolan and Ralph Metcalfe finished so nearly even for first and second places that several judges disputed the result. Lawson Robertson, coach of the American team and of high jumper Jean Shiley, thought it was Metcalfe by a close margin. Tolan himself, thinking he had lost, went over to congratulate Metcalfe. The crowd of 60,000 sat in unbelieving silence after the announcement of Tolan as the winner.[15]

Although electrical timers had been used in the men's West Coast Olympic trials, the IAAF rules committee chose to continue using handheld stopwatches as the official Olympic timing devices. At a meeting in July, the committee did approve semiofficial use of the new Kirby photoelectric timer.[16] Known to the athletes as the "Kirby camera," this primitive device probably created or prolonged more controversy than it prevented or resolved.

No controversy attended the fencing competition in the armory that summer. The venerable sport had few adherents in the United States, and in 1932 they could be found mainly in New York, Boston, and California.[17]

In viewing sports for women in the 1920s, American social observers and critics had found them either worthy or wanting. Swimming enjoyed popular acceptance as an entertaining, glamorous sport, while track and field had been judged harshly and termed dangerous or "blue collar" by critics. To extend this sort of categorizing, fencing was the aristocrat—the crème de la crème. Prior to 1928 fencing had been the province of society's elite; New York's Mrs. Stuyvesant Fish, for example, had regularly contended for women's foils championships.[18]

The 1928 United States Olympic team moved American fencing out of the elitist mold. Marion Lloyd, a telephone company clerk, headed the team. She had learned to fence in the company's recreation program, and within two years had won the women's national foils title. Though eliminated in the semifinals at Amsterdam, Lloyd had the distinction of dealing the only defeat to gold medalist Helene Mayer.[19]

European mastery of Olympic fencing continued until 1948. Maria Cerra placed fourth for the United States that year in London, and Janice York followed with a fourth-place finish at Helsinki in 1952. No other American woman has matched their accomplishments. On Tuesday afternoon, August 2, 1932, however, Marion Lloyd, who became mentor and inspiration for both Cerra and York, broke new ground.[20]

Again heading the U.S. team, with four victories and three defeats in the first elimination round, Lloyd became the first American to reach the finals in Olympic fencing. The next day she finished ninth, with two victories and seven defeats. Helene Mayer, the favorite coming in, placed fifth. The gold medal went to Ellen Preis of Austria and silver to Britain's Heather Guinness after the two had fenced off a tie of eight wins and one loss each. Erna Bogen from Hungary claimed the bronze medal.[21]

At the same July 27 meeting that ruled on timing devices, the Olympic rules committee dealt another setback to sprinters. They voted to continue the ban on starting blocks, which had been under discussion since Amsterdam and used successfully at the men's trials.[22] So Tuesday afternoon, finalists in the women's 100-meter race carried their trowels to the track at four o'clock and dug their own starting holes.

Two American sprinters reached the finals—Wilhelmina von Bremen and Elizabeth Wilde. They took their marks with Canada's Hilda Strike, Great Britain's Eileen Hiscock, Germany's Marie Dollinger, and Poland's Stella Walsh.[23]

Having set a record the day before, Walsh was picked to win easily. Strike took the lead at the gun and held it for the first 40 meters. Walsh, arms and legs working like pistons, drew even with the Canadian and the two battled to the 80-meter mark. In third place, shifting her smooth, graceful stride into overdrive, von Bremen fought to close on them. With a mere inch or two separating Strike and Walsh over the last 20 meters, an upset appeared to be in the making. Then Stella drew on her famous finishing kick to hit the wire half a yard in front. Hilda Strike won the silver medal, but she had extended Walsh far more than anyone had expected, forcing her to repeat her newly set record of 11.9 to win the gold. Billie von Bremen crossed the finish line not quite even with Strike, to take the bronze medal. Elizabeth Wilde tied with Dollinger for fifth behind Britain's Hiscock.[24]

Stella Walsh had been on the track circuit for several years. Most 1932 Olympians knew her and considered her a very private person. She kept to herself, coming to meets already dressed for competition and leaving immediately afterward. Following her gold-medal triumph, "she sneaked off from the stadium before her [Polish] team-mates did," according to reporter Muriel Babcock. Some considered her a rather tragic figure, always on the fringes, but her abrupt switch to the Polish team had left most athletes perplexed. They could not understand why or how she could run for another country. She went on to win the 100-meters silver medal for Poland at the 1936 Games, behind Helen Stephens of the United States, and made an unsuccessful Olympic comeback bid in 1956. The lonely and puzzling life of Stella Walsh ended in the winter of 1980 in Cleveland, Ohio. An innocent by-stander, she was shot during a store robbery attempt. A postmortem report divulged that she had male sex organs. As Olympic chronicler David Wallechinsky put it, "All the while that Walsh had been setting 11 world records, winning . . . two Olympic medals, she was, in fact, a man."[25]

Based on the performances he saw in Evanston, George Vreeland felt the American team was strong in the discus. However, Boston columnist Edward Bulger saw difficulty ahead and, even with a nod of respect toward Lillian Copeland, he wondered who could edge out Poland's Jadwiga Wajs or Greta Heublein of Germany. Heublein, who placed fifth at Amsterdam, had recently thrown an eighth of an inch longer than Ruth Osburn's record breaker in Evanston. Ten athletes met to settle the matter at 2:30 on Tuesday—three Germans, two Poles, one Japanese, and Americans Copeland, Jenkins, and Osburn.[26]

Ruth Osburn had the speed, strength, balance, and agility that the discus demands, and she still carried Coach Fred Schwengel's advice: "Give it all you've got on the first throw, you may not have a second." As she stepped into the circle just in front of the coliseum's south stands, every expression and movement telegraphed her intention to do just that. Holding the discus lightly in her right hand, she slowly swung it back and forth, and went into her throw. Spinning once and three-quarters, she gained momentum and released the discus with a snap of her arm. It was a beautiful throw. The discus hummed straight across the field, passed directly over a small Polish flag, and landed about 2 feet beyond it. The flag marked the Olympic record set in 1928 by Halina Konopacka (129 feet 11¾ inches). Ruth's throw of 131 feet 8 inches was hailed as the world record, and she appeared to have a lock on Olympic gold.[27]

For 30 minutes no one approached that mark. Lillian Copeland knew her last throw that day would be her final Olympic effort, and she summoned up a reserve of strength, resolve, and concentration. Her well-grooved windup flowed into a smooth spin across the circle and she released the disc with explosive force. It sailed out, actually hit the flag, and glided past the marker where Ruth's great toss had landed. Lillian Copeland had won her gold medal.[28]

She and Ruth Osburn had won gold and silver for the United States, and Jadwiga Wajs the bronze for Poland. Greta Heublein once again placed fifth, behind her German teammate Tillie Fleischer.[29]

Old friends rejoiced for Copeland. Dean Cromwell, men's USC and 1936 Olympic track coach, said she deserved unusual praise for proving "that women can make comebacks." He thought she had been at the peak of her form in Amsterdam when she placed second in the discus and marveled that she had decided to try for the Olympic team after starting her first year in law school.[30]

While she must surely have been disappointed, Ruth Osburn graciously accepted the outcome. She said, "I did my best and I am glad an American won. I've got the next Olympics four years from now, ahead of me." Margaret Jenkins did not place that day, but she stole onto the field and retrieved the discus Lillian used in her victory. She concealed it under her shirt, and later gave it to her longtime friend and rival as a trophy.[31]

Judging for the discus and javelin in 1932 was straightforward and uncontroversial. Once the measuring tape was read, the outcome was not in dispute. The Games organizers had tried to provide similar certainty by buying the finest in Swiss watchmaking technology for the timed events. Thirty 21-jewel watches, each costing six thousand 1932 dollars, were graduated for tenth-of-a-second timing and certified by the Swiss government.[32] Scientific precision was supposed to give comfort and assurance, but human hands controlled the watches, and fallible human eyes sighted along the finish lines.

Protests and complaints about Olympic judging had a long history. They date back at least to the contentious 1908 Games in London, where officials ordered a rerun of the 400-meter dash because of a disputed first heat. Notable official bungling in the Xth Olympiad included allowing runners to go one lap too many in the men's steeplechase. The infamous Tolan-Metcalfe finish lives in memory, along with that of the men's 5,000-meter race. In the latter, the crowd roared in outrage when the judges gave first place to world record–holder Lauri Lehtinen of Finland. Lehtinen had twice swerved in front of Ralph Hill, blocking the Oregonian's attempts to pass during the last 50 meters. The judges' decision in the 5,000 meters finally came after a two-hour delay.[33]

Some of the most amusing satire of the summer of 1932 came at the expense of the Olympic judges. Will Rogers considered everyone fair game, from Herbert Hoover on down. He regularly commented on the Games, and his column on Thursday, August 4, targeted the judges.

> I have been a patron of these games now all summer, and there is something that I think should be rectified. . . . I think that the judges should be notified in some way who wins the various events, so they will know it on the day it happens. As things are now they have to go to the movies at night and see the pictures to see who won, now I think that they should know who these winners are as soon as the audience does. . . .
>
> If the judges will just watch the [photographers] they will find out who wins, the cameramen rush to the winners right away, so it might not be a bad idea to have the cameramen tell the judges. . . .[34]

By ironic coincidence, Rogers' comments appeared in the *Los Angeles Times* on the day of the most disputed of the women's events—the final of the 80-meter hurdles.

Preliminary hurdle heats the day before had produced times below the record of 12.2 seconds set by South Africa's Marjorie Clark at Durban in 1930. The first heat pitted Clark against Babe Didrikson and Simone Schaller of the United States, Canada's Betty Taylor, and Michi Nakanishi of Japan. Clark was away first. Nakanishi fell at the second hurdle. At the halfway mark, Simone led, while Babe, with her usual slow start, was fourth. With one hurdle left, Didrikson and Schaller were even. They cleared the barrier together and broke the tape virtually tied at 11.8. Photographs of the finish show them dead even, but press accounts implied that Babe had won handily. The two American hurdlers first met uneventfully in Evanston. They had spent some time together congenially in Los Angeles—including the afternoon when

Simone took Babe downtown to help her find new shoes. This semifinal heat was Schaller's first on-track brush with the Didrikson mystique.[35] ·

Evelyne Hall, well aware of Babe's power and ploys, ran in the next heat with Canada's Alda Wilson, Britain's Violet Webb, Poland's Felicja Schabinska, and Mie Muraoka of Japan. Evelyne and Alda Wilson were even at 40 meters, then Violet Webb moved past Wilson for second place. With finesse and skill over the hurdles, and with a stronger finishing drive than Webb's, Evelyne broke the tape in 12 seconds flat—also below Clark's record time.[36]

At 3:30 Thursday afternoon, August 4, the hurdle finalists came onto the track; they measured and dug starting holes. Evelyne was in the inside lane, Babe next to her, then Marjorie Clark, Alda Wilson, Schaller, and Webb. On their marks, mounting tension broke when Babe shot off in a false start; one more and she was out. Again on their marks, the gun sent them off, Evelyne in the lead with a good start. Cautious after jumping once, Babe started even more slowly than usual. Evelyne was well in the lead over the first hurdle and Violet Webb was next over, a good foot ahead of Babe and Marjorie Clark. A less polished hurdler, Babe made up time between the barriers and forged into the lead. Hall flew along in the adjoining lane and Babe's lead began to slip. Evelyne pulled even and they crossed the last hurdle together. They were absolutely even when their forward feet touched the ground just before the finish line. As they hit the tape together, Babe threw up her arm; on the train from Evanston, she had confided this trick to Evelyne as a way of making the officials think her the winner.[37]

Evelyne caught the tape neck-high with enough force to sustain an abrasive cut that drew blood. In the words of the *Dallas Morning News,* "It looked almost like a dead heat but the judges decided in Babe's favor without much delay." Arthur Daley of the *New York Times* called it an "eye-lash victory," and judged it "quite comparable to the Tolan-Metcalfe 100-meter battle." Damon Runyan wrote, "They hit the tape apparently right together." Photographs and movie film footage do not provide proof beyond a doubt. One enduring still photo, taken from Evelyne's side of the track, clearly shows a tie. The judges, positioned on the side of the track that put Didrikson first in their line of sight, took nearly half an hour to make their decision.[38]

Many in the crowd of spectators thought Evelyne had won or at

least tied. She recalled returning toward the tunnel, going past the officials still in conference, and hearing the other athletes "all cheering and
clapping and saying, 'You won, you won, you won.' " When the officials
finally ruled, the gold medal went to Babe and the silver to Evelyne.
Accounts by those journalists and historians who did not consider it a
dead heat set Babe's margin of victory anywhere from 2 to 6 inches.
Curiously, the officials registered the time for each as 11.7 seconds,
new world and Olympic records.[39]

Damon Runyan went on to say, "There is no doubt in [Babe's]
mind about the result, whatever any one may think. She waves her
hand at the stands after the finish." Thoroughly dejected and discon-
solate, the usually effervescent Evelyne Hall returned to a quiet Chapman Park Hotel, where little sound of the controversy echoed. Muriel
Babcock once again caught the essence of Babe's brash arrogance, a
condescending confidence that rankled others. When she asked about
the finish, Babe told her, "Sure, I slowed up a little, . . . I just wanted to
make it a good race. Win the next event? Well, I hope so. That's what
I'm here for."[40]

The memory of those few seconds in 1932 remained distinct and
clear for Evelyne. In the autumn of 1990, she recounted the entire
episode once again and speculated on instant replay and what might
have been:

> But you know—a race like that is very, very fast. Of course, if
> they'd had the instant camera—. . . But the Kirby camera—it was
> the first time they used a camera like that but it wasn't official. A
> week later . . . they had this big meeting . . . [at] the Biltmore—
> and they had the American officials there. They showed the race
> [films] with Tolan and Metcalfe and with me . . . [on] a regular size
> screen. . . . And all the officials were around and they had pointers
> and they were trying to figure where Didrikson was and where I
> was—and also they did the same with Tolan and Metcalfe. They
> said if the camera had been official it could have been otherwise—
> that at least it was a tie.[41]

The United States might easily have laid claim to the bronze
medal in the hurdles as well as gold and silver. Attention to an equally
close finish for third and fourth disappeared in that given to first and
second place. Simone Schaller had hit a hurdle in practice a few days
earlier and she ran in the finals with a still tightly wrapped and sore left

knee. Pictures indicate another photo finish between her and Marjorie Clark. They were neck-and-neck at the tape, but foot positions suggest Schaller reached the line first. She later said she might have beaten Clark, adding, "but who cared. Everyone was watching Babe Didrikson. They didn't care about anybody else." She took it in stride, and later said, "I wasn't too disappointed though. I was just glad to get in the finals."[42]

The next women's events took place the following Sunday, August 7, the concluding day for track and field. The high jump began at 2:30 and the 4 × 100-meter relay at 3:00. The return of the official Olympic band that day brought back some of the emotional stir and excitement, color and delight of the Opening Ceremony. It entertained another near-capacity crowd in the coliseum as the high jumpers trooped onto the field that afternoon.[43]

The official program listed eight sprinters eligible for the American relay team: Mary Carew, Evelyn Furtsch, Ethel Harrington, Tidye Pickett, Annette Rogers, Louise Stokes, Wilhelmina von Bremen, and Elizabeth Wilde. When the United States failed to take the gold medal in the 100-meter event, Coach George Vreeland became absolutely determined to win the relay. He sought the four fastest runners while looking for the quickest start, the strongest finishing drive, and the surest baton handling. For two weeks, all eight ran trial sprints. Billie von Bremen had the fastest times; Annette Rogers ran a close second. With only one false start allowed, Vreeland coached everyone to avoid jumping the gun.[44]

Mary Carew consistently got off the mark faster than anyone. She remembered spending "hours and hours passing that baton" and Vreeland's telling them not to look back at the runner passing it but to "dig in and start running—it's up to her to get it into your hand." He was a stickler about baton passing, certain they would need three perfect exchanges to win. Evelyn Furtsch's speed and dexterity with the baton won her the fourth relay spot.[45]

On Sunday, August 7, the quartet of Carew, Furtsch, Rogers, and von Bremen ran in lane number four. They took aim at the first and only Olympic mark for the relay—48.4 seconds, set by Canada in 1928. Five other teams started—Holland, Germany, Great Britain, Japan, and Canada.[46]

From the opening gun it was a two-team race. Mary Carew bolted off first on the start against Canada's Mildred Frizzell to put the U.S. team slightly ahead in the first 100 meters. The baton went smoothly to Evelyn. She ran it a bit farther out in front and handed off to Rogers. As they swung around the curve on the third leg, Mary, the second of Canada's sprinting Frizzell sisters, regained a little ground. The hours of baton drill paid off 100 meters from home. Annette passed perfectly to Billie von Bremen, while Mary Frizzell could manage only a fair exchange with Hilda Strike. Billie started the anchor leg almost on even terms with Strike. Her long stride grew stronger as they went, and she carried the tape away at the finish with about a yard to spare. They had covered the 400 meters in a record-breaking 47 seconds. They actually did it in 46.9, but for some reason, women's relays were not recorded in tenths of seconds in 1932. Their time is now listed in Olympic records as 46.9.[47] Great Britain placed third, the Netherlands fourth, Japan fifth, and in sixth place came Germany's by now familiar quartet—Heublein, Braumuller, Fleischer, and Dollinger.

With an enormous crowd screaming approval, one-tenth of a second mattered little that afternoon. Evelyn said, "We didn't give Wilhelmina much of a chance to catch her breath before Mary Carew, Annette and I swarmed all over her." Reflecting on the race later, she decided, "We must have made three perfect passes."[48]

Vreeland's strategy and preparation had reaped a valuable dividend. After the brief, tumbling victory celebration, Annette Rogers returned to the high jump, where the action had started at 2:30.

That neither African American sprinter ran in the relay raises the question of race and fairness in choosing the team, which rested with Coach George Vreeland. Separate explanations of Vreeland's priorities and selection process offered by team members decades later are virtually identical; they form the basis of the account above.

In 1984, asked about her Los Angeles summer, Tidye Pickett recalled, "The athletes as a whole were wonderful, and the coaches, too." As for not running in the Games, she said, "But times were different then. Some people just didn't want to admit that [Louise Stokes and I] were better runners."[49] Given the telegram from the NAACP, Vreeland surely grasped the importance of objectivity. Given the prevailing racial attitudes and practices of 1932, the possibility of discrimination, however subtle, makes a final answer to the question unlikely.

★　★　★

High jump, last of the women's events, provided another enduring example of official timidity, uncertainty, and some ineptitude. It was soon after arriving in Los Angeles that Babe Didrikson had told the omnipresent Muriel Babcock about the trials in Evanston: "I'm the only girl, as far as I know, that jumped western style, like the boys."[50] That style, the Western Roll, represented an early try for greater vertical lift over the bar. Most women still used the classic scissors jump in 1932. The scissors, better at keeping the head or shoulder from crossing the bar in advance of the feet, allowed less chance for fouling. This fundamental rule—that the feet must cross first—still held for women. The high jump controversy of the Xth Olympiad may have been a prime factor in the elimination of that rule the following year.

Another near capacity crowd followed the jumping closely— Babe was going for an unprecedented third individual gold medal. Six nations entered high jumpers. Carolina Gisolf of the Netherlands came to defend her record set in Amsterdam, and Germans Ellen Braumuller and Helma Notte threatened to break it. Yayeko Sagara and Yuriko Hirohashi represented Japan. South Africa's Marjorie Clark rated as a challenger along with Canada's Eva Dawes. Annette Rogers, Babe, and Jean Shiley carried hopes and expectations for the United States.[51]

Coach Lawson Robertson had equipped Jean with physical and mental skills that set records, and he discouraged her from experimenting with the Western Roll. He also prescribed some measures that now seem quaint, to say the least. He ordered what sounds like several days of bed rest leading up to major meets. He absolutely insisted that Jean stay off her feet, to "preserve the spring in her legs." In Los Angeles that summer, in her days of seclusion before Sunday, August 7, a growing number of athletes sought out Shiley's room in the Chapman Park. They implored her to beat Babe; high jump would be the last opportunity.[52] The incessant drumbeat of boastful hype, capped by the 80-meter hurdles outcome, had definitely become exasperating.

The jumping continued on through Sunday afternoon. One by one the jumpers went out—Annette Rogers at 5 feet 2 inches, to place sixth. Toronto's Eva Dawes cleared the bar at 5 feet 3 inches to claim the bronze medal. Only Jean and Babe remained. Both bettered Gisolf's world record of 5 feet 3¾ inches. The bar went up to 5 feet 5 inches and Jean cleared it. Babe missed her first try at this height, but made it on the second. They next tried with the bar at 5 feet 6 inches and Jean missed. Babe sailed over, but her foot hit the standard, knocking the bar off to register a miss. The bar went back to 5 feet 5¼ inches for a jump-off. Both cleared this height again, and then the judges entered the picture. They said Babe's head crossed before her feet when she rolled over the bar, and they ruled her jump a dive. This foul put Babe out. Jean Shiley won the gold medal. Babe received the silver medal and a share of the world record set that day.[53]

The whole affair was misunderstood, and many accounts both then and since imply that Babe was "robbed" of a third gold medal. One jumper had protested Babe's style in Evanston, and throughout the jump-off in Los Angeles the Canadian and German jumpers had repeatedly urged Jean to protest. Babe said she had never been called for diving in a meet, adding, justifiably, "I think they should have at least warned me earlier in the jumping."[54]

And so the judging cast another cloud. By the time the Olympic judges finally ruled Babe's style illegal, as Jean said decades later in marvelous understatement, it was "a very bad time to call a foul."[55]

The Official Program of the Games carried an account of the event the next day, which ended with, " 'The Babe,' who seems to have won the hearts of all Olympic fans, was not quite able to claim her third world title. Jean just outjumped her."[56]

The competition had begun one week before on the high note of Babe Didrikson's gold medal–winning javelin throw. It had been an incredibly successful week for the American women. In all, they won five gold medals in the six events, setting an Olympic record with each. They also won three silver medals and one bronze.

In his official report to the American Olympic Committee, team manager Fred Steers noted that women in Europe had competed in track and field long before American women had. Then he proudly hailed his seventeen trail-blazing athletes for "clearly outclassing the combined Women's Track and Field Teams of the world."[57]

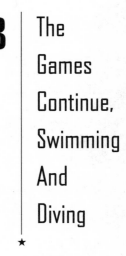

8 | The Games Continue, Swimming And Diving

★

When the action shifted to the swimming stadium, the Olympics drew closer to Hollywood, or vice versa. At some point during the Games, rumor had many if not most swimmers headed for movie contracts.

The glamour-girl label had stuck. One Associated Press writer implied that they flaunted it. In the florid style of the day he wrote:

> They strut—and strut. . . . [The] sprinters, jumpers and weight heavers never appeared until time to do their stuff, and disappeared immediately afterward, [but] the femmes who gain fame . . . in aqua, are never out of sight. . . . [M]any of them make a habit of parading—and then parading some more.[1]

Perhaps they did parade and flaunt, but they considered themselves serious competitors. The paradox of glamour girl and serious athlete may have sent mixed signals to press and public and to some of the swimmers themselves.

Eleanor Holm told Muriel Babcock, "My appearance is more important to my life as a woman than any swimming championship." She even went so far as to say, "If I had to choose between swimming cups and honors, and loss of looks . . . I'd give up the championship." Yet she was a fierce competitor and considered it "a great thrill to compete in the Olympics." She later said of 1932, "nothing was going to stop me," and in 1936 she made a deadly serious effort to work back into shape and land a spot on a third Olympic team.[2]

Hollywood columnist Louella Parsons saw both sides of the seeming contradiction. She pointed out that they fought hard to win even as she said "film producers ought to take a look at this crop of youth and beauty right on Los Angeles' very door step."[3] Parsons did not separate beauty and prowess, and she did not disparage women's records.

Few men in the working sports press could resist the glamour angle. Grantland Rice, staunch champion of Babe Didrikson, tried and almost succeeded when he wrote:

> [Swimming and diving stars] will take the play away from the men—as far as crowd excitement goes. One reason is that they are easier to look at, . . . Another reason is that most of the leading women swimmers and divers have all the skill a man can show, even if they lack the physical drive. This isn't true in most track and field sports, where . . . [i]t will take another generation or two to make any large improvement. . . . [But in swimming] the women will break just as many of their records as the men will break.[4]

Without the glamour label for track and field athletes, male journalists had fallen back to comparing their times and distances to those of men and proclaiming the women inferior. For the swimmers, they added sex and glamour to their specious argument. Columnist Paul Gallico insisted that sex appeal alone brought the huge crowds to women's meets, which always drew better than those of the men. He also discounted women's swimming accomplishments because they did not match the men's records.[5] Grantland Rice, a somewhat less patronizing observer, may have foreseen that the women could save the day in Olympic swimming for the United States.

The only serious casualty to hit the entire United States team struck the swimmers on Saturday, July 30—the day of the Opening Ceremony. Louisa Robert, the Atlanta backstroker whose trip to Los Angeles had barely won last-minute approval from her parents, reported to the team nurse that morning with what she thought was a cold. Later that day she underwent an emergency appendectomy—not minor surgery in 1932. By evening, the hospital report had her "getting along nicely," but this unexpected turn of events forced abandonment of her Olympic medal hopes.[6]

Louisa's mother had flown to Los Angeles earlier that week to be on hand for the Games, and her father was to join them on August 1. Once the shock and concern had passed, the whole misfortune assumed a festive air. The Roberts took a bungalow on the grounds of the Ambassador Hotel and more or less held open house for the swimming team. With a galaxy of stars around, their parties highlighted the rest of the stay for everyone.[7]

The other swimmers had a full week longer to prepare for their stint in the Games than their track and field counterparts had. During that week, when training schedules allowed, they would drift into the coliseum and cheer on the others.

Every team had time slots assigned for training in the Stadium pool, and the Los Angeles Playground and Recreation Department set aside mornings for Olympic use at such sites as Griffith Pool on Riverside Drive near Griffith Park and West Los Angeles Pool on Stoner Avenue. Some teams practiced in the private pools of the athletic clubs and the Ambassador Hotel. The swimmers' clothing allotment, most of which was donated by manufacturers, did not include warmups. The women nearly froze at early morning workouts in the outdoor pools, but clearly, the facilities in 1932 were superior to those at the previous Games.[8]

Swimming events began Saturday, August 6. Men's 100-meter freestyle preliminaries led off at 9 a.m., and the trial heats for women's 200-meter breaststroke followed at 9:30.

European swimmers had always claimed the Olympic breaststroke title. With Americans Jane Cadwell and Anne Govednik both literally unknown and untested, United States hopes for a breaststroke medal in 1932 rode with Margaret Hoffman. The new American record Hoffman set in the trials at Jones Beach buoyed those hopes considerably. She had not begun training until the end of the college term that spring. Even so, Yale's Robert Kiphuth, head coach of the U.S. swimming team, considered her overtrained and held her out of practice for three days during their first week in Los Angeles.[9]

The draw for trial heat number one put Hoffman with Clare Dennis of Australia. The second heat had Anne Govednik and Else Jacobsen of Denmark. Jane Cadwell swam in the third, which included

Japan's Hideko Maehata. Earlier that year Jacobsen had set a world record of 3:03.4 for the distance, and she came to Los Angeles the clear favorite to break the Olympic record of 3:11.4.[10]

Record breaking in swimming began as early as it had in javelin the week before—in the first heat of the first event. This time the honor went to 16-year-old Claire Dennis, whose broken toe proved no impediment. She stroked the 200 meters in 3:08.2; Peg Hoffman followed at 3:14.7 to qualify. World record–holder Jacobsen took the second heat, with Anne Govednik close behind to reach the finals. Heat number three went to Japan's Maehata, but Jane Cadwell posted the third best overall time to claim a spot in the finals.[11] In a historic first, three Americans had reached an Olympic breaststroke final, but they knew from the numbers they would not have an easy time on August 9.

From the instant the starter's gun sounded, the final was a duel between Dennis and Jacobsen. They were even at the first turn and Hideko Maehata slowly caught up with them. As they neared the finish, Dennis inched ahead to win by an eyelash in 3 minutes 6.3 seconds; Maehata finished next (3:06.4), with a sagging Jacobsen in third. After Jacobsen came Britain's Margery Hilton, then Hoffman, Govednik, and Cadwell.[12]

Margaret Hoffman's fifth place time of 3:11.8 was 5.5 seconds off the pace but 7.4 seconds better than her fifth-place finish in 1928. Govednik's 3:16 flat put her in sixth—the first time that two breaststrokers from the United States placed in the Olympics. Hoffman later said ruefully that breaststroke was not one of the better events for Americans in her era, adding, "I was the best that we had in this country, and I was only fifth." Hideko Maehata won the gold medal in Berlin four years later, but Europeans continued to dominate 200-meter breaststroke. No American placed higher in the event than Margaret Hoffman did in Los Angeles until Claudia Kolb brought home the silver medal from Tokyo in 1964.[13]

Everyone had expected the American swimmers to face heavy odds in breaststroke, but not in 100-meter freestyle. Not since 1920, when Australia's Fanny Durack won it in Antwerp, had an American failed to take that gold medal. Helene Madison held every freestyle record from 100 yards to the mile; surely the 100-meter gold was a given.

Madison took her world record of 1:06.6 for the distance into the swimming stadium on Saturday, August 6. By 3:30 that afternoon when the preliminary heats ended, disbelief had set in. The Olympic record of 1:11 had been broken three times. Britain's Joyce Cooper was the first to do it, cutting it by a full two seconds in heat number two. Madison clipped off another tenth of a second in the third, and in the fourth Eleanor Saville lowered it further to 1:08.5, the day's best time.[14]

Failing to post the best time in a preliminary heat was hardly cause for alarm, but Helene did not appear her usual confident self in the semifinals the following day. She easily outdistanced the others for 50 meters but appeared to tire badly on the home stretch. Willemijntje den Ouden of the Netherlands cut the Olympic time still further to 1:07.6 in the semifinals. Some observers thought it would be no surprise to see Madison trail den Ouden or Garatti Saville, or both, in the finals.[15] Willie den Ouden reached the final with the best mark, and the fourteen-year-old Dutch girl looked impressive doing it. Saville had beaten Madison in a 50-meter exhibition race in Pasadena two weeks before.

The stage was set at 3 p.m., Monday, for the greatest challenge of Madison's swimming career and she nearly missed it. Helene sauntered out onto the pool deck at exactly 3:00; she suddenly realized she was late, jumped into the pool to get wet, and popped back out just in time to get in position.[16] The starter held the swimmers on the mark for what seemed an eternity, but no one broke in a false start. All six hit the water almost simultaneously. Madison was out in front immediately, with den Ouden a close second. The rhythmic power of Madison's stroke put her a body length ahead at 25 meters, but den Ouden cut the lead to 2 feet at the turn. Eleanor Saville battled Australia's Frances Bult for third place, 6 feet behind the frontrunners.[17]

Helene regained her earlier lead and seemed on the verge of running away with the race at the 75-meter mark when she veered into the right side lane divider and slowed noticeably. Willie den Ouden quickly closed on her and they covered the last 20 meters neck-and-neck. Madison returned to the center of the lane, and the stroke that had made her a champion carried her in at 1:06.8 for her first gold medal. The diminutive den Ouden had pushed Helene to an Olympic record, and her own time (1:07.8) was the second best ever.

Eleanor Saville, third by a body length at 1:08.2, took the bronze to go with the silver medal she won for the 100-meters at Amsterdam. Jo McKim followed closely to place fourth in 1:09.3.[18]

After it was over, Helene cried tears of both joy and relief when she said, "I have been pointing for this race for two years."[19] (Australia's Dawn Frazier was the first to take the 100-meter mark under a minute, to 59.5, at Tokyo in 1964.)

Tuesday morning, August 9, was one more picture-perfect day in Southern California, and another capacity crowd was in place by 10:00 at the swimming stadium. The women backstrokers took the deck for the 100-meter trials.

Maria Braun Phillipsen, Olympic champion from the Netherlands, came to Los Angeles to defend her Amsterdam time of 1:21.6. Eleanor Holm now held the world record, 1:18.2, set three weeks earlier in the rough water at Jones Beach. Both Australia's Bonnie Mealing and Britain's Phyllis Harding had recently bettered Phillipsen's 1928 time. Veteran observers were certain they would see the fastest Olympic backstroke time ever, and most expected Eleanor Holm to swim it.[20]

In the first heat that morning Holm, Mealing, and Harding went head to head. Joan McSheehy swam in heat two, which included two versatile freestylers—Elizabeth Davies of Britain and the scrappy den Ouden, fresh from her strong challenge of Madison the day before. In the third, but for an uncooperative appendix, Louisa Robert would have met the defending champion.[21] American swimmers had specialized, and by 1932, unlike the Europeans, each competed in only one stroke.

Holm drew the outside lane and had to contend with the backwash, but she took the lead at the gun and never trailed. Bonnie Mealing soon claimed second place. Holm pulled through the water with graceful precision and had a lead of more than a body length at the finish. She had clocked an amazing 1:18.3 and set a new Olympic record.[22] Holm, Mealing, and Harding moved into the finals.

The other trial heats bordered on the anticlimactic. Joan McSheehy moved on to the finals along with Phillipsen. By the time of the finals two days later, the field of seven backstrokers had shrunk to six. Just after placing second in the 400-meter freestyle trials in the interim, Phillipsen suffered a serious insect bite that escalated into a case of blood poisoning and forced the defending champion to with-draw from the remaining competition.[23]

The backstroke final came late in the afternoon; an overflow crowd of 12,000 jammed the stadium. Hundreds more were turned away. Eleanor Holm, the woman who "turned down a contract from Ziegfeld," now drew better than ever.[24] The six swimmers held firmly to the overflow trough and waited for the start. At the crack of the gun, they were on their way with a burst of power. Eleanor swam a champion's race all the way, keeping an eye on Bonnie Mealing for the first 50 meters. With a yard lead at 75 meters she launched a sprint finish that clinched first place by a body length in 1:19.4. The huge, partisan Los Angeles crowd roared an ovation when she swung up onto the deck. Dripping wet and flashing her wide smile, she accepted an enormous bouquet of flowers.[25] She had reached her four-year goal of an Olympic gold medal.

The decisive victory came over a strong field. Bonnie Mealing took the silver in 1:21.3, Elizabeth Davies won the bronze medal in 1:22.5, with Phyllis Harding close behind. Joan McSheehy (1:23.2) placed fifth.[26]

Springboard divers took center stage at 8:30, Wednesday morning, the day between the record-setting backstroke thrillers. Another bizarre intervention by judges delayed the diving competition. Dr. Leo Donath, the judge from Hungary and president of the International Swimming Federation, said the suits worn by Jane Fauntz and Georgia Coleman exposed too much of their backs and sent them out to change. The early crowd grumbled at the decision and delay, but both divers had to find acceptable replacement suits.[27]

Coleman had no spare, so she borrowed a suit from Margaret Hoffman. It fit the lean, five-foot-seven-inch Hoffman better than the chunky, compact Coleman, but Georgia did not let that hamper her on the board.[28]

When Fauntz later discussed the Hungarian judge's personal and arbitrary decision, she recalled that the regulation Olympic suit "was only cut down six inches in the back," and had a restrictive skirt. Her own suit had, she said, "a nice low cut back and it didn't have a skirt. It was a little cotton suit and it looked like silk when I dove." It had never crossed her mind that she "was not decently dressed."[29]

When the diving finally began, Fauntz claimed first place through the required dives, with Georgia next and Katherine Rawls close behind. Coleman, always supreme in the optional dives, where she elected the most difficult, overtook Fauntz in the last few dives. Elegantly graceful, Jane Fauntz had true star presence on the board; she chose to end with her favorite optional running full twist, which had scored "10s" at the Nationals. This time, however, she forgot one of her own cardinal rules—"Don't watch the other divers"—and lost her concentration. She later recounted the painful episode:

> I was overly confident, a tiny bit, and my timing was off ever so much. I went up in the air and I knew I had misjudged my take-off. So when I came down, my usual knife entry wasn't there and my legs splashed over from the knees down. . . . It was the worst [dive] I had ever done. . . . I didn't even want to come up from the bottom of the pool. . . . I went from first to third. Georgia went on to nail her gainer one-and-a-half.[30]

Swimmer Helen Johns recalled being in the stands that day. She agreed it was a bad dive and added that "it seemed she would never come up out of the water."[31]

With points totalling 87.52, Georgia Coleman won the gold medal. Jane Fauntz slipped to third place with 82.12 points for the bronze. Katherine Rawls stayed barely ahead of her and, with her 82.56, took the silver. It was an American sweep, with Olga Jordan of Germany, Canada's Doris Ogilvie, and Magdalene Epply of Austria following in that order.[32]

The American springboard trio was a favorite subject for photographers. In the center they always put fourteen-year-old Katherine Rawls, short, slight, with her hair in a "boyish bob." They posed Coleman, sturdy and athletic, on one side and tall, slender, more sophisticated Fauntz on the other.

Diving exhibitions were crowd-pleasing favorites in 1932. There had been one the morning before, and that same afternoon the three medal winners returned to the pool to give yet another.[33]

Three days of competition remained, and another large freestyle field answered the 400-meters call at 10:00, Thursday morning, August 11. No delay unsettled the crowd in the once again sold-out stadium;

swimming judges apparently had a less puritanical yardstick for women's suits. Damon Runyan described Helene Madison's as "a black silk suit of a scanty cut that would have given the beach authorities of the effete East chills and a fever a few years back."[34]

The first trial heat that morning went routinely, with the Los Angeles Athletic Club's Norene Forbes moving to the next round. After easing her way along in the second heat, Helene Madison had to race ahead to beat a surging Maria Braun-Phillipsen: this was just before the latter's poisonous insect bite. The big news came in the third heat, where Lenore Kight lived up to her press billing, acquired at Jones Beach, as the one to watch. Her 5:40.9 broke the Olympic record (5:42.8) set by America's Martha Norelius at Amsterdam. The last heat sent Denmark's Lilli Anderson and Jennie Maakal from South Africa on to the semifinals; Yvonne Godard posted the third fastest time overall to round out the semifinal slate.[35]

Friday morning brought another ideal day for a full schedule in the Olympic pool. Platform diving began at 9:00, followed by the 400-meter freestyle semifinals at 9:45. The freestyle 4 × 100-meter relay went at 4:35 that afternoon.

The 400-meter semifinal races showed the clear dominance of the United States in freestyle. All three Americans—Forbes, Kight, and Madison—advanced to the finals to meet Cooper, Godard, and Maakal. Neither race in the semis produced any times out of the ordinary, and Lenore Kight was well off her pace of the day before.[36] Saturday's 400-meter final would be the last event for women, and even without another record breaker on Friday, it promised to end the Xth Olympiad with a bang.

The divers came out early Friday morning. This time, no judge found anything wrong with the suits they wore, and diving began on schedule for another packed crowd of 12,000. Georgia Coleman, the springboard gold medal already hers, joined fellow Californians Dorothy Poynton and Marion Dale Roper to try for platform gold as well. In 1932, competition called for two dives from the 5-meter platform and two from 10 meters.

The press reported that Poynton had sprained her back in practice the day before and competed "with her body strapped heavily with adhesive tape." She herself recalled being hurt in one of the diving exhibitions that proved so popular that summer. She did spend the night in the hospital, but next morning after a dive from 5 meters, she knew she would be all right. She was determined that her parents would see her compete because they had missed her springboard silver medal performance in Amsterdam.[37]

Poynton, proving to be more than all right, scored highest in all four dives. In the running swan off the 5-meter platform, she netted 9.68 points to Georgia Coleman's 8.80. Her standing swan dive from 10 meters rated 9.46 to keep her ahead of Coleman, who scored 9.24. Her running swan from 10 meters, with a perfect approach and take-off and an entry that scarcely rippled the surface, brought waves of applause from the festive crowd and 10.8 points from the judges. Her last dive, a back jackknife off the 5-meter stand, almost as perfect as the swan, scored 10.32 points, giving her a total of 40.26 and the gold medal.[38]

"Gorgeous Georgia," as Damon Runyan invariably called Coleman, stayed a close second to Poynton until her running swan, to claim second place and the silver medal (35.56 total). Marion Dale Roper consistently finished behind Poynton and Coleman in Los Angeles area competition. She had placed third at a meet in June; one observer insisted that she was "a much better performer than the judges gave her credit for being." Her best Olympic dive was the final 5-meter back jackknife, which rated 9.6 points. Her total of 35.22 points came very close to Coleman and garnered the bronze medal.[39] As they had in springboard, the American women again swept the field.

The women's 4 × 100-meter freestyle relay, Friday's last race, went at 4:35. Eligible swimmers had vied for two weeks for the undecided place on the team. In the final selection, Coach L. DeB. Handley named Helen Johns to swim the number two lap. Working with Handley, Helen had improved her stroke while continually posting the fastest times in training.[40] Josephine McKim won the lead-off spot, Eleanor Garatti Saville was to swim third, and Helene Madison would anchor the team. They expected the strongest opposition to come from Britain and the Netherlands.

Madison had been in the 400-meter freestyle semifinals that morning. Her personal coach from Seattle, Ray Daughters, hoped she would not have to overcome any lead in the relay. He planned to instruct her "not to sacrifice her chances in the 400 in order to win the relay." He considered the 400-meter title more important to the United States.[41] Whatever the importance of the two events, or Daughters's priorities, he need not have worried about overcoming any lead.

Jo McKim hit the water with a fast start, staked the team to an early lead, and her 1:09 for the first 100 meters sent Helen Johns off at very nearly the same pace to keep them in front. Johns reached the halfway mark in 1:09.2, sending Eleanor Saville off on the third lap. She covered the distance in 1:10, and gave Madison a comfortable lead for the anchor leg. Helene did the last 100 meters in 1:09.8.[42] The women of the United States had another gold medal.

The American team eclipsed the 1928 record of 4:47.6 by more than nine seconds. They covered the distance in 4:38 flat to set Olympic and world records. Each U.S. freestyler swam her leg of the relay below the individual 100-meter Olympic record of 1:11 set in Amsterdam.[43]

From the crack of the gun until the final touch, the Americans had kept the lead. With Willie den Ouden swimming anchor, the team from the Netherlands (4:46.5) took second ahead of Great Britain (4:52.4), and Canada nosed out Japan to place fourth.[44]

With one event each for both women and men remaining on Saturday, the women swimmers were the toast of the town. They had won every gold medal so far except in breaststroke. They had swept all three medals in both springboard and platform diving. Friday's *Boston Transcript* wryly observed, "The swimmers are swimming morning and afternoon. The Japanese and Helene Madison are doing nicely." While the men from the United States had also taken all six diving medals, the swimmers had only the gold medal Buster Crabbe won in 400-meter freestyle.[45] The Japanese had virtually frozen out everyone else and, with only 200-meter breaststroke and 1,500-meter freestyle to go for the men, things did not change.

Helene Madison had claimed gold medals in the relay and for 100 meters, but through the semifinals she had looked vulnerable at 400 meters. Distractions escalated during the week, with continuous speculation about a Madison movie career and a constant demand for interviews. The day before the 400-meter final, Royal Brougham, sports editor of Seattle's *Post-Intelligencer*, took her in tow. He arranged dinner at the Biltmore for her with Arthur Brisbane, Hearst's national political columnist. In the front-page piece that grew out of this, Brisbane heaped lavish praise on her appearance and her championships. He wrote, "Helene Madison is the right kind of an 'old fashioned girl.' She might have been a character in Louisa Alcott's 'Little Women.' " He went on to say:

> This Seattle girl is not only a champion of all woman champions, but also very beautiful and extremely intelligent. Her eyebrows would have been worth a million francs in the days of Louis XV.

And he had a 1932 man's advice for the "extremely intelligent" champion of champions: "Helene Madison, who is 19, should now marry and help one of ten sons to become president."[46]

Earlier in the week, her father had granted a long interview to Muriel Babcock. If Helene saw it in the *Los Angeles Times,* it must surely have caused some distraction. Four hours before the 100-meter finals, Charles Madison announced that his daughter would retire from swimming at the end of the Games. He told Babcock, "Whether she wins or loses, . . . she is through." He did not hesitate to speak for her, saying:

> She's fed up herself with all of it. I don't think she has the same zest for racing that she used to have. She's hit her peak. She's won her records, got them all practically, and now it's time she did something else.

When Babcock suggested that it must be tremendous to have a great champion in the family, Madison thought back over the last two years and replied:

> Well . . . it hasn't been what you might think. The house has sort of revolved about this swimming business. . . . It got so it was nothing but receptions and luncheons for her. . . . Got to be pretty arduous. . . . There's the money angle, too. It costs something to have a champion in the family. . . . Ye-es, it's quite a business, this amateur swimming. I'd like to see her get something out of it.[47]

Olympic success meant few if any returns in that era, but possibilities loomed. Helene had several definite offers, including a swimming movie, vaudeville appearances, and exhibition tours as a professional swimmer. She said she would welcome a role in pictures, but
only feature films. Speaking for herself, and unlike her father, she said
nothing else would lure her from amateur ranks.[48] By week's end she
had accepted no offer, and winning the 400-meter gold medal was her
top priority.

No foreign swimmer had come near Helene's world record of 5 min-
utes 31 seconds for 400 meters freestyle. Before the Games, Britain's
Joyce Cooper and Yvonne Godard of France appeared to be her main
competition. They all met in the finals, along with Jennie Maakal of
South Africa and the other two Americans, Norene Forbes and Lenore
Kight.[49] By breaking the old Olympic record at the Jones Beach trials,
Kight had stirred enormous interest in herself and in this last race of
the Games.

On Saturday, as for most of the week, a capacity crowd packed the
stands. Tension and excitement began to build the minute the swimmers moved into position. Madison went out fast at the starter's gun
and broke loose from the rest of the field—all but Lenore Kight. No
more than a foot ever separated the two Americans as they stroked the
length of the pool eight times. The crowd, on their feet throughout,
screamed and shouted in a thunderous roar. At 50 meters the two leaders hit the turn together, but Helene gained 6 inches on the push-off.
Kight battled back on each length, only to lose ground to the taller
Madison on the turns. They were dead even with half a pool length to
go. Five meters from the finish, no one could tell who led. The judges
conferred at length and ruled Helene the winner—by a split second
and a quick touch, it would seem.[50]

The record books list Madison's time as 5:28.5 and Kight's as
5:28.6, both well under the Olympic and world records. Jennie Maakal
clinched the bronze medal for South Africa and the next three places
went to Joyce Cooper, Yvonne Godard, and Norene Forbes.[51]

The press praised Kight for giving Madison the hardest race of
her career. They admired her sportsmanship and said she was even
greater in defeat. Lenore herself could only say, "I gave everything I
had. I did my best. Helene is certainly a wonderful swimmer."[52]

Grantland Rice called that race "one of the most amazing performances of the entire Olympic Games." Lenore recalled it decades later as the only close finish in the swimming events and said:

> They actually didn't know who the heck won it, you know, and it
> took them so long to decide—and Helene was national champion,
> so she deserved it—they wouldn't have a tie.[53]

She forced Madison to set a new world record, to win by a fingertip, and broke the old one herself in doing it.

The champion, now holder of three Olympic gold medals, found herself caught up in an even greater whirl of publicity and rumor after that victory. Almost before her hair was dry, she said it had been her final race, confirming her retirement from amateur swimming. That evening she gave a nationwide radio interview and held the limelight at the Ambassador's Coconut Grove. Jane Fauntz recalled dancing at the Ambassador that night and said, "[W]ho should come dancing by but Helene Madison, dancing with no less than Clark Gable. Helene was a pretty good half-head taller. . . ."[54]

Helene stayed in Los Angeles for another two weeks. She made more public appearances amid movie rumors, and her photograph was everywhere. One newspaper photo showed her stylishly dressed, wearing a hat, a corsage, and a wide smile, and the caption beneath summed it up:

> Having broken all the swimming records a girl can break, "Queen
> Helene" Madison dons her street clothes and smiles coyly at the
> movie magnates who dangle tempting contracts in her direction.[55]

Sportswriter Royal Brougham had reported and promoted her career from its start on Seattle's beaches; he now painted a fairy tale ending. He wrote that within the week Helene would "sign a contract which will bring her glory and gold. . . . She is finding the pot of gold at the end of the rainbow."[56]

By two o'clock, Sunday, August 14, a crowd estimated at 100,000 had filled the coliseum for the Closing Ceremony. Because so many athletes had left Los Angeles earlier, encouraged by the Olympic Committee in order to save the cost of their room and board, a parade of the nations' flags replaced the parade of athletes. There was, however, no lessening of dramatic effect on what Grantland Rice termed "one of those emotional thrills that come rarely in any human's life." With the blue and white of Greece in front, the full complement of flags flew on the field just at sunset. Trumpet fanfare and artillery salute marked the lowering of the five-ringed Olympic flag, which was consigned to Los Angeles Mayor John Porter for safekeeping until it would rise in Berlin in 1936. The huge crowd then joined the massed bands and thousand-voice chorus in a last emotion-filled moment, singing "Aloha" while the sun dropped below the horizon toward the Pacific rim.[57]

The Olympic Games of 1932, begun in doubt, ended in triumph. A large part of that triumph belonged to the American women athletes. For two weeks they thrilled, entertained, and inspired unprecedented Olympic crowds. They rewrote the record book in virtually every event. Some may have gone to Los Angeles unaware of what the Games were all about, but they departed Olympians. They took with them every track and field gold medal except that for the 100-meter race, and the gold in every swimming and diving event but 200-meter breaststroke. The entire nation came to embrace them by way of sports page, movie newsreels, and fledgling network radio. They offered to young women of competitive bent across the country positive evidence and hope that they, too, might excel in athletics. They helped give Americans a brief and colorful diversion from the burdens of the Depression, and they had an unforgettable summer of their own.

Epilogue

After the Games ended many of the athletes moved on to post–Olympic meets. The British Empire–United States track meet lured runners to San Francisco's Kezar Stadium the next week. Swimmers and divers went to Agua Caliente in Mexico to give a series of exhibitions.

Some track and field team members had left the Chapman Park almost immediately after their events. Babe Didrikson flew home from Los Angeles on Wednesday, August 11. She arrived in Dallas the next morning and bounded from the plane at Love Field for a reception that rivaled Lindbergh's. The fire chief's car headed a procession into downtown Dallas with Babe perched on top of the back seat waving to thousands of cheering fans who lined the long route. After a stop at the municipal building for another official welcome, it was on to the Adolphus Hotel for a civic luncheon. Five hundred admiring Texans cheered her and speakers praised her lavishly for putting Dallas on the map.[1]

They threw a theater party in her honor that night, but first came the inevitable press conference. She fielded a question about the high jump decision and declined the opportunity to complain about it. When pressured about Fred Steers, she reportedly said he continued to harass her in Los Angeles and had not given her "the same treatment he did the other girls, including a negro [sic] member of the team."[2]

Amid talk that she would turn professional, rumors of endorsements and offers for Babe to perform ran rampant. She entered one more track meet late in August, but publicity following that Chicago meet centered more on golf than track. Her public identification with golf began during the Games in Los Angeles, where she posted a score of 82 and claimed it to be only her tenth round of golf. Following her ill-starred high jump competition she went immediately to the coliseum press box. There, to test her boastful golf claims, Paul Gallico arranged a round for her with his colleagues Grantland Rice, Westbrook Pegler, and Braven Dyer, who was sports editor of the *Los Angeles Times.* After the match at the Brentwood Country Club, Dyer reported that she stepped up to the first tee and outdrove all of them.[3] The other writers helped build the Didrikson legend and keep it alive.

Babe went on to find her greatest glory in golf, but it came after controversy over her amateur status, a stint in vaudeville, and a long string of exhibition barnstorming tours. She brought her booming tee shots and showmanship to women's golf and became a gallery favorite. She was the first American to win the British Ladies Amateur title, and by 1947 had won every other major amateur championship. Women's golf changed forever in 1948, the year Babe and five other charter members, including standouts Patty Berg, Betty Hicks, and Betty Jameson, formed the Ladies' Professional Golf Association (LPGA).[4]

Babe married professional wrestler George Zaharias in December 1938, and Colorado eventually became their home. In April 1953, persistent fatigue and general malaise sent her to the hospital for a checkup. Radical surgery, including a colostomy, followed the diagnosis of rectal cancer. During her days of recovery Babe's fans flooded the hospital room with cards and flowers. Only fourteen weeks later she played a tournament at Tam O'Shanter outside Chicago. She was fifteenth that day, but she had returned to tournament play against incredible odds. She finished out the season and won the Ben Hogan Comeback of the Year award. Babe's illness gained the upper hand again after the 1954 season. In the years since the Olympic Games in Los Angeles, the woman, the legend, and her life's victories had been woven into the national fabric. When Babe died on September 27, 1956, her passing was lamented by a fellow golfer of note, Dwight Eisenhower, in a presidential press conference.[5]

★   ★   ★

Regardless of all the talk of "turning pro," professional sports offered little future for women in 1932. Even Babe Didrikson, with enormous publicity and promotion, had an uphill battle for what scant early success she had. One other member of the Olympic track team went on to play for a time as a professional athlete—Babe's mismatched roommate from the Chapman Park, Ruth Osburn.

Ruth never considered track and field her sport and competed only one more year. Basketball and softball ranked first and second with her, and back at home in Missouri she played semipro softball. She never again worked at discus or shot as she might have. In 1936, coach Fred Schwengel persuaded her to train for the Berlin Games, but she realized her heart was not in it and quit after three weeks.[6]

At about that same time, C. M. Olson of Cassville, Missouri, started a women's professional basketball team. He owned a chain of seven beauty salons in Missouri and Arkansas, and the basketball team was a promotional vehicle for them.[7] Whatever Olson's motives for entering the women's sports picture, his All American Red Heads team offered talented women athletes a chance to play for pay.[8]

A henna rinse turned Ruth Osburn's dark brown hair to auburn, and she became a Red Head. The team toured the country and played against local teams much as the Harlem Globe-Trotters do. A high point for the team was its three-month tour of the Philippines in the spring of 1940. After their return, Ruth became player/manager of an Olson farm team in Arkansas—The Ozark Hill Billies. Both teams disbanded a week or so after the December 7, 1942, attack on Pearl Harbor. Ruth joined the war effort and went to work in an ordnance plant in Iowa.[9]

Fellow Missourian Elizabeth Wilde left Los Angeles after the last track event in 1932 on the same train with Ruth Osburn. Loretto Academy packed Kansas City Union Station with well-wishers to welcome her home. That fall, with what was essentially an athletic scholarship based on her Olympic experience, she entered Webster College. That small school near St. Louis, supported by the Sisters of Loretto, encouraged sports competition.[10]

At Webster she played basketball and ran track in a successful college athletic career. She also met Richard Kinnard, a student in accounting at St. Louis University, and they were married in July 1935. After the birth of their son the following year, she played semiprofessional basketball with "the little boy running around on the sidelines." She also formed a track team that competed in meets in the surrounding towns. The Kinnards moved to Kansas City in 1943. Their daughter was born there and when she was about three years old Elizabeth began teaching. During a long and successful career, she handled the entire program of physical education at Notre Dame Sion, a small parochial school.[11]

One 1932 Olympian who truly had her heart set on the 1936 Games was Jean Shiley. Following the British Empire meet in San Francisco, she returned home to Pennsylvania and a rousing reception in Haverford Township. Economics forced Jean to teach swimming briefly in the summer of 1933, the year she graduated from Temple University. She still held the Olympic and world high jump records and had every intention of training for another Olympic team. It was not to be, however hard she pleaded her case in New York with Dan Ferris of the Olympic Committee. Ferris ruled that teaching swimming two summers before had made her a professional athlete, and he barred her from the team.[12]

The country remained mired in the Depression and when Jean graduated from Temple she could not find a job. She always said, "Thank God for the WPA." The local Works Progress Administration office hired her as a substitute typing teacher—she taught herself before the first class—and then as a secretary. During World War II she served as an officer in the Navy. While stationed as an administrative officer on Navy contracts at Bausch & Lomb in Rochester, New York, Jean met physicist Herman Newhouse. They were married November 11, 1945. Over time, they and their three children lived in a variety of places associated with physics research, including a stay at Los Alamos in New Mexico. Whenever Babe Didrikson Zaharias played near the Newhouse home on the golf circuit, the two rivals from 1932 would have a reunion.[13]

Others from the summer of '32 had better luck with the Olympic Committee. Track and field athletes who did go on to the 1936 Olympic team included Tidye Pickett, Annette Rogers, Simone Schaller, and Louise Stokes.

★ ★ ★

Simone Schaller went to the British Empire meet following the Games in Los Angeles. With a brisk San Francisco breeze behind her in Kezar Stadium, she cut a tenth of a second from the 80-meter hurdle record just set by Babe Didrikson. She said this record did not count because the wind was blowing, and added, "but that's the story of my life." She had narrowly missed the bronze medal at Los Angeles, and misfortune followed her to Berlin, where she again made it into the finals of the 80-meter hurdles. Simone was set to run for a medal when the Italians lodged a protest over her semifinal heat of the day before. The results were altered, Schaller's place in the final went to an Italian runner, and Simone was out. This time there was no Kirby camera; she saw no pictures and had no recourse. A subsequent three-day trip to Switzerland to visit her grandfather in Bern partially eased the bitter disappointment.[14]

Simone played basketball between Olympic years. She risked possible disqualification playing on an El Monte city team unsanctioned by the AAU. She did not compete in track and field after 1936, and tennis became her sport. Simone married Joseph Kirin in 1937. They remained in the Los Angeles area, where they raised their three children—daughter Constance and sons Robert and James.[15]

Neither Tidye Pickett nor Louise Stokes ran in the 4 × 100-meter relay in Los Angeles although both qualified for selection to the team. The disappointment stayed with both young African American sprinters. In recalling that summer, Pickett said, "The girls liked me very much. We weren't any different as far as the other girls were concerned. . . . [The] athletes as a whole were wonderful, and the coaches, too." That did not include Babe Didrikson, who, Pickett said, "just plain didn't like me, didn't want me on the team." She came close to agreeing with Babe on Fred Steers, though, recalling that the team manager caused Tidye and Louise "quite a lot of concern."[16] Still running for the Chicago Park District, Pickett took the indoor 50-meter hurdles title in 1936. Both sprinters secured places on the Olympic team that year, but Pickett broke her foot in the 80-meter hurdle semifinals in Berlin and Stokes was not chosen for the relay. Once again, neither young woman ran for a medal in the Games.

On her return to Malden, Massachusetts, Louise Stokes received a civic welcoming parade from the hometown that had helped to send her to Europe. She planned to try for the 1940 Games scheduled for Tokyo, but World War II canceled the Games and ended Louise's Olympic chances. She married Wilfred Fraser and they lived in both Malden and neighboring Medford at various times. She worked for the postal service and remained an active leader in community youth sports. In September 1987, Malden again honored its famed athlete daughter. Wilfred, Jr., represented his mother's family at the dedication of a memorial statue in the Louise Stokes Fraser Courtyard of Malden High School.[17]

Tidye Pickett went back to Chicago after the Berlin Games. She earned a master's degree from Northern Illinois University and had a long career in education. She married a fellow teacher, Frank Phillips, and raised three daughters. She was a teacher and elementary school principal in the East Chicago Heights school district, and when she retired as a principal, the district named the Tidye A. Phillips School in her honor.[18]

Annette Rogers returned home to Chicago from Los Angeles in 1932 and entered Northwestern University. She continued to train with the Illinois Women's Athletic Club and won national championships in high jump and 100- and 200-meter sprints. By 1936, Rogers and the corps of young athletes who had comprised the Athletic Club's relay team were sponsored by the Illinois Catholic Women's Club.[19]

Annette appreciated the pageantry and spectacle of the Berlin Games. She never forgot Adolf Hitler's charismatic presence in the Olympic Stadium and his impact on the crowd. One lasting impression of Germany was that of regimentation, even among the children. Politics had at first seemed remote to her, but she recalled that as time passed the young woman assigned as her interpreter "got my confidence and she started telling me how scared they were . . . and how they had to do this and that and if they didn't they would be put in a concentration camp. She was really scared—she was about my age." They corresponded for the first year after the Games, "and suddenly it stopped—and I've never heard from her [since]."[20]

The Americans won the 4 × 100-meter relay, and Annette won a second Olympic gold medal. The highly favored German team had a lead when its anchor runner proved the soundness of George Vreeland's 1932 coaching—she dropped the baton on the hand-off. While sports historians will say, "We can never know,"[21] Annette Rogers remained firmly convinced that even a smooth transfer would not have won for the Germans. She said of the American anchor, "Helen Stephens would have caught that girl and passed her up in nothing." Rogers also competed in the high jump, placing sixth, and in the 100-meter race, where she ran fifth.[22] Forty-eight years passed before another sprinter won back-to-back gold medals in the 400-meter relay.

When Annette graduated from Northwestern in 1937, she took the job offered by the Chicago Board of Education in physical education and began a long and satisfying career in teaching. She married Peter J. Kelly, and continued teaching as they raised two sons and a daughter. Looking at technological improvements in track, she recalled digging their own starting holes on cinder tracks decades earlier. Then, comparing runners' times today with theirs in the thirties, she concluded "we weren't that bad."[23]

Evelyne Hall would have given almost anything for a visit to Pickfair in 1932, but the gregarious Chicago hurdler had to leave Los Angeles before Pickford and Fairbanks entertained the Olympic teams. She cashed in the train ticket provided by the Olympic Committee to finance the trip home in their well-worn Buick for herself, her husband Leonard, and her mother-in-law.[24]

Evelyne maintained her AAU ties and continued to compete through 1936. Olympic funding was difficult that year and she had no backing for the trip to Berlin. Her fortunes took an upward turn, however, when she received a scholarship to Chicago's American College of Physical Education. She began work as a recreation director for the Chicago Park District while she was in school and, running under its sponsorship, claimed the 1935 national 50-meter hurdles title. She continued working there through World War II. In addition to regular sports, dance, and craft activities, she coached track for all age levels and took teams to meets around the country.[25]

In 1946, the family, which now included a daughter, moved to Glendale, California, where Evelyne became the city's first woman recreation supervisor. She organized the programs for women and children, and they included AAU competition. Track teams remained a top priority for her in the face of opposition from the area's college physical education leaders. She was coach/manager of the American women's team for the inaugural Pan American Games in 1951. She left the Glendale parks when her son was born, but continued work with handicapped children—with the Easter Seal Society and the Special Olympics.[26]

The Games of 1932 left an indelible mark on Evelyne. She became a true Olympic advocate, ally, and patron and was involved in founding the Southern California Olympians. Even as she cherished 1932, the cheerful optimist looked ahead with her philosophy that "you don't look back—what happened yesterday is gone. It's tomorrow that I'm thinking about."[27] She found one thing from that early Olympic summer hard to consign to the past, though—the 80-meter hurdles final haunted her for a long time.

Margaret Jenkins did not stay for long in Los Angeles after the discus event that summer. She had to get on to the fabulous fishing at Lake Tahoe, where she had built a cabin in the mid-twenties. When school began in the fall she returned to town and to teaching in the Santa Clara school district. She spent World War II as an officer in the Navy. Margaret returned to the Bay Area when her terminal leave was up in January of 1946 and decided to take early retirement from teaching. She always said, "My teaching career was nothing special." Shrewd investing left her in a position to enjoy what truly interested her: her mountain home, artwork, fishing, the outdoor life, and traveling. The pioneer California athlete shared generously in women's history projects and concerns of Northern California Olympians. She often wondered, "When did I find time to teach!!!"[28]

A victorious Billie von Bremen returned home from Los Angeles to a San Francisco welcome and to run in the British Empire meet. She resumed her job in the Emporium's accounting office, and later that fall the tall blonde sprinter was chosen "Miss California." By the time she married attorney Robert Asch in October 1935, she had become "one of the Western Women's Club's brightest lights." The Asches lived in Palo Alto, and while raising their son she continued to play tennis avidly. She suffered a fatal heart attack on July 23, 1976, while she and her husband were spectators at a professional tennis match in Oakland.[29]

★   ★   ★

Following the American relay triumph, the tiny Orange County town of Tustin honored two of its favorite products—Evelyn Furtsch and avocados. Evelyn, by far the more important, was named "Calavo Queen" and feted by her hometown. Her winning smile and gold medal brought the town more glory than the avocado crops did in 1932.[30]

Evelyn did not continue with the Los Angeles Athletic Club and had no track affiliation after the Games. During two years at Santa Ana College she played basketball and other sports. She married fellow student Joe Ojeda in 1934. Coach Humeston approached her about training for the 1936 Games, but the birth of a daughter in 1935 ruled it out.[31]

In that same year, controversy escalated over whether the United States should send Olympic athletes to a Berlin which offered mounting evidence of abhorrent anti-Semitism and harbingers of the Holocaust to come. Many who customarily supported American Olympians refused to support the Games that they considered legitimation of the odious Nazi regime. The Committee on Fair Play in Sports led an American movement to boycott the Games. That committee of nationally prominent figures ranged from Francis Biddle to James M. Curley and Norman Thomas, from journalist Heywood Broun to Freda Kirchwey, editor and publisher of the *Nation,* and from theologians Drs. Harry Emerson Fosdick and Reinhold Niebuhr to Dr. Mary Woolley, president of Mount Holyoke College. Evelyn Furtsch joined other athletes of conscience who lent their names in opposition to participating in what is now often called "The Nazi Olympics."[32] When asked about her stand later, she cited the influence of coach and history teacher Vincent Humeston.

Only Annette Rogers from the 1932 relay team made it to Berlin for the Games, but the quartet apparently had an admirer in Germany. Late in World War II, while a friend of Evelyn's was moving toward the Rhine with the United States Third Army, he came across a picture of the relay team taken from a German language book on the 1932 Olympics. He found it tacked to the wall of a deserted German billet, "liberated" it, and sent it home for Evelyn.[33]

After a few years with J. C. Penney in Santa Ana, the Ojedas moved the few miles to Tustin and opened their own market, which Evelyn described as "a little grocery store on the main highway." By now son Roland had joined daughter Barbara. In 1950 her husband went into the real estate business with her uncle in Garden Grove, and when development boomed in Southern California he opened his own office just south of Disneyland. Evelyn secured her own license and spent thirty years herself working in real estate.[34]

Mary Carew ran in the British Empire meet in San Francisco after the Games in Los Angeles and then boarded the train for home with other Olympians. The long trip back to Boston was punctuated with station stops where crowds came to cheer them. They reached Cleveland in time for an introduction at the National Air Races. The city of Medford turned out en masse at Boston's South Station to greet her and swimmer Helen Johns, whose train arrived just behind Carew's. In September, Medford staged a "Mary Carew Day" celebration in her honor and presented her with a scholarship. She returned for her sophomore year at the Posse-Nissen School of Physical Education.[35]

She married William Armstrong in 1938. He had followed her career for years at all the meets in Boston. She said their daughter and two sons grew up in stadiums. Later on, going to night school, Mary earned a degree from Boston University and began a teaching career that ranged from middle school to kindergarten.[36]

She had continued to run for the Medford Girls Club after the 1932 Games, and always thought perhaps she should have competed in 1936. She served as a timer at the trials in Providence, Rhode Island, and thought she could have made the team. The comradely bond of Olympic athletes gripped Mary in Los Angeles, and she said, "It lasts all your life. It's very important, it's very friendly, and it's very special . . . you'd have to be made of stone not to shed a tear" at the sight of an American woman on the victory stand.[37]

Fencer Marion Lloyd repeated as an Olympian in 1936. In the face of intense European competition, however, she did not place in her third Olympiad. She remained the foremost woman fencer in the United States, inspiring and fostering the careers of later Olympians. She married her New York fencing master, Joseph Vince, and after World War II they moved to Los Angeles, where he opened another Salle. The motion picture industry relied on fencing experts and a number of film personalities came to Vince for instruction. Marion taught children and assumed her husband's other classes when he gave full time to a major picture. In addition to three Olympic teams, Marion Lloyd was a member of nine Amateur Fencing League of America national championship teams. After her death in 1969, the AFLA fittingly named its Women's Foil Under-19 event the Marion Lloyd Vince Memorial.[38]

Even for the glamour girls of swimming, financial benefits stemming from their Olympic accomplishments were rare. With radio in its infancy and television still years in the future, 1932 medal winners had no prospects as sports color commentators. Before the day of athletes' agents, few product endorsements came their way, but Jane Fauntz and Helene Madison both made cereal and Camel cigarette endorsements. Dreams of motion picture careers sprang from the success of Olympic swimmer Johnny Weissmuller, who went from winning gold in 1924 and 1928 to stardom as the movies' Tarzan.

Louella Parsons wrote that a female Weissmuller in adventure films should be a box office success, and mentally cast Helene Madison in the role. Helene did sign a contract and made one movie that she later called "terrible." After Los Angeles she returned to Seattle's West Green Lake Beach—as a hotdog vendor. With three Olympic gold medals and every freestyle record in the world, she could not circumvent park department rules barring women from teaching swimming. She entered training as a nurse and in March 1937, just short of becoming an R.N., she married L. C. McIver, a power company executive. Their one child was born the following year—a daughter known as Helene Madison, Jr., and fondly called "Junie" by her mother's friends.[39]

  She resumed her place in the Seattle aquatic scene in 1950 with the opening of the Helene Madison Swim School. The McIvers divorced in 1958, and when the swim school closed soon after, she returned to the field of nursing. In the mid-1960s a diagnosis of throat cancer followed an earlier one of diabetes. When the press brought her plight to national attention, people responded generously to help with soaring medical expenses; total strangers remembered "Queen Helene" and the summer of 1932.[40]

  Never moving far from sight of the beach where it all began, she died on November 25, 1970. When the International Swimming Hall of Fame had honored Helene Madison in 1966, the Washington Athletic Club sent her to Fort Lauderdale to receive the honor.[41] It was perhaps the least her old sponsor could do for the woman whose teenage exploits had brought such glory during its fledgling years in the Great Depression.

Eleanor Holm fared better in the world of show business. Warner Brothers signed her to a seven-year contract just after the Los Angeles Games, intending to cast her in conventional roles rather than as a swimmer. She said, "They paid me four hundred and fifty dollars a week, and they sent me to school to lose my Brooklyn accent." She had one major role in a picture, a 1937 Tarzan movie opposite Glenn Morris, decathlon gold-medalist at the Berlin Games. She married bandleader Art Jarrett, star at the Coconut Grove, after the 1932 Olympics and stayed in Los Angeles to sing with Jarrett's band. Eleanor Holm endeared herself to the young swimmers whom she helped whenever she was at the Los Angeles Athletic Club.[42]

In 1936 she left the band and nightclub circuit to train for a third Olympic team. It was an important goal. When she was removed from that team for drinking and breaking shipboard training rules on the way to Berlin, it hurt deeply. She said, "I was dead. I was heartbroken." Art Jarrett was ready to sue until fantastic offers generated by the publicity began to roll in. Thinking back, she said, "I did all right after I won in 1932, but 1936 made me a *star*—it made me a glamour girl! Just another gold medal would never have done *that!*" She divorced Jarrett and went on to swim in Billy Rose's Aquacades at the 1939 New York World's Fair and elsewhere. She married Rose in 1939. That marriage ended in 1954 in a prolonged and celebrated divorce action dubbed "The War of the Roses" by the press. She later moved to Florida and into a career as an interior decorator.[43]

Eleanor Holm entered the International Swimming Hall of Fame as a Charter Honoree in 1965. The tough, proud competitor with the enormous glamour girl smile soon became the Hall's "Grande Dame." William O. Johnson interviewed her a few years later and wrote, "She said with that incandescent smile alight, 'Life owes me nothing—I've had a *ball!*'"[44]

In March 1937, Joan McSheehy signed to join good friend and teammate Holm in the "Water Follies of 1937," with plans to tour New

England and the East Coast. She had competed for another two years after the 1932 Games, and in 1933 took the national title to interrupt Eleanor's six-year reign in 100-yard backstroke. That same year she swam on the Women's Swimming Association team that won the 300-yard medley relay championship. The witty and popular McSheehy put her swimming career aside and married Wilson Huffman of Baltimore. Spinal meningitis struck her in the spring of 1948, and she died at the Johns Hopkins Hospital on April 15 that year.[45]

Hollywood tapped into the popular water follies and aquacades and adapted elements of them for the movies. The swimming film became popular about a decade too late for the young women of 1932, but one other medalist from that summer had a brief career in motion pictures.

After her springboard triumph Georgia Coleman seriously considered an offer to tour Australia, diving in exhibitions that were also to feature Eleanor Holm. Possibilities of that sort detoured her from plans for college that fall. Her widely reported romance with diver Mickey Riley finally faded from newsreels and press accounts, but only after false reports of their marriage at the end of the Games in Los Angeles. The trip Down Under did not materialize, and Georgia retired from competition. She taught swimming and diving, helped Fred Cady's young divers at the Los Angeles Athletic Club, and in 1936 went to New York to lend moral support during the Olympic trials.[46]

The following year she was cast in *The Beachcomber,* a film with Elsa Lanchester and Charles Laughton. Georgia contracted polio while shooting the picture in the South Pacific. At that time the dread disease usually meant an end to swimming, diving, or even walking. The determined two-time Olympian made a phenomenal recovery, however, and even returned to swimming and teaching. In late summer 1939, she suffered a recurring infection, and she died September 14, 1940. The eternally happy blonde had remained everyone's favorite, and in 1966 the International Swimming Hall of Fame named her an Honor Diver. Georgia Coleman's sure and assertive gymnastic diving style had turned women's diving onto a new competitive direction.[47]

After the exhibitions in Mexico that Olympic summer, an agent of Howard Hughes contacted Jane Fauntz. No movie contract resulted from the meeting, but later Jane did a little modeling. In addition to Wheaties and Camels endorsements, she appeared on the cover of

Ladies' Home Journal. In the fall of 1932 Jane opted to return to the University of Illinois for her junior year, and she dived professionally at the Chicago World's Fair's Streets of Paris in the summer of 1933. After graduating from the university she worked as a bathing suit designer.[48] Considering her brush with the Olympic judge from Hungary, who better to create new styles?

In 1936 she married Ed Manske, All-American football player at Northwestern who played professionally with the Philadelphia Eagles and Chicago Bears. They moved to Berkeley, California, after World War II, where he joined the University of California coaching staff. When their three daughters were well along in school Jane began her teaching career. She moved from teaching second grade to high school art, and found her true calling. She became an accomplished portrait painter and sculptor. In 1984 she received a commission to create an award to be given by FINA (Fédération Internationale de Natation Amateur). When diver Greg Louganis received it that year at the second Olympics to be held in Los Angeles, Jane Fauntz could almost claim a third Olympiad. She had seen her first as a swimmer, her second as bronze-medalist diver, and the third as an honored artist.[49]

Following the swimmers' 1932 foray to Agua Caliente, Helen Johns returned to the reception at Boston's South Station. Back in Medford, a welcoming parade ended at the Johns home with a mayoral address from their flower-decked front porch. She had one more Olympic moment before entering Brown University's Pembroke College in September. President Hoover had skipped the Games, but he found time at the height of his reelection campaign to invite Olympians to the White House rose garden. Few of the athletes could accept the invitation, but her father, who had happily supported her swimming every inch of the way, sent Helen and her sister down to Washington on the train. They were the only women in attendance.[50]

Helen graduated from Brown in 1936, having majored in psychology and economics. In a pattern familiar to generations of New England college women, she went on to spend a year at the Katherine Gibbs School in order to acquire secretarial skills. In 1937 she married Eugene Carroll, a textile industry executive. Their two daughters were born while they were living in Swansee, Massachusetts. The textile plant moved to Sumter, South Carolina, in 1957, and so did the Carrolls. Helen earned a Master of Education degree from the University of South Carolina and subsequently taught in the Sumter schools' programs for the handicapped. Her competitive swimming career lasted only a short time, but it included the Olympic experience that lasts a lifetime. She echoed others decades later when she recalled the awards ceremony and the Olympic victory stand and said, "I still get a lump in my throat thinking about it."[51]

After her second Olympic summer, Margaret Hoffman returned to Mount Holyoke as a senior and completed a degree in economics. Then, as an economist for the federal government, she joined the legion of bright young people who swept into Washington to staff newly created New Deal agencies. After World War II, in a complete change of scene and pace, she worked as a timber buyer for a western lumber company. In her third and lasting career move, she taught mathematics at the Shipley School in Philadelphia.[52]

Eleanor Garatti Saville, another two-time Olympic swimmer, went back up the coast to San Francisco after the Games in Los Angeles. She resumed the life of a city matron, which she had abandoned when she came out of retirement to train for the trials at Jones Beach. Both Los Angeles and Amsterdam remained vividly alive for her, and she cherished the friendship of the swimmers from both years.[53]

A third veteran of Amsterdam and Los Angeles went on to her third Olympic team in 1936. Dorothy Poynton claimed another gold medal in platform diving at Berlin, and another bronze in springboard to go with the medal from 1928. She later said those 1936 Games were the hardest of all, with more pressure. She had already made some unsigned commitments for endorsements, and had she failed in Berlin, "all that would have been gone." She returned to the endorsements and to tour with a variety of swimming shows.[54]

The Dorothy Poynton Swim Club opened in West Los Angeles in 1952. In the course of its eighteen-year run Dorothy taught an untold number of screen stars' children, including Michael and Maureen Reagan. With a true competitor's mindset, she said she couldn't do anything unless she did it "better than anyone else." She expressed a champion's philosophy when she added, "You know, you only take this route once. . . . It's great having been the world's best in something."[55]

The Berlin Games marked the last Olympic competition for all of the women from the summer of 1932, and the end of their Olympic era. World War II saw to that. Three others from the Los Angeles team competed in 1936—Katherine Rawls, Anne Govednik, and Lenore Kight.

Katherine Rawls went on from Los Angeles to become a versatile record holder—in the pool and on the board. She took Eleanor Holm's individual medley title in 1932 and kept it for eight years. In all, she held thirty national titles in swimming and diving. When she qualified in both freestyle and springboard diving in 1936, she became the only person to win a double place on an Olympic team. Ironically, she never did win an Olympic gold medal but, had the individual medley been added during the 1930s, it could well have been otherwise. In Berlin she won the springboard silver medal, and swam the first leg on the bronze medal–winning 400-meter relay team.[56]

Disappointed by the cancellation of the 1940 Games, Rawls retired from competitive swimming in 1939 and discovered a new love —flying. She was among the original pilots in the WAFS (Women's Auxiliary Ferrying Squadron), and during World War II flew planes to various theaters of combat for the Air Transport Command. After the war she went back to swimming and taught for more than twenty years at the resort in White Sulphur Springs, West Virginia. In 1965 the International Swimming Hall of Fame tapped her as a Charter Honoree—along with her 1932 Olympic teammate Eleanor Holm. She returned home to Florida, where she died of cancer on April 8, 1982.[57]

When the people of Chisholm, Minnesota, welcomed Anne Govednik home from Los Angeles on August 20, 1932, they sent the high school band and a delegation of 200 to Duluth to meet her. With a state highway patrol escort, the caravan picked up more cars along the eighty miles or so back to Chisholm. Bands from three towns led the parade to an official welcome at the Community Building that bulged with a turn-away crowd of 5,000. In the history of Chisholm, with good reason, 1932 became "The Anne Govednik Summer."[58]

In 1936 the community again rallied and sent Anne to the Olympic trials; again she qualified. Swimming against the dominant Europeans, no American breaststroker placed in Berlin. Anne went on to college, and with a degree from St. Cloud State she began her teaching career in physical education. She married Wheeler VanSteinburg in 1941. While their two sons were growing up she continued to teach, including four years at the University of Minnesota-Duluth. In the spring of 1974, Chisholm honored her once more in ceremonies re-dedicating the swimming facility at the junior high school and naming it the Anne Govednik Pool.[59]

Lenore Kight's close brush with gold in the 400 meters at Los Angeles prompted Grantland Rice to write, "No second-place competitor deserves more fame than Lenore Kight. . . . Her coronet should be just as bright as that of the winner." The Homestead, Pennsylvania, city council more than agreed and passed resolutions praising its favorite daughter. Lenore continued to swim on the town's Carnegie Library team and in the next four years won a total of twenty national freestyle titles in distances ranging from 100 yards to the mile. She won the 400-meter freestyle bronze medal at the Berlin Games, and did not forget feeling the distinct chill of political repression and regimentation in Germany in 1936.[60]

In 1935 Lenore married school administrator Cleon Wingard. They made their home in Cincinnati, where they raised a son and a daughter. When Lenore left the amateur swimming ranks in 1936, she won the Toronto and Cleveland Marathons and garnered a few commercial endorsements. She taught swimming at a private pool for twenty years, and never dreamed of competing again. Her son persuaded her to enter the Masters swimming program, and fifty years after her great performance in Los Angeles she promptly broke her age group's freestyle records for 50, 100, and 200 yards. Of her two Olympiads, she preferred the Los Angeles Games, saying, "That's what I call the last *real* Olympics. There weren't any political problems at all."[61]

No Olympiad has ever been totally free from politics, but perhaps the Games of 1932 did present an innocent, more naive perspective on Olympic competition. As Olympic political history has unfolded, that tenth Olympic gathering in Los Angeles stands as a landmark on the road to acceptance for women athletes. Popular medalists, appealing challengers, close finishes, and timing and judging controversies put women's events in the news. Press photos, radio interviews, and movie newsreels made women competitors a positive attraction across the country and around the world. Superior performances by the women of 1932 virtually assured the place of women's events in the Olympic Games of the future.

Critics of athletic competition for girls and women continued to play on fears and apprehensions. But as early as the mid-twenties, 1932's women Olympians had been undaunted by criticism. For the most part they had a clear sense of who they were and reveled in the sports they loved. After their Olympic years, even though hemmed in by the traditional role assigned to women, by and large they avoided the conventional mold. They continued to compete; they taught and coached other competitors; they pioneered in the armed forces and incipient professional sports; they had careers, which many who married continued during and after marriage and motherhood. Each in her own way and in her own locale offered an example for girls and younger women in the years before a resurgent women's movement made the possibility of becoming an athlete more acceptable and desirable.

In that simpler time before boycotts, blatant national subsidies, and full-time, nearly professional training, in 1932 an amateur athlete could come from obscurity and secure a spot on the Olympic team. That year, women provided the artistry of fencing, the glamour and excitement of swimming's sisterhood, and the wonder and joy of unknown track and field competitors bursting onto the national scene.

The fun, glory, pride, satisfaction, loyalty, and friendship bridged the years. In 1968, Eleanor Holm summed it up, when she wrote to Helene Madison: "It seems so long ago, our swimming days. We really had the world by a string . . . you and I had our day in the sun."

Notes

INTRODUCTION

1. Major scholarship in the 1980s and '90s focuses on gender issues in attitudes toward women's athletic participation and competition. Some studies that explore the burden of gender that is still being experienced by women athletes, include, for example: Bryson, "Challenges to Male Hegemony in Sport"; Cahn, *Coming on Strong;* Helen Lenskyj, *Out of Bounds: Women, Sport and Sexuality;* Leigh, "The Enigma of Avery Brundage and Women Athletes"; Kane, "Sport Typing: The Social 'Containment' of Women in Sport"; Park, "Physiology and Anatomy Are Destiny!?"; Park and Mangan, *From Fair Sex to Feminism;* Squires, "Sport and the Cult of True Womanhood"; Theberge, "Making a Career in a Man's World: The Experiences and Orientations of Women in Coaching"; Twin, *Out of the Bleachers: Writings on Women and Sport.* A biographical work incorporating gender issues and orientation is Susan E. Cayleff, *Babe: The Life and Legend of Babe Didrikson Zaharias.*

2. Kane, 77.

CHAPTER I

1. Twin, xviii. Twin's introduction provides a good summary of women's progress toward acceptance in the world of sports. See Park, "Physiology and Anatomy are Destiny!?"

2. For the history and importance of women's basketball, see Joan S. Hult and Marianna Trekell, eds., *A Century of Women's Basketball: From Frailty to Final Four* (Reston, Va.: American Alliance for Health, Physical Education, Recreation and Dance, 1991). Paula Welch looks at basketball as an irritant for non-competitive

college administrators that extends to the 1960s in "Interscholastic Basketball: Bane of Collegiate Physical Educators," in Howell, ed., *HerStory in Sport*.

3. Twin, xxix (quotation, emphasis added). Lears presents a broader view pertinent to the sportswoman and advertising in "American Advertising and the Reconstruction of the Body." For a look at the sportswoman as both fact and symbol, see Gregory K. Stanley, "Redefining Health: The Rise and Fall of the Sportswoman. A Survey of Health and Fitness Advice for Women, 1860–1940," Ph.D. diss. (University of Kentucky, 1991).

4. Lucas and Smith, *Saga of American Sport,* 307.

5. Ibid., 346.

6. Himes, "The Female Athlete," 224–237; Wallechinsky, *Complete Book of the Olympics,* 430; Rader, *American Sports,* 336; for a contemporary's account of the Ederle saga, see Gallico, *The Golden People,* 49–65.

7. Donald J. Mrozek, "The 'Amazon' and the American 'Lady': Sexual Fears of Women as Athletes" in Park and Mangan, 285–287. See also Leigh, "Evolution of Women's Participation," 145, 149. Kathy Peiss has done provocative work on working-class women's recreation, *Cheap Amusements.* While Peiss deals with dance halls, movie theatres, and amusement parks, there is relevance for athletics.

8. Author's interviews with Marjorie Bouve, 26 January and 22 February 1952 (quotation). Marjorie Bouve was a founder of both the Boston School of Physical Education and the Bouve-Boston School. She was a graduate of the prototype Boston Normal School of Gymnastics and a devoted disciple of its director, Amy Morris Homans. For the importance of Amy Morris Homans, see Betty Spears, "The Influential Miss Homans," in Howell, ed., *HerStory in Sport.* For the Boston Normal School, see Martha H. Verbrugge, *Able Bodied Womanhood: Personal Health and Social Change in Nineteenth-Century Boston* (New York: Oxford University Press, 1988).

9. Lucas and Smith, 349; Allen Guttmann, *Women's Sports,* 136–140.

10. Korsgaard, "A History of the Amateur Athletic Union," 279, 280, 284.

11. Ibid., 279, 283–284; Lucas and Smith, 350.

12. Sefton, *The Women's Division National Amateur Athletic Federation,* 2–3; Lucas and Smith, 351–353.

13. Leigh, "Evolution of Women's Participation," 54, 55; Guttmann, *Women's Sports,* 163.

14. Wallechinsky, 429, 544, 550, 551. Tennis was reinstated before the 1988 Games in Seoul.

15. Ibid., 429, 449, 451.

16. Ibid., 267–270.

17. Leigh, "Evolution of Women's Participation," 172–174, 179.

18. Welch, "Emergence of American Women in the Summer Olympic Games," 57–58.

19. Gallico, *Farewell to Sport,* 242, 243.

20. Sefton, 55; Leigh, "Evolution of Women's Participation," 183–188; Welch, 58, 64, 65.

21. Lucas and Smith, 356; Leigh, "Evolution of Women's Participation," 183–187; Guttmann, *The Games Must Go On,* 58–60, 194–195. Factors other than Brundage's appreciation of female athletic performance entered into the decision, see Leigh, "Enigma of Avery Brundage," 12, 13.

CHAPTER 2

1. Korsgaard, 284; *AAU Official Track and Field Handbook,* 192–197.

2. Jean Shiley Newhouse interview, 4 September 1990; *Chicago Herald Examiner,* 9 August 1932.

3. Shiley Newhouse interview, 4 September 1990. Basketball was one common denominator in the lives of women athletes. Many of the 1932 women excelled in the sport, and more than one lamented that it had not been an Olympic sport in their era.

4. Jean Shiley Newhouse, interview by George A. Hodak, September 1987, transcript, Amateur Athletic Foundation Library, Los Angeles, 3 (quotation); *Philadelphia Inquirer,* 29 August 1932; Shiley Newhouse interview, 4 September 1990.

5. Shiley Newhouse interview, Hodak transcript, 3 (quotations); Shiley Newhouse interview, 4 September 1990; *Philadelphia Inquirer,* 8 August 1932.

6. Shiley Newhouse, Hodak transcript, 4, and interview, 4 September 1990; *Chicago Herald Examiner,* 29 August 1932.

7. Shiley Newhouse interview, 4 September 1990.

8. Ibid.

9. Ibid.; *Philadelphia Inquirer,* 8 August 1932.

10. Shiley Newhouse interview, Hodak transcript, 5, and interview, 4 September 1990.

11. Shiley Newhouse interview, 4 September 1990; *Philadelphia Inquirer,* 8 August 1932; *Report of the American Olympic Committee, Ninth Olympic Games, Amsterdam, 1928,* 161.

12. Jean Shiley Newhouse interview, 20 October 1992.

13. Shiley Newhouse interviews, 4 September 1990 and 20 October 1990.

14. *AAU Official Track and Field Handbook,* 195, 201.

15. Shiley Newhouse interviews, 4 September 1990 (first quotation), 20 October 1990, and Hodak transcript, 13 (second quotation). For women in medicine and physical education, see Margaret Rossiter, *Women Scientists in America: Struggles and Strategies to 1940* (Baltimore: Johns Hopkins University Press, 1982).

16. Margaret Jenkins, letter to author, 26 November 1990.

17. Ibid.; Jean Newton, "Athletes Exchange Bloomers for Skinsuits," *Los Altos Town Crier,* 4 April 1989. In telegraphic meets, athletes perform in their respective facilities. Results are telegraphed to a central meet headquarters where final results are calculated.

18. Margaret Jenkins, interview with author, 27 November 1990; Mardi Bennett, "Local Women Pioneers Paved Way for Success," *San Jose Mercury News,* 1 March 1989.

19. Jenkins interview, 27 November 1990; Yvonne Jacobson, "Margaret Jenkins: Living the Competitive Spirit," *Santa Clara County Broadcaster,* December 1990 (quotation).

20. Jenkins interview, 27 November 1990; Jacobson, "Margaret Jenkins: Living the Competitive Spirit," *San Jose Evening News,* 23 May 1927.

21. Jenkins letter, 26 November 1990 (first quotation); Jacobson, "Margaret Jenkins" (quotation re Templeton); for more on Mosher, see Carl Degler, "What Ought to Be and What Was: Women's Sexuality in the Nineteenth Century," *American Historical Review* (December 1974), 1480.

22. Margaret Jenkins, letters to author, 26 November 1990 and 16 April 1991.

23. Margaret Jenkins, letter to the author, 15 November 1990 (quotations); Jacobson, "Margaret Jenkins."

24. *Report of the American Olympic Committee, 1928,* 159; Margaret Jenkins, telephone conversation with the author, 25 April 1991.

25. Jacobson, "Margaret Jenkins."

26. Margaret Jenkins letter, 26 November 1990.

27. Starr, *Material Dreams,* 68, 69; Slater, *Great Jews in Sports,* 41.

28. Slater, 41; *AAU Official Track and Field Handbook,* 196–197.

29. Evelyne Hall Adams, interview with author, 19 October 1990; Mary Carew Armstrong, interview with author, 5 November 1990; Margaret Jenkins interview, 27 November 1990; Shiley Newhouse interview, 4 September 1990; Evelyn Furtsch Ojeda, interview with author, 16 October 1990; *Los Angeles Times* (hereafter, *LAT*), 3 August 1932.

30. Starr, 151–153; *AAU Official Track and Field Handbook,* 196–197.

31. *LAT,* 3 August 1932; Jacobson, "Margaret Jenkins" (quotation).

32. Velma Dunn Ploessel, interview with author, 17 October 1990; Simone Schaller Kirin, interview with author, 13 November 1990.

33. Simone Schaller Kirin, interview by George A. Hodak, August 1988, transcript, Amateur Athletic Foundation Library, Los Angeles, 2.

34. Ibid., 1; Schaller Kirin, interview with author, 5 March 1991; *LAT,* 4 August 1932.

35. Schaller Kirin interview, 13 November 1990.

36. Ibid.; Schaller Kirin interview, Hodak transcript, 2.

37. Aileen Allen, letter to V.W. Humeston, 4 May 1931 (photocopy in author's possession); Furtsch Ojeda interview, 16 October 1990.

38. Furtsch Ojeda, interview by George A. Hodak, transcript, Amateur Athletic Foundation Library, Los Angeles, 3.

39. Furtsch Ojeda interview, 16 October 1990; *United States Census, 1930, Vol. I,* 131.

40. Furtsch Ojeda, interview with the author, 29 January 1991; Paul Zimmerman, "Evelyn Furtsch Ojeda: A Star Is Rediscovered," *LAT,* 10 April 1984 (Humeston quotation).

41. Furtsch Ojeda interview, 16 October 1990, and Hodak transcript, 1.

42. Furtsch Ojeda interview, 16 October 1990.

43. Zimmerman, "Star Rediscovered," *New York Times* (hereafter, *NYT*), 26 July 1931; Furtsch Ojeda interview, 16 October 1990.

44. *LAT,* 13 and 20 June 1932.

45. Carew Armstrong interview with the author, 5 November 1990; Helen Johns Carroll, interview with the author, 7 November 1990.

46. Carew Armstrong interview, 5 November 1990.

47. Carew Armstrong, telephone interviews with the author, 5 November 1990 and 18 February 1991.

48. Carew Armstrong interview, 5 November 1990.

49. Ibid.

50. Carew Armstrong interview, 18 February 1991.

51. *AAU Official Track and Field Handbook,* 192, 198; *NYT,* 26 July 1931.

52. Carew Armstrong interview, 5 November 1990; *Malden Evening News,* 29 August 1972; *United States Census, 1930, Vol. III, part 1,* 1085.

53. *Malden Evening News,* 29 August 1972 and 31 December 1931.

54. Carew Armstrong interview, 5 November 1990.

55. *NYT,* 26 July 1931; *Boston Transcript,* 1 July 1932; *Malden Evening News,* 31 December 1931 and 29 August 1972 (Stokes quotation).

56. Annette Rogers Kelly, interview with the author, 13 November 1990; Elizabeth Robinson Schwartz, interview with the author, 22 February 1991; Hall Adams interview, 19 October 1990.

57. Rogers Kelly interview, 13 November 1990 (quotations); Hall Adams interview, 19 October 1990.

58. *NYT,* 26 July 1931.

59. *Boston Transcript,* 30 July 1932; Robert Paul, telephone conversation with the author, 20 March 1991; Wallechinsky, 429, 437; Hall Adams interview, 19 October 1990; Shiley Newhouse interview, 20 October 1990.

60. Robert Paul conversation, 20 March 1991; Wallechinsky, 147; *NYT,* 26 July 1931; *Boston Transcript,* 30 July 1932; *AAU Official Track and Field Handbook,* 210; Hendershott, *Track's Greatest Women,* 226.

61. Hall Adams interview, 19 October 1990; Rogers Kelly interview, 13 November 1990; *Boston Transcript,* 30 July 1932.

62. Rogers Kelly interview, 13 November 1990; *Boston Transcript,* 19 July 1932; *NYT,* 26 July 1931.

63. Rogers Kelly, letter to the author, 5 November 1990, and telephone conversation with the author, 26 April 1991.

64. Rogers Kelly letter, 5 November 1990, and interview, 13 November 1990.

65. Rogers Kelly, telephone interviews with the author, 13 February 1991 and 13 November 1990.

66. *AAU Official Track and Field Handbook,* 195; *Boston Transcript,* 30 July 1932.

67. Hall Adams interview, 19 October 1990.

68. Ibid.; Evelyne Hall Adams, interview by George A. Hodak, September 1987, transcript, Amateur Athletic Foundation Library, Los Angeles, 12, 2.

69. Hall Adams interview, 19 October 1990, and Hodak transcript, 2 (quotation).

70. Hall Adams interview, 19 October 1990 (first quotation), and Hodak transcript, 2–3 (second quotation).

71. Hall Adams interview, 19 October 1990.

72. *AAU Official Track and Field Handbook,* 195; Hall Adams interview, Hodak transcript, 4, 5; Hall Adams interview, 19 October 1990, and telephone conversation with the author, 20 February 1991.

73. Hall Adams interview, 19 October 1990, and Hodak transcript, 4; *AAU Official Track and Field Handbook,* 194, 199.

74. Hall Adams interview, 19 October 1990, and Hodak transcript, 8; *NYT,* 26 July 1931.

75. Johnson and Williamson, *Babe Didrikson Story,* 65 (quotation).

76. George White, "The Sport Broadcast," *Dallas Morning News,* 8 July 1932; Johnson and Williamson, 62.

77. Johnson and Williamson, 62; White, *Dallas Morning News,* 8 July 1932; Hendershott, 2.

78. Johnson and Williamson, 53, 55, 58, 61; *Current Biography 1947,* 699.

79. Johnson and Williamson, 63, 64, 72; *Current Biography 1947,* 699.

80. Zaharias, *This Life I've Led,* 41, 42; Johnson and Williamson, 68.

81. *NYT,* 26 July 1931.

82. Johnson and Williamson, 80 (quotations); Hendershott, 45.

83. *Dallas Morning News,* 14 July 1932; Jenkins interview, 27 November 1990; Hall Adams interview, 19 October 1990; Johnson and Williamson, 80 (quotation).

84. Johnson and Williamson, 79.

85. Ibid.; Schoor, *Babe Didrikson,* 47–49; *Dallas Morning News,* 8 July 1932.

86. Gallico, "Farewell to Muscle Molls," *Farewell to Sport,* 239.

87. *Dallas Morning News,* 12 July 1932.

88. Ibid., 14 July 1932.

89. *LAT,* 4 July 1932; Evelyn Furtsch Ojeda, telephone interview with the author, 29 January 1991.

90. *Chicago Herald Examiner,* 12 July 1932.

91. Eleanor Garatti Saville, telephone interview with the author, 20 February 1991; Margaret Jenkins, letter to the author, 29 January 1991.

92. Robert Paul conversation, 20 March 1991; Jenkins interview, 27 November 1990; *AAU Official Track and Field Handbook,* 197.

93. Jenkins interview, 27 November 1990; Ruth Osburn, telephone interview with the author, 9 January 1991.

94. *San Francisco Chronicle,* 25 March 1932.

95. Ibid.

96. Ibid.; *Boston Transcript,* 19 July 1932; taped copy of film showing von Bremen's running style, Amateur Athletic Foundation Library, Los Angeles; Carew Armstrong interview, 5 November 1990, inter alia.

97. Maxwell Bond, "The Chicago Board of Education Playgrounds and the Colored Child," *The Playground,* 20 (1926): 211.

98. Allan H. Spear, *Black Chicago: The Making of a Ghetto, 1890–1920* (Chicago: University of Chicago Press, 1967), 14.

99. *Northern Illinois University Alumni News* (Summer 1984), 1.

100. Ibid.

101. Fred Schwengel, telephone interview with the author, 19 April 1991.

102. Ibid.; Ruth Osburn interview, 9 January 1991.

103. Osburn interview, 9 January 1991.

104. *Boston Transcript,* 26 July 1932.

105. Osburn interview, 9 January 1991; *Boston Transcript,* 26 July 1932.

106. Osburn interview, 9 January 1991; *Boston Transcript,* 26 July 1932; *Shelby County Herald,* 29 June 1932.

107. Osburn interview, 9 January 1991.

108. Elizabeth Wilde Kinnard, telephone interview with author, 6 March 1991.

109. Wilde Kinnard interview; *Kansas City Journal-Post,* 17 July 1932.

110. *Boston Transcript,* 19 July 1932; Wilde Kinnard interview.

111. Wilde Kinnard interview.

112. Carew Armstrong interview, 5 November 1990; Shiley Newhouse interview, 4 September 1990.

CHAPTER 3

1. *Chicago Herald Examiner,* 3 July 1932.

2. Ibid.

3. *Chicago Tribune,* 10–27 July 1932.

4. Ibid., 7–16 July 1932.

5. *Boston Transcript,* 9 July 1932; Wallechinsky, 126; *NYT,* 13 July 1932.

6. *Chicago Herald Examiner,* 21 July 1932; *LAT,* 30 July 1932 (quotation).

7. *Chicago Tribune,* 12 July 1932; *Seattle Times,* 15 July 1932; *NYT,* 16 July 1932 (quotations).

8. *The Summer Northwestern,* 15 July 1932.

9. Ibid.

10. *Dallas Morning News,* 12 July 1932.

11. *Official Athletic Rules and Official Handbook of the Amateur Athletic Union of the United States* (New York: American Sports Publishing Co., 1932), 100.

12. Korsgaard, 287 (Minutes of the 1926 AAU annual meeting), 297; Schwengel interview; *Dallas Morning News,* 3 July 1932.

13. *Dallas Morning News,* 20 July and 12 August 1932.

14. Zaharias, 47–48.

15. *Chicago Tribune,* 16 July 1932; *Chicago Herald Examiner,* 14 and 15 July 1932.

16. *Philadelphia Inquirer,* 17 July 1932; Shiley Newhouse interview, 20 October 1990; Jenkins interview, 27 November 1990.

17. *Philadelphia Inquirer,* 17 July 1932; *The Summer Northwestern,* 19 July 1932 (quotation).

18. *Kansas City Journal-Post,* 17 July 1932; Hall Adams interview, 19 October 1990, and Hodak transcript, 10 (quotation).

19. Schaller Kirin interview, 13 November 1990.

20. *LAT,* 23 July 1932. In the Fosbury Flop, introduced at the 1968 Games in Mexico City by Dick Fosbury, jumpers go over the bar headfirst and backwards.

21. AAU, *Official Handbook (1932),* 84; Shiley Newhouse interview, 20 October 1990; Rogers Kelly interview, 13 November 1990.

22. Shiley Newhouse interview, 20 October 1990; Rogers Kelly interview, 13 November 1990.

23. Rogers Kelly interview, 13 November 1990; *Dallas Morning News,* 20 July 1932 (re: protest); *AAU Official Track and Field Handbook,* 195.

24. *AAU Official Track and Field Handbook,* 197; *LAT,* 17 July 1932.

25. *Boston Transcript,* 19 July 1932.

26. Osburn interview, 9 January 1991 (quotations); Schwengel interview; *LAT,* 17 July 1932.

27. Shiley Newhouse interview, Hodak transcript, 16.

28. *Kansas City Journal-Post,* 17 July 1932; *Chicago Herald Examiner,* 17 July 1932; Rogers Kelly letter, 5 November 1990.

29. Wilde Kinnard interview.

30. *Kansas City Journal-Post,* 17 July 1932; *Chicago Tribune,* 17 July 1932.

31. Ibid.

32. Ibid; *LAT,* 10 April 1984; *Dallas Morning News,* 20 July 1932 (first quotation); Furtsch Ojeda interview, 16 October 1990 (second quotation).

33. *Chicago Defender,* 23 July 1932. For the influential role of the *Chicago Defender,* see James R. Grossman, *Land of Hope: Chicago, Black Southerners, and the Great Migration* (Chicago: University of Chicago Press, 1989).

34. Johnson and Williamson, 74–75.

35. See, e.g., *NYT,* 17 July 1932, and *Seattle Post-Intelligencer,* 17 July 1932.

36. George White, "Sport Broadcast," *Dallas Morning News,* 31 July 1932.

37. Furtsch Ojeda interview, 16 October 1990.

38. Annual minutes, 1916, cited in Korsgaard, 281.

39. *LAT,* 10 April 1984; Dunn Ploessel interview, 18 October 1990; Furtsch Ojeda interview, 16 October 1990.

40. Rogers Kelly interview, 13 November 1990.

41. Wilde Kinnard interview.

42. Schwengel interview; Osburn interview, 9 January 1991.

43. Rogers Kelly letter, 5 November 1990.

44. *NYT,* 21 July 1932; Shiley Newhouse interview, Hodak transcript, 16, and interview, 4 September 1990.

45. Shiley Newhouse interview, 4 September 1990; Carew Armstrong interview, 5 November 1990; *Northern Illinois University Alumni News* (Summer 1984); *Chicago Sun-Times,* August 1984.

46. Hall Adams interview, 19 October 1990.

47. Shiley Newhouse interview, 4 September 1990, and Hodak transcript, 16; Evelyne Hall Adams, telephone conversation with the author, 20 February 1991; Johnson and Williamson, 85.

48. *Seattle Post-Intelligencer,* 23 July 1932 (Shiley quote); *Philadelphia Inquirer,* 23 July 1932 (Didrikson quote).

CHAPTER 4

1. *NYT,* 27 July 1931.

2. Korsgaard, 282.

3. Ibid., 285.

4. AAU, *Official Swimming Handbook,* 130, 131, 136.

5. Evans, "Status of the American Woman in Sport," 114.

6. Krieg, ed., *Robert Moses,* 135.

7. *Seattle Times,* 17 July 1932 (first quotation); *Seattle Post-Intelligencer,* 22 July 1932 (Dawn Gilson returned to Seattle and remarked further, "It was a wonder to me that they broke records on the course at all"); Garatti Saville interview (last quotation).

8. *LAT,* 9 August 1932.

9. Besford, *Encyclopedia of Swimming,* 90; Sally Guard, "Still Very Much in the Swim," *Sports Illustrated* (July 1992); Johnson, *All That Glitters,* 186 (quotation).

10. Carlson and Fogarty, *Tales of Gold,* 91.

11. AAU, *Official Swimming Handbook,* 133; Carlson and Fogarty, 91, 92; "washer-woman" statement by Holm in *New York Herald Tribune,* 2 July 1948, quoted in Donald E. Fuoss, "An Analysis of the Incidents in the Olympic Games from 1924 to 1948," 178.

12. American Olympic Committee, *Ninth Olympic Games,* 309; Carlson and Fogarty, 92 (quotation).

13. AAU, *Official Swimming Handbook,* 132–134, 147–149; *LAT,* 2 May 1932; Besford, 90; International Swimming Hall of Fame, *Yearbook,* 92 (Rawls quotation).

14. Lenore Kight Wingard, telephone interview with the author, 1 February 1991.

15. AAU, *Official Swimming Handbook,* 32; American Olympic Committee, *Ninth Olympic Games,* 23, 301.

16. Wallechinsky, 434; AAU, *Official Swimming Handbook,* 130–132.

17. Young, *Los Angeles Athletic Club,* 125; *Seattle Post-Intelligencer,* 14, 16, 17 March, and 4 July 1930; AAU, *Official Swimming Handbook,* 134.

18. Robert Paul conversation, 20 March 1991; Helen Johns Carroll, telephone interview with the author, 7 November 1990; Garatti Saville interview; Gallico, *Farewell to Sport,* 239. Gallico held typical male journalists' views on sports for women and women in sports. He was greatly enamored of the swimmers— as women. He disparaged the popularity of their sport as little more than the appeal of beautiful women in swimsuits; since their times fell short of those turned in by male swimmers, they could not be taken seriously as athletes.

19. Elizabeth Hoffman, telephone interview with the author, 17 January 1991.

20. Ibid.; *Boston Transcript,* 8 August 1932.

21. *Boston Transcript,* 8 August 1932 (quotation); Wallechinsky, 441.

22. Elizabeth Hoffman interview.

23. Ibid.

24. *Boston Transcript,* 8 August 1932; Elizabeth Hoffman interview.

25. Ainsworth, *History of Physical Education in Colleges for Women,* 37–39; Elizabeth Hoffman interview.

26. AAU, *Official Swimming Handbook,* 133, 148; Elizabeth Hoffman interview.

27. Jane Fauntz Manske, interview by George A. Hodak, July 1987, transcript, Amateur Athletic Foundation Library, Los Angeles, 4.

28. Ibid., 1.

29. Ibid., 2, 3.

30. Ibid., 2, 3.

31. Ibid., 4, 5.

32. Ibid., 7–17.

33. Ibid., 7–17.

34. Fauntz Manske interview, Hodak transcript, 18–20; AAU, *Official Swimming Handbook,* 148, 150; *Seattle Post-Intelligencer,* 15 March 1930.

35. Fauntz Manske interview, Hodak transcript, 20 and 21.

36. AAU, *Official Swimming Handbook,* 145; *San Francisco Chronicle,* 11 February and 1 March 1925.

37. *San Francisco Chronicle,* 11 February and 1 March 1925.

38. Ibid., 4 March 1926; AAU, *Official Swimming Handbook,* 130, 145.

39. Garatti Saville interview; American Olympic Committee, *Ninth Olympic Games,* 310; Wallechinsky, 430, 445.

40. Eleanor Garatti Saville, letter to the author, 25 February 1991, and interview; *San Francisco Chronicle,* 16 May 1930; *San Rafael Marin Journal,* 5 June 1930.

41. Garatti Saville interview.

42. Ibid.

43. AAU, *Official Swimming Handbook,* 150 and 135; Young, 84.

44. Carlson and Fogarty, 122.

45. Ibid., 122.

46. Ibid., 122; American Olympic Committee, *Ninth Olympic Games,* 301, 309.

47. *LAT,* 17 April 1932; Young, 128.

48. Dunn Ploessel interview, 18 October 1990.

49. Young, 67, 83, 92.

50. Young, 111; Swimming Hall of Fame, *First Anniversary Yearbook,* 28 (quotation) and 36.

51. Robert Paul conversation, 20 March 1991; *LAT,* 11 August 1932.

52. Swimming Hall of Fame, *First Anniversary Yearbook,* 28; *Report of the American Olympic Committee, 1928,* 301, 309; Fauntz Manske interview, Hodak transcript, 7.

53. AAU, *Official Swimming Handbook,* 135, 151; *LAT,* 17 April 1932; Besford, 50.

54. *LAT,* 17 April 1932; Dunn Ploessel interview, 18 October 1990 (quotation).

55. Dunn Ploessel interview, 18 October 1990.

56. *Seattle Times,* 7 July 1932; *Chicago Herald Examiner,* 6 July 1932; *Philadelphia Inquirer,* 3 July 1932 (e.g., of photo).

57. *Chicago Herald Examiner,* 6 July 1932. For the general state of transcontinental air travel at the time, see Robert J. Serling, *Eagle: The Story of American Airlines* (New York: St. Martin's/Marek, 1985).

58. *Chicago Herald Examiner,* 6 July 1932; *Seattle Post-Intelligencer,* 6 July 1932.

59. *LAT,* 15 October 1982; Young, 130.

60. *LAT,* 11 August 1932 (quotation); *Boston Transcript,* 23 July 1932; International Swimming Hall of Fame, photocopies of clippings from Rawls file in correspondence with the author, 16 January 1991.

61. Swimming Hall of Fame, *Fifth Anniversary Year Book,* 92; *Boston Transcript,* 2 August 1932.

62. *NYT,* 21 July 1931.

63. *Census, 1930, Vol. I,* 571; Belluzzo, *History of CHS Sports,* 110.

64. Petition for Naturalization by Martin Govednik, in U.S. Department of Labor Naturalization Service, Naturalization Records, 1909–1967, photocopy in possession of the author; *Chisholm Free Press,* 17 January 1974.

65. Belluzzo, 67, 68, 111.

66. *Mesaba Miner,* 7, 21, 28 April 1932; AAU, *Official Swimming Handbook,* 148.

67. Belluzzo, 111; *Tribune* quotations reprinted in *Mesaba Miner,* 19 May 1932.

68. *Virginia Daily Enterprise,* 8 July 1932.

69. *Detroit News,* 2 July 1933; Detroit Yacht Club, *Main Sheet,* March 1932, 12, and June 1932, 15; AAU, *Official Swimming Handbook,* 148.

70. DYC, *Main Sheet,* June 1932, 10, 15, and August 1932, 10.

71. Ibid., August 1932, 10.

72. Ibid., July 1932, 13.

73. *Atlanta Constitution,* 5 July 1932.

74. Ibid., 5, 10, 17 July 1932.

75. Ibid., 1, 5, 7, 10 July 1932.

76. Johns Carroll interview, 7 November 1990.

77. *Atlanta Constitution,* 13 July 1932; Johns Carroll interview, 7 November 1990; Garatti Saville interview ("entity" quotation).

78. *Worcester Evening Gazette,* 16 April 1948; *Worcester Telegram,* 16 April 1948.

79. *Worcester Evening Gazette,* 16 April 1948; *Worcester Telegram,* 16 May 1928; *Boston Herald,* 16 May 1928; *NYT,* 16 April 1948.

80. *Worcester Telegram,* 16 May 1928; AAU, *Official Swimming Handbook,* 147.

81. Johns Carroll interview, 7 November 1990; Carlson and Fogarty, 93.

82. *Boston Globe,* 8 March 1930; Johns Carroll interview, 7 November 1990.

83. Johns Carroll interview, 7 November 1990.

84. Ibid.; Helen Johns Carroll, letter to the author, 19 December 1990.

85. Johns Carroll letter, 19 December 1990, and interview, 7 November 1990.

86. Johns Carroll interview, 7 November 1990.

87. Ibid.

88. Ibid.; AAU, *Official Swimming Handbook,* 130.

89. *Boston Transcript,* 8 July 1932; Johns Carroll letter, 19 December 1990, and interview, 7 November 1990.

90. AAU, *Official Swimming Handbook,* 134.

91. *Cincinnati Enquirer,* 17 August 1986; Lenore Kight Wingard, telephone interview with the author, 1 February 1991.

92. Kight Wingard interview, 1 February 1991.

93. *Seattle Post-Intelligencer,* 15 August 1932 (Gallico quotation); Kight Wingard interview, 1 February 1991.

94. Kight Wingard interview, 1 February 1991.

95. Ibid.

96. *Seattle Post-Intelligencer,* 11 August 1932.

97. Ibid., 23 March 1930.

98. Ibid., 23, 24 March 1930.

99. *LAT,* 9 August 1932; *Seattle Times,* 17 May 1966.

100. Katherine Wolfe, Madison's high school physical education teacher, on her will to win, *Seattle Post-Intelligencer,* 28 March 1930. Teammates concurred; she hated to lose.

101. AAU, *Official Swimming Handbook,* 30–132, 146, 147; *Seattle Post-Intelligencer,* 15 March 1930.

102. *Seattle Post-Intelligencer,* 28 March 1930.

103. AAU, *Official Swimming Handbook,* 130–132, 146, 147.

CHAPTER 5

1. International Swimming Hall of Fame, *Fifth Anniversary Yearbook,* 49.

2. International Swimming Hall of Fame, *Tenth Anniversary Yearbook,* 12; Slater, 51. In 1914, coverage of the AAU umbrella, seen as desirable and beneficial for the future of women's swimming, was not easily obtained.

3. Garatti Saville interview; Johns Carroll interview, 7 November 1990 (first quotation); Margaret Hoffman, telephone interview with the author, 17 January

1991; Kight Wingard interview, 1 February 1991.

4. Frederick Rubien, ed., *Report of the American Olympic Committee, Games of the Xth Olympiad* (hereafter, Olympic Committee Report), 1932, 194.

5. *Chicago Herald Examiner,* 6 July 1932.

6. *Seattle Times*, 8 and 11 July 1932; *Seattle Post-Intelligencer,* 11 July 1932.

7. Belluzzo, 114; Helen Johns Carroll, letter to the author, 11 March 1991.

8. Johns Carroll interview, 7 November 1990.

9. *NYT,* 15 July 1932; Belluzzo, 112.

10. *NYT,* 15 and 16 July 1932; *Seattle Times,* 22 July 1932; *Seattle Post-Intelligencer,* 22 July 1932; Garatti Saville interview.

11. *NYT,* 21 July 1931.

12. Ibid., 16 July 1932; *Boston Transcript,* 19 July 1932.

13. *NYT,* 16 July 1932; *Philadelphia Inquirer,* 16 July 1932; *LAT,* 20 July 1932; *Boston Transcript,* 16 July 1932.

14. *NYT,* 17 July 1932; *Seattle Post-Intelligencer,* 17 July 1932.

15. *NYT,* 17 July 1932.

16. *Seattle Times,* 16 July 1932.

17. *NYT,* 17 July 1932; *Atlanta Constitution,* 17 July 1932; *Seattle Post-Intelligencer,* 17 July 1932.

18. *NYT,* 17 July 1932.

19. *Seattle Post-Intelligencer,* 17 July 1932; *NYT,* 17 July 1932.

20. Ibid., 16 July 1932.

21. Ibid., 17 July 1932; *LAT,* 20 July 1932; *Philadelphia Inquirer,* 16 July 1932.

22. *NYT,* 24 July 1932.

23. Johns Carroll interview, 7 November 1990.

24. *NYT,* 15 and 19 July 1932; *LAT,* 21 July 1932; *Seattle Post-Intelligencer,* 20 July 1932.

25. *Philadelphia Inquirer,* 22 July 1932.

26. Maria Cerra Tishman, telephone interview with the author, 5 April 1991; *NYT,* 26 July–22 August 1931.

27. *NYT,* 19 July 1932; *Chicago Herald Examiner,* 6 July 1932 (quotation); *LAT,* 21 July 1932; *Seattle Post-Intelligencer,* 20 July 1932.

28. Johns Carroll interview, 7 November 1991; *Seattle Post-Intelligencer,* 29 July 1932 (quotations).

29. *LAT,* 22 and 23 July 1932.

CHAPTER 6

1. *Census, 1930, Vol. I*, 128; Starr, 79–82.

2. Zimmerman, *Los Angeles the Olympic City*, 2; Mary Pickford, tape transcription of Olympic speech, 6 July 1932, copy in possession of the author; *LAT*, 7 July 1932.

3. *Chicago Herald Examiner*, 25 July 1932; *NYT*, 21 and 24 July 1932; *Seattle Post-Intelligencer*, 17 July 1932.

4. *LAT*, 17 July 1932.

5. *Report of the Organizing Committee: The Games of the Xth Olympiad*, 292–294 (hereafter, *Report of the Organizing Committee*).

6. *LAT*, 24 July 1932; *Report of the Organizing Committee*, 294.

7. *Report of the Organizing Committee*, 294; *Chicago Defender*, 6 August 1932; Shiley Newhouse interview, 4 September 1990.

8. *LAT*, 10 July 1932.

9. *Chicago Herald Examiner*, 9 July 1932; *NYT*, 20 July 1932; *Chicago Tribune*, 22 July 1932.

10. *LAT*, 18 July 1932; *NYT*, 15 July 1932; *Chicago Herald Examiner*, 20 July 1932.

11. *LAT*, 19 July 1932.

12. Ibid., 22 July 1932.

13. Ibid., 23 July 1932.

14. Ibid., 24 July 1932.

15. Ibid., 3 July 1932.

16. Ibid., 24 July 1932.

17. Ibid., 25 July 1932; *Chicago Herald Examiner*, 20 and 27 July 1932.

18. *LAT*, 25 July 1932; *Seattle Post-Intelligencer*, 25 July 1932; *NYT*, 25 July 1932.

19. *LAT*, 30 July 1932.

20. Fauntz Manske interview, Hodak transcript, 25.

21. *LAT*, 30 July 1932.

22. Fauntz Manske interview, Hodak transcript, 26; Margaret Hoffman interview.

23. Shiley Newhouse interview, 4 September 1990; Hall Adams interview, 19 October 1990; Carew Armstrong interview, 5 November 1990 (quotation).

24. Ruth Osburn interview, 9 January 1991; Fred Schwengel interview.

25. This sentiment was universal among the team members interviewed.

26. Shiley Newhouse interview, 20 October 1990, and Hodak transcript, 26

and 27; Carew Armstrong interview, 5 November 1990; Furtsch Ojeda interview, 16 October 1990.

27. *Xth Olympiad Committee of the Games, General Regulations and Program of the Olympic Games,* 12.

28. *Dallas Morning News,* 20 July 1932 (Didrikson quotation); Ruth Osburn interview, 9 January 1991.

29. Johns Carroll interview, 7 November 1990.

30. Shiley Newhouse interview, 4 September 1990; Hall Adams interview and Hodak transcript, 13; Wilde Kinnard interview; Los Angeles City Directory, 1932 (n.p.), (re: state societies).

31. Shiley Newhouse interview, 4 September 1990; Wilde Kinnard interview; Hall Adams interview and Hodak transcript, 13. All team members interviewed had great memories of the social life in Los Angeles during the Games.

32. *Chicago Herald Examiner,* 5 August 1932; Hall Adams, Carew Armstrong, Osburn, Garatti Saville, Johns Carroll interviews, inter alia.

33. Wallechinsky, 12; Osburn and Hall Adams interviews, inter alia; Pickford speech, tape transcription.

34. Starr, 209; Hall Adams, Osburn, Garatti Saville, Johns Carroll interviews, inter alia.

35. Louella Parsons, "American Girl Swimmers Potential Candidates for Screen," *Seattle Post-Intelligencer,* 29 July 1932.

36. Wilde Kinnard interview; Shiley Newhouse interview, 4 September 1990.

37. Henstell, *Los Angeles,* 200, 201; *LAT,* 28 July 1932.

38. *Chicago Defender,* 6 August 1932.

39. *LAT,* 28 July 1932; *Chicago Tribune,* 29 July 1932 (quotation); Kight Wingard interview, 1 February 1991.

40. Fauntz Manske interview, Hodak transcript, 22.

41. *LAT,* 31 July 1932.

42. Ibid., 23 July 1932.

43. Ibid., 26 July 1932.

44. Shiley Newhouse interview, 4 September 1990, and Hall Adams interview, inter alia.

45. "The Sportlight," *Dallas Morning News,* 30 July 1932.

46. *Boston Transcript,* 29 July 1932.

47. *LAT,* 29 July 1932; *NYT,* 30 July 1932.

CHAPTER 7

1. *NYT,* 31 July 1932; *Chicago Tribune,* 1 August 1932.

2. *NYT,* 24 and 31 July 1932; *Philadelphia Inquirer,* 31 July 1932; *Chicago Herald Examiner,* 31 July 1932.

3. *NYT,* 31 July 1932; *Official Program, Xth Olympiad,* 30 July 1932; "Occidental College Fifty Year Club News" (n.d., n.p.), Bill Henry Papers, Occidental College Library, Los Angeles, California; *Chicago Herald Examiner,* 31 July 1932.

4. *Chicago Tribune,* 31 July 1932; interviews with participants, including Hall Adams, Schaller Kirin, Shiley Newhouse, Kight Wingard, inter alia. Olympians took marching seriously before TV camera close-ups of the parades provided the opportunity for individualism.

5. *NYT,* 31 July 1932; *Official Program, Xth Olympiad,* 30 July 1932; *Chicago Herald Examiner,* 31 July 1932 (quotation).

6. *Official Program, Xth Olympiad,* 31 July 1932; *Chicago Herald Examiner,* 1 August 1932; *NYT,* 1 August 1932.

7. *Chicago Tribune,* 1 August 1932.

8. *LAT,* 1 August 1932; *Official Program, Xth Olympiad,* 31 July 1932, 21; *Chicago Tribune,* 1 August 1932 (quotation).

9. Wallechinsky, 147.

10. *LAT,* 1 August 1932.

11. Ibid., 29 July 1932; *Boston Transcript,* 7 July 1932; *NYT,* 30 July 1932.

12. *Seattle Post-Intelligencer,* 24 July 1932; *Boston Transcript,* 1 August 1932; *Chicago Herald Examiner,* 2 August 1932.

13. *Philadelphia Inquirer,* 2 August 1932; *Boston Transcript,* 1 August 1932; *Chicago Herald Examiner,* 2 August 1932; *Official Program, Xth Olympiad,* 1 August 1932, 13, and 2 August 1932, 11.

14. *Philadelphia Inquirer,* 2 August 1932; *Official Program, Xth Olympiad,* 2 August 1932, 11.

15. *Philadelphia Inquirer,* 2 August 1932.

16. *LAT,* 6 and 28 July 1932.

17. Eleanor Cass *Book of Fencing* (Boston: n.p.), 1930, 319–320; Cerra Tishman interview, 5 April 1991.

18. Cerra Tishman interview, 5 April 1991.

19. Ibid.; American Olympic Committee, *Ninth Olympic Games,* 210, 211; Wallechinsky, 267–270.

20. Janice York Romary, telephone interview with the author, 21 February 1991; Cerra Tishman interview, 5 April 1991; Wallechinsky, 267–269.

21. Olympic Committee Report, 1932, 151, 156; *Philadelphia Inquirer,* 5 August 1932.

22. *LAT,* 28 July 1932.

23. *Official Program, Xth Olympiad,* 2 August 1932, 11.

24. *Boston Transcript,* 3 August 1932; *NYT,* 3 August 1932; taped copy of film of the 1932 women's 100-meter final, Amateur Athletic Foundation Library, Los Angeles.

25. Carew Armstrong, Hall Adams, and Shiley Newhouse interviews, inter alia; *LAT,* 12 August 1932 (Babcock quotation); Wallechinsky, 127 (second quotation).

26. *Boston Transcript,* 1 August 1932; *Official Program, Xth Olympiad,* 2 August 1932, 6.

27. *Official Program, Xth Olympiad,* 3 August 1932, 3; Report of the Organizing Committee, 474.

28. *LAT,* 3 August 1932; *Official Program, Xth Olympiad,* 3 August 1932, 3.

29. Olympic Committee Report, 1932, 127.

30. *LAT,* 3 August 1932.

31. Ibid., 3 August 1932 (quotation); Jenkins interview, 27 November 1990. The medal-winning discus is now in the Olympic artifacts collection of the Amateur Athletic Foundation, Los Angeles.

32. Lucas, *The Modern Olympic Games,* 121.

33. Korsgaard, 190; Olympic Committee Report, 1932, 104.

34. *LAT,* 4 August 1932.

35. *Official Program, Xth Olympiad,* 13; *LAT,* 4 August 1932; *NYT,* 4 August 1932; Schaller Kirin interview, 13 November 1990.

36. *Official Program, Xth Olympiad; NYT,* 4 August 1932; *Chicago Herald Examiner,* 4 August 1932.

37. *NYT,* 5 August 1932; Johnson and Williamson, 104–105; *Dallas Morning News,* 5 August 1932; *Philadelphia Inquirer,* 5 August 1932; taped copy of 1932 film of 80-meter hurdles final, Amateur Athletic Foundation Library, Los Angeles; Hall Adams interview and Hodak transcript, 16–17.

38. Hall Adams interview; *Dallas Morning News,* 5 August 1932; *NYT,* 5 August 1932; *Chicago Herald Examiner,* 5 August 1932 (Runyan quotation); Shiley Newhouse interview, 4 September 1990.

39. Hall Adams, Jenkins, Schaller Kirin, Furtsch Ojeda, Rogers Kelly, Shiley Newhouse, and Carew Armstrong interviews with the author; Hall Adams interview, Hodak transcript, 16 (quotation); *Philadelphia Inquirer,* 5 August 1932; *Dallas Morning News,* 5 August 1932; Wallechinsky, 134.

40. *Chicago Herald Examiner,* 5 August 1932 (Runyan quotation); Schaller Kirin, Shiley Newhouse, Carew Armstrong, and Wilde Kinnard interviews with the author; *LAT,* 5 August 1932 (Didrikson quotation).

41. Evelyne Hall Adams interview.

42. Schaller Kirin interview, 13 November 1990 (first quotation), and Hodak transcript, 7 (second quotation).

43. *Official Program, Xth Olympiad,* 7 August 1932, 2, 5.

44. Ibid., 7; Jenkins interview, 27 November 1990; Rogers Kelly interview, 13 November 1990; Wilde Kinnard interview.

45. *LAT,* 10 April 1984; Carew Armstrong interview, 5 November 1990 (quotations); Furtsch Ojeda interview, 16 October 1990; Shiley Newhouse interview, 4 September 1990.

46. Mary Carew Armstrong, telephone interview with the author, 18 February 1991; *LAT,* 8 August 1932.

47. *LAT,* 8 August 1932; *Chicago Herald Examiner,* 8 August 1932; *Philadelphia Inquirer,* 8 August 1932; *Official Program, Xth Olympiad,* 7 August 1932; Olympic Committee Report, 1932, 125 (re tenths of seconds); Wallechinsky, 134.

48. Furtsch Ojeda interview, 16 October 1990 (first quotation); *LAT,* 10 April 1984 (second quotation).

49. *Northern Illinois University Alumni News* (Summer 1984), 1.

50. *LAT,* 23 July 1932.

51. *Official Program, Xth Olympiad,* 7 August 1932, 5.

52. Watson, *Xth Olympiad,* 129; Shiley Newhouse interviews, 4 September 1990 and 20 October 1990; Johnson and Williamson, 106–107; Hall Adams interview.

53. Olympic Committee Report, 1932, 126; *LAT,* 8 August 1932; Johnson and Williamson, 106–107; Shiley Newhouse interviews, 4 September and 20 October 1990 and Hodak transcript, 19–23; Wallechinsky, 140.

54. Shiley Newhouse interview, 4 September 1990; *LAT,* 8 August 1932 (quotation).

55. Shiley Newhouse interview, 4 September 1990.

56. *Official Program, Xth Olympiad,* 8 August 1932, 3.

57. Olympic Committee Report, 1932, 121.

CHAPTER 8

1. Frank G. Menke, Associated Press item, *Seattle Post-Intelligencer,* 12 August 1932 (quotation). The label was indelible. Sixty years later, more than one '32 track and field athlete volunteered the comment, "The swimmers were the glamour girls."

2. *LAT,* 10 August 1932; Carlson and Fogarty, 92.

3. *Seattle Post-Intelligencer,* 29 July 1932.

4. Grantland Rice, "The Sportlight," *LAT,* 29 July 1932.

5. Gallico, *Farewell to Sport,* 250.

6. *Chicago Herald Examiner,* 31 July 1932.

7. *Atlanta Constitution,* 22 July 1932; Johns Carroll interview, 7 November 1990; Garatti Saville interview.

8. *Report of the Organizing Committee,* 313; Johns Carroll interview, 7 November 1990.

9. Elizabeth Hoffman interview.

10. *Official Program, Xth Olympiad,* 6 August 1932, 16.

11. Olympic Committee Report, 1932, 204; *LAT,* 7 August 1932; *Boston Transcript,* 7 August 1932.

12. *Boston Transcript,* 10 August 1932; *LAT,* 10 August 1932; Olympic Committee Report, 1932, 204; Wallechinsky, 441.

13. Margaret Hoffman interview; Wallechinsky, 440–442.

14. Olympic Committee Report, 1932, 202.

15. *Boston Transcript,* 8 August 1932; Olympic Committee Report, 1932, 202; *LAT,* 8 August 1932.

16. *LAT,* 9 August 1932.

17. *NYT,* 9 August 1932.

18. *NYT* and *LAT,* 9 August 1932; Olympic Committee Report, 1932, 202.

19. *LAT,* 9 August 1932.

20. *Boston Transcript,* 28 July 1932.

21. Olympic Committee Report, 1932, 203.

22. Ibid., 203; *NYT,* 10 August 1932.

23. Olympic Committee Report, 1932, 203; *LAT,* 12 August 1932.

24. *LAT,* 12 August 1932 (Ziegfeld quote); *NYT,* 12 August 1932.

25. *LAT, NYT,* and *Philadelphia Inquirer,* 12 August 1932.

26. Olympic Committee Report, 1932, 204.

27. *Seattle Post-Intelligencer* and *LAT,* 11 August 1932; Fauntz Manske, Hodak transcript, 27.

28. *LAT* and *Chicago Herald Examiner,* 11 August 1932.

29. Fauntz Manske interview, Hodak transcript, 27.

30. Ibid., 28, 29; taped copy of 1932 film of Olympic diving, Amateur Athletic Foundation Library, Los Angeles.

31. Johns Carroll interview, 7 November 1990.

32. Olympic Committee Report, 1932, 206.

33. *Official Program, Xth Olympiad,* 10 August 1932, 2.

34. *Chicago Herald Examiner,* 9 August 1932.

35. Olympic Committee Report, 1932, 204; *Boston Transcript,* 12 August 1932.

36. *NYT,* 13 August 1932; Olympic Committee Report, 1932, 204.

37. *NYT,* 13 August 1932 (quotation); Carlson and Fogarty, 124.

38. *NYT,* 13 August 1932; Olympic Committee Report, 1932, 207; *Report of the Organizing Committee,* 651.

39. Damon Runyan, *Chicago Herald Examiner,* 13 August 1932, inter alia; *NYT,* 13 August 1932; *Report of the Organizing Committee,* 651.

40. Johns Carroll interview, 7 November 1990.

41. *Seattle Post-Intelligencer,* 12 August 1932.

42. *NYT* and *LAT,* 13 August 1932.

43. Wallechinsky, 430 and 446; *NYT,* 13 August 1932.

44. *LAT,* 13 August 1932; Wallechinsky, 446.

45. *Boston Transcript,* 12 August 1932.

46. *Chicago Herald Examiner,* 14 August 1932.

47. *LAT,* 9 August 1932.

48. *Seattle Post-Intelligencer,* 13 August 1932.

49. *Official Program, Xth Olympiad,* 13 August 1932, 17.

50. *NYT, Philadelphia Inquirer,* and *LAT,* 14 August 1932.

51. *Olympic Committee Report, 1932,* 205.

52. *LAT,* 14 August 1932.

53. Rice, "The Sportlight," *Philadelphia Inquirer,* 14 August 1932; Kight Wingard interview, 1 February 1991.

54. *Seattle Post-Intelligencer,* 14 August 1932; Fauntz Manske interview, Hodak transcript, 26.

55. *LAT,* 15 August 1932.

56. *Seattle Post-Intelligencer,* 14 August 1932.

57. *Philadelphia Inquirer,* 15 August 1932 (Rice quotation); *Chicago Herald Examiner,* 15 August 1932; Olympic Committee Report, 1932, 65.

EPILOGUE

1. *LAT* and *Dallas Morning News,* 12 August 1932.

2. *Dallas Morning News,* 12 August 1932.

3. *LAT,* 9 August 1932.

4. Johnson and Williamson, 186.

5. Ibid., 204–219.

6. Ruth Osburn interview, 9 January 1991.

7. Ibid.

8. Ibid.

9. *Cassville Republican,* 18 April 1940; Ruth Osburn interview, 9 January 1991.

10. Wilde Kinnard interview.

11. Ibid.

12. Shiley Newhouse interview, 20 October 1990.

13. Ibid.; Shiley Newhouse interview, Hodak transcript, 32 and 33.

14. Schaller Kirin interview, 13 November 1990 (quotation); Schaller Kirin interview, Hodak transcript, 14–16.

15. Schaller Kirin interview, 13 November 1990; Schaller Kirin interview, Hodak transcript, 9.

16. *Northern Illinois University Alumni News* (Summer 1984), 1 (first and second quotations); *Chicago Sun Times,* 10 August 1984 (last quotation); *AAU Official Track and Field Handbook,* 1953–52, 200.

17. *Malden Evening News,* 9–12 September 1936 and 14 September 1987.

18. *Northern Illinois University Alumni News* (Summer 1984), 5.

19. Rogers Kelly interview, 13 November 1990; *AAU Official Track and Field Handbook,* 193–195.

20. Rogers Kelly interview, 13 November 1990.

21. Richard K. Mandell, *The Nazi Olympics* (Urbana: University of Illinois Press, 1987), 214.

22. Rogers Kelly interview, 13 November 1990 (quotation); Wallechinsky, 127, 140.

23. Rogers Kelly, letter to the author, 5 November 1990, and interview, 13 November 1990 (quotation).

24. Hall Adams interview, 19 October 1990.

25. Ibid. and Hodak transcript, 20.

26. Hall Adams interview, 19 October 1990, and Hodak transcript, 23.

27. Hall Adams interview, 19 October 1990 (quotation), and Hodak transcript, 24.

28. Margaret Jenkins interview, 27 November 1990 (first quotation), and letter to the author, 26 November 1990 (second quotation).

29. *San Francisco Chronicle,* 21 September 1935 (quotation) and 25 July 1976; *Palo Alto Times,* 24 July 1976.

30. *LAT,* 9 August 1932.

31. Furtsch Ojeda interview, 16 October 1990, and Hodak transcript, 9.

32. Committee on Fair Play in Sports, *Preserve the Olympic Ideal: A Statement of the Case Against American Participation in the Olympic Games in Berlin* (New York, 20 Vesey Street [1935]), 62 and 44. For coverage of the 1936 boycott and controversy, see Guttmann, *The Games Must Go On* and *The Olympics.*

33. Furtsch Ojeda interview, 16 October 1990; undated clipping from Ojeda collection, copy in the author's possession.

34. Furtsch Ojeda interview, 16 October 1990.

35. Carew Armstrong interview, 5 November 1990, and telephone interview with the author, 18 February 1991.

36. Carew Armstrong interview, 5 November 1990.

37. Ibid.

38. Interviews with Janice York Romary, 21 February 1991, and Maria Cerra Tishman, 4 April 1991; Jeffrey Tishman, letter to the author, 17 March 1991.

39. *Seattle Post-Intelligencer,* 15 August 1932, 7 March 1937, and 22 December 1966; Helene Madison McIver Ware, interview with the author, 22 August 1990.

40. Helene Ware interview; *Seattle Post-Intelligencer,* 22 December 1966.

41. *Seattle Post-Intelligencer* and *Seattle Times,* 26 November 1970; International Swimming Hall of Fame, *Fifth Anniversary Yearbook,* 74; Helene Ware interview.

42. Johnson, *All That Glitters Is Not Gold,* 187 (quotation); *Philadelphia Inquirer,* 23 August 1932; Velma Dunn Ploessel interview, 18 October 1990.

43. Johnson, 188 (quotation); Carlson and Fogarty, 94–95.

44. International Swimming Hall of Fame, *Fifth Anniversary Yearbook*, 53, and Yearbook, 1973 (n.p.); Johnson, 189 (quotation).

45. *Worcester Telegram*, 31 March 1937; AAU, *Official Swimming Handbook*, 147–149; *Worcester Telegram*, 16 April 1948; *NYT*, 16 April 1948.

46. *LAT*, 11 August 1932; *NYT*, 6 September 1940; Dunn Ploessel interview, 18 October 1990.

47. *The Diver*, undated, 14, from the files of the International Swimming Hall of Fame, Fort Lauderdale, Fla.; *NYT*, 16 September 1940.

48. Fauntz Manske interview, Hodak transcript, 32–41.

49. Ibid., 32–41; Hall Adams interview, 19 October 1990.

50. Johns Carroll interviews, 7 November 1990 and 15 February 1991; *Boston Globe*, 8 September 1932.

51. Johns Carroll interviews, 7 November 1990 and 15 February 1991.

52. Elizabeth Hoffman interview.

53. Garatti Saville interview.

54. Wallechinsky, 452; Carlson and Fogarty, 125–126.

55. Carlson and Fogarty, 126.

56. AAU, *Official Swimming Handbook*, 133; Wallechinsky, 430–450; International Swimming Hall of Fame, *Fifth Anniversary Yearbook*, 71; Fact Sheets from files of the Swimming Hall of Fame.

57. International Swimming Hall of Fame, *Fifth Anniversary Yearbook*, 71; Fact Sheets from the files of the Swimming Hall of Fame.

58. Belluzzo, 116–118.

59. *Chisholm Free Press*, 17 and 24 January 1974; Mary Govednik Sega, telephone conversation with the author, 18 July 1991; Belluzzo, 120.

60. *LAT*, 14 August 1932 (quotation); AAU, *Official Swimming Handbook*, 130–132 and 146–147; Kight Wingard interview, 1 February 1991.

61. Kight Wingard interview; *Hamilton & Fairfield (Ohio) Journal-News*, 16 February 1984; *Cincinnati Enquirer*, 20 July 1984 (quotation).

Rosters

TEAM ROSTER FENCING

Muriel Guggolz	Salle Vince, New York
Dorothy Locke	Salle Vince, New York
Marion Lloyd	Salle Vince, New York

TEAM ROSTER SWIMMING AND DIVING

Jane Cadwell	Detroit Yacht Club
Georgia Coleman	Los Angeles Athletic Club
Jane Fauntz	Illinois Women's Athletic Club, Chicago
Noreen Forbes	Los Angeles Athletic Club
Anne Govednik	Chisholm, Minnesota
Margaret Hoffman	Scranton Swimming Association, Pennsylvania
Eleanor Holm	Women's Swimming Association, New York
Helen Johns	Women's Swimming Association, Brookline, Mass.
Lenore Kight	Carnegie Library Club, Homestead, Pennsylvania
Helene Madison	Washington Athletic Club, Seattle
Josephine McKim	Los Angeles Athletic Club
Joan McSheehy	Women's Swimming Association, New York
Dorothy Poynton	Los Angeles Athletic Club
Katherine Rawls	Fort Lauderdale, Florida
Louisa Robert	Atlanta Athletic Club
Marion Dale Roper	Los Angeles Athletic Club
Eleanor Garatti Saville	Western Women's Club, San Francisco

ALTERNATES

Dorothea Dickinson	Women's Swimming Association, New York
Anna Mae Gorman	Carnegie Library Club, Homestead, Pennsylvania
Edna McKibben	Washington Athletic Club, Seattle

TEAM ROSTER TRACK & FIELD

Mary Carew	Medford Girls Club, Massachusetts
Lillian Copeland	Los Angeles Athletic Club
Mildred Didrikson	Employers' Casualty Company, Dallas, Texas
Evelyn Furtsch	Los Angeles Athletic Club
Nan Gindele	Illinois Women's Athletic Club, Chicago
Evelyne Hall	Illinois Women's Athletic Club, Chicago
Ethel Harrington	Illinois Women's Athletic Club, Chicago
Margaret Jenkins	Western Women's Club, San Francisco
Ruth Osburn	Shelbyville, Missouri
Tidye Pickett	Chicago, Illinois
Annette Rogers	Illinois Women's Athletic Club, Chicago
Gloria Russell	Western Women's Club, San Francisco
Simone Schaller	Los Angeles Athletic Club
Jean Shiley	Meadowbrook Club, Philadelphia
Louise Stokes	Onteora Club, Melrose, Massachusetts
Wilhelmina von Bremen	Western Women's Club, San Francisco
Elizabeth Wilde	Loretto Academy, Kansas City, Missouri

List of Interviews

All interview subjects are 1932 Olympians unless otherwise noted.

Adams, Evelyne Hall. Oceanside, California, 19 October 1990; telephone interview, 20 February 1991.

Armstrong, Mary Carew. Telephone interviews, 5 November 1990 and 18 February 1991.

Carroll, Helen Johns. Telephone interviews, 7 November 1990 and 15 February 1991.

Jenkins, Margaret. Telephone interviews, 27 November 1990 and 25 April 1991.

Hoffman, Elizabeth (Margaret Hoffman's sister). Telephone interview, 17 January 1991.

Hoffman, Margaret. Telephone interview, 17 January 1991.

Johnson, Doris Buckley (teammate of Helene Madison). Edmonds, Washington, 2 August and 21 October 1990.

Kelly, Annette Rogers. Telephone interviews, 13 November 1990 and 26 April 1991.

Kinnard, Elizabeth Wilde. Telephone interview, 6 March 1991.

Kirin, Simone Schaller. Telephone interviews, 13 November 1990 and 5 March 1991.

Mucha, Olive McKean (teammate of Helene Madison and 1936 Olympian). Troutdale, Oregon, 1 May 1992.

Newhouse, Jean Shiley. Los Angeles, 4 September and 20 October 1990.

Ojeda, Evelyn Furtsch. Tustin, California, 16 October 1990; telephone interview, 29 January 1991.

Osburn, Ruth. Telephone interviews, 9 January and 18 September 1991.

Ploessel, Velma Dunn (1936 Olympian). Los Angeles, 17 October 1990.

Romary, Janice York (1952 and 1956 Olympic fencer). Telephone interview, 21 February 1991.

Saville, Eleanor Garatti. Telephone interview, 20 February 1991.

Schwartz, Elizabeth Robinson (1928 and 1936 Olympian). Telephone interview, 22 February 1991.

Schwengel, Fred (Ruth Osburn's coach). Telephone interview, 19 April 1991.

Sega, Mary Govednik (Anne Govednik's sister). Telephone interview, 18 July 1991.

Skok, Mary Lou Petty (1936 Olympian). Telephone interview, 14 December 1993.

Tishman, Maria Cerra (1948 Olympic fencer). Telephone interview, 5 April 1991.

Ware, Helene McIver (Helene Madison's daughter). Marysville, Washington, 22 August 1990.

Wingard, Lenore Kight. Telephone interview, 1 February 1991.

Yeomans, Patricia Henry (daughter of Bill Henry, technical director of the 1932 Olympic Games). Los Angeles, 6 September 1990.

Bibliography

Ainsworth, Dorothy S. *The History of Physical Education in Colleges for Women.* New York: A. S. Barnes, 1930.

Amateur Athletic Union. *The AAU Official Track and Field Handbook: Rules and Records.* New York, 1953.

American Olympic Committee. *Report of the American Olympic Committee, Ninth Olympic Games, Amsterdam, 1928.*

Barry, James P. *The Berlin Olympics.* New York: Franklin Watts, Inc., 1975.

Belluzzo, Lawrence. *Wherever I May Be: History of CHS Sports, 1925–1941.* Chisholm, Minn.: n.p., 1991.

Besford, Pat. *Encyclopedia of Swimming.* London: Robert Hale & Co., 1971.

Braine, Tim, and John Stravinsky. *The Not So Great Moments in Sports.* New York: William Morrow, 1986.

Browne, Frederick Granger, ed. *The Games of the Xth Olympiad, Los Angeles, 1932: Official Report.* Los Angeles, 1933.

Bryson, Lois. "Challenges to Male Hegemony in Sport," in Michael A. Messner and Donald F. Saho, eds., *Sport, Men and the Gender Order: Critical Feminist Perspectives.* Champaign, Ill.: Human Kinetics Books, 1990.

Cahn, Susan K. *Coming On Strong: Gender and Sexuality in Twentieth-Century Women's Sport.* New York: The Free Press, 1994.

Carlson, Lewis H., and John J. Fogarty. *Tales of Gold.* New York: Contemporary Books, 1987.

Cayleff, Susan E. *Babe: The Life and Legend of Babe Didrikson Zaharias*. Urbana: University of Illinois Press, 1995.

Espy, Richard. *The Politics of the Olympic Games*. Berkeley: University of California Press, 1979.

Evans, Virginia L. "The Status of the American Woman in Sport, 1912–1932." Ph.D. diss., University of Massachusetts, 1982.

Finley, M. I., and H. W. Pleket. *The Olympic Games: The First Thousand Years*. London: Chatto & Windus, 1976.

Fuoss, Donald E. "An Analysis of the Incidents in the Olympic Games from 1924 to 1948." Ed.D. diss., Teachers College, Columbia University, 1951.

Frommer, Harvey. *Olympic Controversies*. New York: Franklin Watts, 1987.

Gallico, Paul. *Farewell to Sport*. New York: International Polygonics, 1990.

————. *The Golden People*. New York: Doubleday, 1965.

Gardiner, E. Norman. *Greek Athletic Sports and Festivals*. London: Macmillan and Co., 1910.

Gerber, Ellen W. *The American Woman in Sport*. Reading, Penn.: Addison-Wesley, 1974.

Guttmann, Allen. *The Games Must Go On: Avery Brundage and the Olympic Movement*. New York: Columbia University Press, 1984.

————. *The Olympics: A History of the Modern Games*. Urbana: University of Illinois Press, 1992.

————. *Women's Sports: A History*. New York: Columbia University Press, 1991.

Hanley, Reid M. *Who's Who in Track & Field*. New Rochelle, N.Y.: Arlington House, 1973.

Hart-Davis, Duff. *Hitler's Games: The 1936 Olympics*. London: Century, 1986.

Hendershott, Jon. *Track's Greatest Women*. Los Altos, Calif.: Tafnews Press, 1987.

Henry, Bill, and Patricia Henry Yeomans. *An Approved History of the Olympic Games*. Sherman Oaks, Calif.: Alfred Publishing Co., 1984.

Henstell, Bruce. *Los Angeles, An Illustrated History*. New York: Alfred A. Knopf, 1980.

Himes, Cindy L. "The Female Athlete in American Society." Ph.D. diss., University of Pennsylvania, 1986.

Holtzman, Jerome. *No Cheering in the Press Box*. New York: Holt, Rinehart and Winston, 1974.

Howell, Reet, ed. *HerStory in Sport: A Historical Anthology of Women in Sports*. West Point, N.Y.: Leisure Press, 1982.

International Swimming Hall of Fame. *Fifth Anniversary Yearbook*. Ft. Lauderdale, 1971.

―――. *Tenth Anniversary Yearbook*. Ft. Lauderdale, 1975.

Johnson, William O. *All That Glitters Is Not Gold: The Olympic Games*. New York: Putnam's, 1972.

―――, and Nancy P. Williamson. *"Whatta Gal": The Babe Didrikson Story*. Boston: Little Brown, 1977.

Kane, Mary Jo. "Sport Typing: the Social 'Containment' of Women in Sport." *Arena Review* 13 (November 1989), 77–96.

Kieran, John, and Arthur Daly. *The Story of the Olympic Games, 776 B.C. to 1972*. New York: J. B. Lippincott, rev. ed., 1973.

Korsgaard, Robert. "A History of the Amateur Athletic Union of the United States." Ed.D. diss., Teachers College, Columbia University, 1952.

Krieg, Joann P., ed. *Robert Moses: Single-Minded Genius*. Interlaken, N.Y.: Heart of the Lakes Publishing, 1989.

Lears, T. J. Jackson. "American Advertising and the Reconstruction of the Body, 1880–1930," in Kathryn Grover, ed., *Fitness in American Culture: Images of Health, Sport, and the Body, 1830–1940*. Amherst: University of Massachusetts Press, 1989.

Leigh, Mary Hanson. "The Evolution of Women's Participation in the Summer Olympic Games, 1900–1948." Ph.D. diss., Ohio State University, 1974.

―――. "The Enigma of Avery Brundage and Women Athletes." *Arena Review* 4 (May 1980), 11–21.

―――, and Therese M. Bonier. "The Pioneering Role of Madame Alice Milliat and the F.S.I. in Establishing International Track & Field Competition for Women." *Journal of Sport History* 4 (Spring 1977): 72.

Lenskyj, Helen. *Out of Bounds: Women, Sport and Sexuality*. Toronto: The Women's Press, 1986.

Lucas, John. *The Modern Olympic Games*. New York: A. S. Barnes & Co., 1980.

―――, and Ronald A. Smith. *Saga of American Sport*. Philadelphia: Lea & Febiger, 1978.

Official Program, Xth Olympiad. 30 July through 14 August 1932.

Park, Roberta J. "Physiology and Anatomy are Destiny!?: Brains, Bodies and Exercise in Nineteenth Century American Thought." *Journal of Sport History* 18, no. 1 (Spring 1991), 41–63.

―――, and J. A. Mangan. *From Fair Sex to Feminism: Sport and the Socialization of Women in the Industrial and Post-Industrial Eras*. London: Frank Cass & Co., Ltd., 1987.

BIBLIOGRAPHY

Peiss, Kathy. *Cheap Amusements: Working Women and Leisure in Turn-of-the-Century New York.* Philadelphia: Temple University Press, 1986.

Pizer, Vernon. *Glorious Triumphs: Athletes Who Conquered Adversity.* New York: Dodd, Mead, 1968.

Rader, Benjamin. *American Sports: From the Age of Folk Games to the Age of Spectators.* Englewood Cliffs, N.J.: Prentice Hall, 1983.

Roxborough, Henry. *Canada at the Olympics.* Toronto: McGraw-Hill Ryerson, Ltd., 3rd ed., 1963.

Rubien, Frederick, ed. *Report of the American Olympic Committee, Games of the Xth Olympiad.* New York: American Olympic Committee, 1933.

Schoor, Gene. *Babe Didrikson: The World's Greatest Woman Athlete.* New York: Doubleday, 1978.

Slater, Robert. *Great Jews in Sports.* Middle Village, N.Y.: Jonathan David Publishers, 1983.

Spalding's Official Athletic Almanac. New York: American Sports Publishing, 1932.

Starr, Kevin. *Material Dreams: Southern California Through the 1920s.* New York: Oxford University Press, 1990.

Twin, Stephanie L., ed. *Out of the Bleachers: Writings on Women and Sport.* Old Westbury, Conn.: Feminist Press, 1979.

Wallechinsky, David. *The Complete Book of the Olympics.* New York: Penguin Books, 1984.

Welch, Paula D. "The Emergence of American Women in the Summer Olympic Games, 1900–1972." Ed.D. diss., University of North Carolina, Greensboro, 1975.

Young, Betty Lou. *Our First Century: The Los Angeles Athletic Club, 1880–1980.* Los Angeles: LAAC Press, 1980.

Zaharias, Babe Didrikson. *This Life I've Led: My Autobiography.* New York: A. S. Barnes, 1955.

Zimmerman, Paul. *Los Angeles the Olympic City, 1932–1984.* Hollywood: Delmar Watson, 1984.

NEWSPAPERS

Atlanta Constitution

Boston Transcript

Cassville [Missouri] Republican

Chicago Herald Examiner

Chicago Tribune

Cincinnati Enquirer

Dallas Morning News

Detroit News

Kansas City Journal-Post

Los Angeles Times

Malden (Massachusetts) *Evening News*

New York Times

Palo Alto Times

Philadelphia Inquirer

San Francisco Chronicle

San Rafael Marin Journal

Shelby (Missouri) *County Herald*

Seattle Post-Intelligencer

Seattle Times

Worcester Evening Gazette

Worcester Telegram

Index